The End of Custer

The End of Custer
The Death of an American Military Legend

Dale T. Schoenberger

hancock

house

ISBN 0-88839-288-5
Copyright © 1995 Dale T. Schoenberger

Cataloging in Publication Data
Schoenberger, Dale T.,1939-1993
    End of Custer
    Death of an American Military Legend

    Includes bibliographical references and index.
    ISBN 0-88839-288-5

    1. Little Big Horn, Battle of the, 1876.   2. Dakota
Indians—Wars, 1876.   3. Indians of North America—
Wars—1866-1895.   R. Custer, Geroge Armstraong, 1839-
1876.   I. Title.
E83.876.S36 1991   973.8'2   C91-091396-x

Cover Art: *Custer's Last Stand* by E. S. Paxson, courtesy of the Buffalo Bill
    Historical Center, Cody, WY
Edited: Herb Bryce
Production: Lorna Lake

Published simultaneously in Canada and the United States by

HANCOCK HOUSE PUBLISHERS LTD.
19313 Zero Avenue, Surrey, B.C. V4P 1M7
(604) 538-1114   Fax (604) 538-2262

HANCOCK HOUSE PUBLISHERS
1431 Harrison Avenue, Blaine, WA 98230-5005
(604) 538-1114   Fax (604) 538-2262

Contents

To Walter Thomas Schoenberger,
    A father and a friend, who started
    it all by introducing me to the
    Battle at the Little Bighorn

Hancock House regrets that author
Dale T. Schoenberger passed away
before this book was published and
that he was unable to do a final proof.

Preface

This work is the result of more than thirty years of study on the subject. The actual writing—and rewriting—of the manuscript took twelve years. I have taken the liberty of pointing out some clarifications for the reader's benefit.

First, many (but not all) of the times given for the afternoon of June 25, 1876, are approximate and could vary as much as ten, fifteen, or twenty minutes on either side of the hour. Most were too preoccupied that hot summer day to take much note of time.

Second, the ages given for the participants in the battle were the ages at the time of the battle regardless of approaching birthdates later in 1876.

Third, I have endeavored to write a descriptive account of the battle as to the actions of the individual officer, trooper, Indian scout, civilian, chief, warrior, and Indian woman in the hope of giving the reader an "on the spot" feeling of being in the battle. In this style, it is hoped, the reader will come to view the heroics and pathos of the individual combatants in this tragic event. To accomplish this purpose, I have allowed the reader to follow many individuals in the battle; to know where they were, at what times, and what they were doing. This is not the story of *one man*, but a story of all who were a part of this historic event.

A final word regarding military ranks in the nineteenth century or Old Army: while in reality Gibbon and Custer were not generals—it was Colonel Gibbon and Lieutenant Colonel Custer—I have arbitrarily referred to both of these officers as holding their highest brevet ranks while, just as arbitrarily I have referred to subordinate officers who had less-than-general brevet ranks as holding their lineal (actual) ranks. In the Old Army of the nineteenth century, it was a point of courtesy and honor for former Civil War generals such as Gibbon and Custer to be addressed as "General."

DALE T. SCHOENBERGER
Within bugle sound of old Jefferson Barracks,
St. Louis County, Missouri 1992

Acknowledgments

In the more than three decades which this book was in progress, countless people have given their valuable time and tireless energy to me in the research of this work. Far too many, I am sorry to say, to list here. But a few, nonetheless, need to be named.

In no special order . . . Walter Mason Camp (1867–1925) without whose indefatigable, grassroots research, which spanned three decades, this book would have been far less a work of history; the staff at the National Archives; the librarians at both Indiana University and Brigham Young University; the past historians and staff at the Custer Battlefield National Monument (CBNM), now known—as of 1992—as the Little Bighorn Battlefield National Monument; the late Custer scholar and author Dr. Lawrence A. Frost, M.D.; the late author-historian John M. Carroll; National Park historian W. Bill Henry who also served at the CBNM; Custer scholar the Reverend Father Vincent A. Heier; author-historian Richard G. "Dutch" Hardorff; LeAnn Simpson of the Custer Battlefield Historical and Museum Association; author-historian Ron Nichols for answering my probing questions about Reno's military battles; Norman Crockett, for his probing questions; author-historian Brian C. Pohanka, for a valuable piece of military combat protocol; and a special thanks to National Park historian, Neil C. Mangum, former historian at the Custer Battlefield for those "unique, in-depth guided tours" of the Custer and Reno battlefields during the summers of 1983 and 1991; and to Dan Martinez of the National Park Service for riding that horse across the Little Bighorn at Reno's retreat crossing (where Hodgson was killed) to show me and others how Reno's panic-stricken troopers did it on that long-ago afternoon. Last, but certainly far from least, a special thanks to fellow author-historian Jim Willert, who, one hot afternoon along Custer Ridge, pointed out several pertinent observations with his keen insight into the battle.

A special thanks to my editor at Hancock House, Herb Bryce, whose expertise at what he does best kept me from my own "Little Bighorn."

Introduction: The Roots of War

The Battle at the Little Bighorn River had its roots in the Fort Laramie (Wyoming) Treaty of 1868. The treaty, in part, resulted from Oglala Sioux Chief Red Cloud's victorious war (1866–1868) against the U.S. Army along the "Bloody" Bozeman Trail in present Wyoming and Montana. The treaty created a "permanent" reservation for the Sioux in part of present South Dakota, west of the Missouri River. (The Oglala Sioux actually were located on the Powder River outside of the Great Sioux Reservation.) The reservation included the Sioux ancestral home, the pine-shrouded Black Hills—called *Paha Sapa* by the Sioux—in western South Dakota and northeastern Wyoming. Entry into the Great Sioux Reservation without tribal consent was prohibited by the Treaty of 1868. The treaty did allow a survey of the reservation if ordered by the President. There was nothing in the treaty pertaining to the Army per se entering the reservation as said surveyor. Article No. 11 of the treaty muddied the waters, however. It allowed for "the construction of railroads, wagon roads, mail stations, and other works of utility or necessity" in Sioux-deeded territory. All of this presumably was with permission of the Sioux since certain chiefs had signed the treaty. In reality, however, it is extremely doubtful if the Sioux even knew of this treaty clause.

The 1874 "Black Hills Reconnaissance," led by Brevet Major General George Armstrong Custer, lieutenant colonel, Seventh United States Cavalry, brought forth the well-publicized fact that the Black Hills were laden with gold deposits. Custer has been criticized by pro-Indian factions as having blazed "The Thieves' Road" into the Black Hills, although it was known as early as 1859 that there was gold there; but in what paying quantities was the unknown factor.

Custer was ambiguous on the subject. He first claimed that Black Hills gold deposits were found "in several places" in "paying quantities," but later he said that "no opinion should be formed" as to the value of the deposits. Still, Custer proclaimed the gold discoveries of his expedition to be "very important and of promising richness." Lieutenant General Philip H. Sheridan concluded,

9

however, that "the Custer [discoveries were] not sufficient to establish [the] existence [of gold] in paying quantities." By the summer of 1875, 800 miners were panning for gold in the Black Hills.

The Thieves' Road notwithstanding, the Treaty of 1868 was a failure almost from its signing. The Sioux had committed wholesale depredations while roaming the unceded lands for bison and a heavy influx of gold seekers into the Black Hills gave Whites effective possession of the *Paha Sapa*. The Sioux also had received treaty goods which were shoddy and meager. The tribe as a whole had grown insolent and defiant by 1875. The treaty was a shambles and the U.S. government faced a dilemma. General in Chief William T. Sherman, as early as 1873, had advocated that the Senate abrogate the treaty and remove the Sioux from the unceded lands (the Powder River basin to the eastern flanks of the Big Horn Mountains). An effort by the government to purchase the Sioux rights to the Black Hills failed.

By the autumn of 1875, the situation had reached the crisis stage. On November 3, in a White House strategy meeting, President Ulysses S. Grant, Secretary of War William W. Belknap, Secretary of the Interior Zachariah Chandler, Commissioner of Indian Affairs Edward P. Smith, among others, decided to force the Sioux from the unceded lands and onto their reservation and to "wink" at the ever-growing influx into the Black Hills. The stage now was set for—war. The Sioux, in violation of the 1868 treaty, raided in the Gallatin River Valley and the upper Yellowstone River in the Montana Territory.

> I am no reservation Indian.
> *Sitting Bull*

> Unless [the Sioux] are caught before early spring, they cannot be caught at all.
> *Lieutenant General Philip H. Sheridan*
> *Commanding Officer, Division of the Missouri*

10

1
The Gathering Storm
December 1875–May 1876

It was an ultimatum that led inexorably to the Sioux War of 1876. On December 6, 1875, Commissioner of the Bureau of Indian Affairs (commonly called the Indian Bureau), Edward P. Smith, acted on a directive from the Secretary of the Interior, Zachariah Chandler. He issued an ultimatum to the now recalcitrant Sioux, via their agents, ordering them to return to their various agencies by January 31, 1876.

The ultimatum went largely ignored and on January 18 the Indian Bureau, with pressure from the War Department, embargoed the movement of guns and cartridges to the tribes for hunting purposes. The need of agency Indians for guns to supplement their agency diet underscored the woeful lack of government food stores for the reservation tribes. The January deadline passed without the agencies being filled by the Winter Roamers. Despite the nearly two months the Sioux had to comply with Commissioner Smith's ultimatum, many of the tribes had failed to receive notice of the deadline. Late in 1875, the Indian Bureau reported that 3,000 Sioux remained off their reservations.[1] Even after the deadline, hundreds of Sioux, and Northern Cheyenne, ignored their agents' warnings and left their reservations. The Indian Bureau wanted these recalcitrants "whipped into subjection."

On February 1, the recalcitrants became the official problem of the War Department (as usual), and more specifically, the jurisdiction problem of the Military Division of the Missouri (commanded by Lieutenant General Philip H. Sheridan) of the Army's geographical command system, "for such action of the Army as deemed proper." The Army's main function was that of a policeman during the period of the Indian Wars (1866–1891). Since 1849, when Congress gave absolute jurisdiction of the Indian problem to the Bureau of Indian Affairs in the Department of the Interior, the Army had been defrocked of formulating Indian policy. The military never had an official policy regarding the tribes after 1849. It merely functioned in the frustrating and thankless task of corralling the recalcitrants.

On January 3 Sheridan wrote General in Chief William T. Sherman that his (Sheridan's) departmental commanders were ready for action. Sheridan's task were formidable. The Sioux, the largest and most dominant tribe on the northern plains, were determined to remain off the reservation all summer. Sheridan was equally determined to have his commanders "strike the unfriendlies" hard.

Sitting Bull (1831–1890), the great inspirational-political leader of the Hunkpapa Sioux, knew well the marked incompatibility between the white man and the red. This fact made Sitting Bull an implacable foe of the white man. To the great Hunkpapa, all white men were perfidious. His famous words, "I am no reservation Indian," became a rallying cry around the council fires of the upper Missouri River country. Sheridan and other generals mistakenly considered Sitting Bull a noninfluential Indian with a small following who owed his truculent reputation to Eastern press agentry.

Another prominent recalcitrant in the hostile camp was Crazy Horse (1842?–1877), a war chief of the Oglala Sioux. Crazy Horse was the flower of the Sioux Nation. He had broken with the great Oglala chief Red Cloud over the latter's signing of the 1868 treaty. Many Oglalas deserted Red Cloud's direction and followed Crazy Horse on the bloody war trail.

***

Sheridan's military expedition against the Sioux was commanded in the field by Brigadier (later Major) General Alfred H. Terry (1827–1890), the gouty-hipped, heavily chin-whiskered commander of the Department of Dakota. A wealthy bachelor-lawyer, the scholarly Terry, a non–West Pointer, was a man of sensitive nature, mild demeanor, and cordiality, all of which made him well liked by his subordinates. Terry's responsibility was seeing that, somewhere among the three large columns of troops which Sheridan had placed in the field for the campaign, they struck the "unfriendlies," hard. Terry, a deskbound administrator, was on his first field campaign.

Early winter intelligence reports had indicated that the various Sioux tribes were gathering in large numbers on the upper Missouri

River. Sitting Bull alone was reported to have between 300 and 600 lodges in his camp. Terry reported to Sheridan on March 24 that a reliable source put the Sioux strength at "not less than 2,000 lodges and that the Indians are loaded down with ammunition." Most of the ammunition had come to the tribes from the Indian agencies before the embargo deadline. This, in effect, had the U.S. government arming both warring parties in the ensuing conflict. Several weeks later, Terry scaled down the Sioux estimates to 1,500 lodges which meant 2,250 warriors. This extremely revisionist fact alone disputes the later-manufactured myth that and the Seventh Cavalry did not realize just how many Indians they were riding to meet. Since Custer met approximately 1,800 warriors, Army intelligence prior to the campaign was reasonably accurate. Terry's figures, which included the Winter Roamers (i.e., those Indians who did not return to their agencies during the winter months), were several times more accurate than those that the agencies had reported. Lost in the concern about the Sioux was the fact that the Northern Cheyenne were allied with them. The Sioux and the Cheyenne had shared the same plains for years in friendship. A common bond—hatred of the white man—had united these two tribes.

Terry would lead one column of troops westward from Fort Abraham Lincoln, in present North Dakota. A second column was to march eastward from Fort Ellis in the Montana Territory. It was to be commanded by Brevet Major General (later Brigadier General) John "Old Poppycock" Gibbon (1827–1896), the testy colonel of the Seventh U.S. Infantry. He was a stodgy, former West Point graduate (class of 1847) with a lame hip and white whiskers. A primary function of Gibbon's column would be to guard the Yellowstone River and keep any hostile Indians from crossing north of the river and escaping, a difficult, if not impossible, task. To accomplish this, Gibbon would keep scouting patrols south of the Yellowstone in search of recalcitrants. The third column was to be commanded by the bushy-whiskered Brigadier (later Major) General George Crook (1829–1890), an ascetic, former West Point graduate (class of 1852) who commanded the Department of the Platte. Crook was to march northward from Fort Fetterman, Wyoming Territory. Crook at times was a most capable officer and Sherman mistakenly considered him the Indian-fighting

Army's best general; but he was an erratic-thinking eccentric who would prove to be the weakest link on the summer's campaign.

Crook was the first in the field, on March 1. His march was slowed by adverse weather. A blizzard struck, dumping several inches of snow and the temperature plummeted below zero. On the frigid morning of March 17, in 25 degrees below zero weather, ten cavalry troops from Crook's command struck the 105-lodge village of Northern Cheyennes and Oglalas near the Powder River in Montana. The village was mistakenly identified as that of Crazy Horse. Northern Cheyenne Chief Two Moons, by his own admission, was in this camp.[2] The attack force was commanded by the white side-whiskered, 54-year-old Brevet Major General Joseph J. Reynolds, colonel and commanding officer of the Third U.S. Cavalry and West Point graduate (class of 1843).

Surprised by the attack on their camp, the Indians at first fled, but then counterattacked Reynolds, who became somewhat befuddled. Reynolds held the abandoned village, had it torched, and gradually withdrew from the field of combat under sporadic hostile gunfire after sustaining only four dead and six wounded. John G. Bourke, then Second Lieutenant, Third Cavalry, later wrote of the Reynolds engagement on the Powder that "we practically abandoned the victory to the savages." Crook blamed the inept Reynolds, who had botched a chance for a brilliant victory. An irate Sheridan agreed, calling Reynolds's blunder "shamefully disgraceful."

After Reynolds's bitter fiasco of the seventeenth, Crook aborted his march because of a shortage of supplies, shortage of horses for his Indian scouts, lack of forage for his troop's horses, and the brutal weather; he returned to Fort Fetterman. He did not take the field again until May 29. In the meantime, Gibbon's command had left Fort Ellis on March 30 and trekked eastward. Terry's column had been delayed because of the late Dakota winter and lack of natural forage and did not leave Fort Lincoln until May 17.

While Terry waited for favorable weather, the intended vice commander of his column of troops, Brevet Major General George Armstrong "Autie" Custer,[3] lieutenant colonel, Seventh U.S. Cavalry, had committed a serious gaffe. The charismatic Custer, a West Point graduate (class of 1861), 36 years old, erstwhile "Boy General" and

14

"Beau Saber" of the Civil War Union Army, had gotten himself into "hot water" with President Ulysses S. Grant. On March 29 and April 4, Custer had blabbed gossip to a U.S. House of Representatives Committee investigating alleged improprieties of recently resigned and maligned Secretary of War William W. Belknap and the latter's alleged selling of post traderships for personal profit. Custer's gossipy testimony was accepted by the committee, which was not encumbered by the modern legalities of evidence. Despite his sincere intentions, Custer also had tied Orvil Grant, the unscrupulous younger brother of the president, to the post tradership scandal. That is, the anti-Grant New York *Herald* had published a telegram and an article (both allegedly written by Custer) besmirching the names of Orvil Grant and Secretary Belknap, respectively. The scandal-plagued Grant Administration was under heavy fire that election year. Embarrassed and angered by Custer's hearsay evidence, Grant, in a pique, ordered Custer "detained" while the Seventh Cavalry (which made up the majority of Terry's command) prepared to march against the Sioux. Grant technically had Custer detained for his failure to clear his congressional testimony with the Adjutant General as per War Department edict. Grant's animosity was understandable, since his long-shot chance for a third term as president had all but died. Grant's slim chance, for a third term, however, was doomed long before Custer's hearsay testimony by the numerous scandals in his corrupt administration. Grant was an honest man, but he was naive enough to believe that because he was honest it followed that his political appointees were burdened with the same scruples.

An eleventh-hour appeal by Custer (through Terry), endorsed by Custer's longtime mentor (since the Civil War), Sheridan, persuaded the soldier in Grant to rescind his order and allow Custer to accompany and command his regiment. Custer, as the Seventh Cavalry's lieutenant colonel since the regiment's organization in 1866, was never the official regimental commander of the Seventh Cavalry. Custer, however, was the Seventh Cavalry's vice commander and its acting commanding officer on every occasion in which the regiment took the Indian campaign trail in Custer's lifetime.

So "Custer's Luck" had carried the day! Grant's change of heart might have been due, in part, to the New York *Herald*'s scathing editorials. The *Herald,* published by Custer's friend James Gordon Bennett, Jr., in its issue of May 6, castigated Grant by accusing the president of disgracing Custer because he would not "crook the pregnate hinges of the knee to this modern Caesar." (Interestingly, neither Sheridan nor Terry seriously considered the Seventh Cavalry's 54-year-old colonel and commanding officer, Brevet Major General Samuel D. Sturgis, West Point (class of 1846), for the campaign. Sturgis's young son, Jack, served as a "shavetail"—second lieutenant—in his father's regiment.)

Terry and Custer arrived at Fort Lincoln a week before the Seventh Cavalry departed the post on May 17. The day before the Seventh marched from Lincoln, Gibbon's Crow scouts found an Indian village of 300-plus lodges eighteen miles from the mouth of Montana's Tongue River. The day of the Terry-Custer column departure, Gibbon was attempting, rather unsuccessfully, to get his command across the swollen Yellowstone. The river was a raging torrent and a frustrated Gibbon abandoned the fording after several of the command's horses had drowned.

***

Custer was eager "to cut loose and swing clear of Terry"—Custer's words to one of Terry's staff officers[4]—on the campaign since Terry was a desk soldier on his first Indian campaign. Custer's critics have used these words to support their collective claim that the glory-hunting Custer had an ego which would not allow him to share an important victory with another commander. Such thinking also has given emphasis to the shopworn myth that Custer needed a brilliant victory against the Sioux so he could capture the Democratic Party's presidential nomination for 1876.[5]

Custer had spent the winter of 1875–1876 on leave in New York City. While there, he'd spent considerable time in the company of his friend Bennett of the *Herald.* Some have assumed that Custer's friendship with the powerful and influential Bennett was for the purpose of touting Custer as a "dark horse" candidate for the Democratic ticket. To think that Custer was any kind of presidential candidate in 1876 is absurd. In a June, 1876, editorial, Bennett commended the character and presidential candidacy of U.S. Senator Thomas F. Bayard of Delaware. The Democratic National Convention was held at St. Louis on June 27–29 but a thorough check of the contemporary St. Louis newspapers before and during that convention has failed to find the slightest mention of Custer. There are those who still stubbornly cling to the notion that there was ample time for Custer to score a big victory on the twenty-fifth, send a courier to the nearest telegraph 175 miles away, and wire the St. Louis convention with the news. Those who believe this whole-cloth myth simply don't understand the campaign process of 1876. If there was any grassroots support for Custer's alleged candidacy, it should have been in the delegation of Custer's adopted home state of Michigan, where one of the prominent delegates was Frederick A. Nims. Nims had served as Custer's aide-de-camp in the Civil War and as a civilian had been with Custer on his Yellowstone River expedition in 1873. On the two ballots cast by the Michigan delegation at the nominating convention, no votes were cast for Custer. A man such as Custer, with a lifelong interest in politics—he was a professed Democrat—might have entertained the idea of high political office at some later date, but not in 1876.

2
Prelude to War
June 17–24, 1876

It had been a cold winter. Local thermometers had dropped to -50 degrees in January. But as the snow slowly melted and the spring grass grew green, the Indian tribes moved slowly westward toward Montana's Rosebud Creek. Slowly, their numbers increased with the passing days. It was mid-June, however, before the summer campaign's first major engagement occurred. Again, it was Crook's column which saw the action. The result was not what Sheridan had expected.

Crook had resupplied his command and had left Fort Fetterman on May 29. The humid morning of June 17 found Crook's more than 1,300-man column in an unsaddled rest halt astride the upper Rosebud, a sluggish, alkaline stream whose banks were dotted with clumps of wild rose bushes and numerous rattlesnakes. At 8:30 A.M., gunfire reverberated in the distance, breaking the laziness of the morning. Through a swale-broken ridge two miles north of Crook's column rode 1,000 screaming, breechclothed Sioux and Northern Cheyenne, led by the celebrated Crazy Horse. The battle was joined.

For the next four hours, the fighting was heavy, but with surprisingly few casualties. The five-company battalion of Lieutenant Colonel William B. Royall, Third Cavalry, was cut off and barely extracted itself from destruction.

At 10:30 A.M., Crook dispatched three companies of Third Cavalry, led by Captain Anson Mills, as a reconnaissance in force—i.e., a military scouting unit capable of striking any enemy it happened across—into the Rosebud's Dead Canyon, a canyon which dropped in elevation and was lined with rocky, tree-dotted bluffs, where Crook believed the Indian village was located. (The village actually was fifteen miles distant.) Crook also dispatched a five-company battalion of Second U.S. Cavalry under Captain Henry E. Noyes, a West Point classmate of G. A. Custer, into the canyon as Mills' support. Two hours later, Crook, fearing his inability to support Mills and Noyes unless he abandoned his wounded, dispatched a courier to fetch both officers and their commands from Dead Canyon.

The battle was one long, continuous maneuver and counter maneuver by each side. Despite the length of the battle and the number of rounds fired, the casualties were surprisingly light on both sides. Finally, at 2:30 P.M., after six hours of fighting, the Indians quit the field. Crook's command had fired 25,000 rounds of ammunition during the battle and had killed only 36 Indians while wounding another 63. That was an incredible 252 rounds fired per Indian casualty. Crook's reported casualties were nine cavalrymen and one Crow Indian scout killed, and one officer, six Crow, and five Shoshone Indian scouts wounded. This total did not include a Shoshone youth who was killed while herding some of the scouts' ponies. Controversy, however, clouds Crook's casualty count at the Rosebud. Some believed that Crook deliberately kept his casualty report figures low. At any rate, lack of cartridges and only four days' rations compelled Crook, again, to desert the field.

Crook always claimed that he had achieved a tactical victory on the Rosebud since he and not the enemy had held the field of combat. But one of Crook's subordinate officers later confessed that the command had "little pride in our achievement."

Sheridan called the Rosebud debacle a "victory . . . barren of results." A decade later, Crook, himself, called his fiasco on the Rosebud "a bad fight."

Crook's failure on the Rosebud had jeopardized the summer campaign and had given the Sioux a taste of victory. For the second time in as many attempts, Crook, short of provisions and cartridges, turned his backsides to the enemy and returned to his supply base at the conflux of Big and Little Goose Creeks on the site of present Sheridan, Wyoming. In gross dereliction of duty, Crook failed to inform Terry of the Rosebud fight. Terry moved on the assumption that Crook was advancing rather than withdrawing. Even as late as July 2, Terry was still "in the dark" as to Crook's operations. Later that summer, Crook again took the field against the Sioux—but much too late to help Custer.

19

1. Reno's Reconnaissance
June 10–20

While camped on the Powder River on June 10, Terry ordered a reconnaissance of the Powder to the mouth of the Little Powder River. From there, the patrol was to move (per Terry's orders) across the headwaters of Mizpah Creek, and descend that stream to its junction with the Powder. In taking this route, the reconnaissance party would cross Pumpkin Creek and the Tongue River. From there, it was to descend the Tongue to its junction with the Yellowstone and again hook up with Terry and the rest of the column.

About 3:30 P.M., after a morning of intermittent drizzle, six companies of Seventh Cavalry—half the regiment—and eight Indian scouts, plus Michel "Mitch" Boyer, a half white, half Sioux scout, assigned as the reconnaissance party, left camp. The reconnaissance was led by the Seventh's junior major and vice commander on the campaign, the 41-year-old, swarthy-complected Marcus Albert Reno, a thickset, syphilis-plagued widower and West Point graduate (class of 1857). Reno was on his first Indian campaign and had never served on a campaign under Custer since joining the regiment in 1868. While Custer was detained by his problems with Grant, Reno had pleaded with Terry to give him command of the Seventh Cavalry in the upcoming summer campaign.

"Why not give me a chance as I feel I will do credit to the Army?" Reno had asked Terry. Reno had also pleaded his case with Sheridan. "Why not give me a chance, giving me instructions what to do with Sitting Bull if I catch him?"[1]

Denied his request, Reno was determined to make the best of his opportunities on the campaign even though Custer had requested one of the regiment's senior majors in Reno's stead. Custer and Reno had known each other during the Civil War and neither had any respect for the other's ability as a soldier. A heavy drinker, Reno was tactless, rude, insensitive, and vicious. He was despised by most of his fellow officers and more than one officer in the regiment considered him "a snipping ass."

***

On June 12, Reno's reconnaissance party struck a week-old campsite of twenty-six lodges. The trail of this village suggested a westward movement. On the fourteenth, Reno's party moved to the divide which separated the Mizpah and Pumpkin creeks. From there, Reno moved down the valley of the Pumpkin. No campsites or trails were found. Shortly after dawn on the sixteenth of June, Reno's party moved eight miles down the Tongue. Reno soon faced a dilemma: continue to follow Terry's orders or disobey them and cut across to the site along Rosebud Creek where Gibbon's Crow Indian scouts had sighted a 400-plus-lodge village on May 27. Gibbon's chief of scouts, First Lieutenant James H. Bradley of the Seventh U.S. Infantry, had stated that "we had no sooner reached the summit [on May 27] than we discovered smoke on the Rosebud River [sic], and, bringing out glasses to bear upon it, found ourselves again in the vicinity of an immense Indian camp." Reno chose (as he should have) the second option. After all, the crux of Reno's reconnaissance was to obtain the latest and most accurate information on the movements of the hostiles so that Terry could formulate a workable strategy. How much input by his guide, Mitch Boyer, influenced Reno to disobey Terry's orders is speculative.

At 8:00 A.M. on the sixteenth, Reno's six companies crossed the Tongue and moved west for nineteen miles. Reno halted his reconnaissance a half hour later while Mitch Boyer,[2] a Sioux who had been detached from Gibbon's command to serve as Reno's guide, and the Arikara (Ree) Indian scouts, who had accompanied the Seventh Cavalry from Fort Lincoln, reconnoitered the valley of the Rosebud some four and one-half miles in the distance. In the valley, the scouts discovered a three-week-old campsite and a lodgepole trail of about 380 lodges. Learning of this fact, Reno decided to follow this clearly marked trail to determine how far up the valley it led, an important piece of intelligence. At 8:30 P.M., Reno began a night march, which covered eight miles. He struck east to the Rosebud about twenty-five miles above its mouth.

The next day, Reno moved several miles up the Rosebud. Several more campsites were found by Reno's party. Boyer informed Reno that the village sites were older than the trails between them. This meant that there was more than one village on the move, which indicated an enormous gathering of Indians. Had Reno moved farther down the valley, he would have learned that the trail turned southward toward the Rosebud's divide, about forty miles away. On June 18, Reno moved down the Rosebud to its mouth and then moved west along the Yellowstone, where he rendezvoused with Terry on the twentieth, after trekking 240.5 miles on the reconnaissance.

Custer, who later rejoined Reno on the Rosebud with the other half of the Seventh Cavalry, met with Terry and Reno aboard the expedition's supply steamer, the *Far West,* on the twentieth, to debrief Reno concerning his reconnaissance. Custer obviously had ambivalent feelings concerning the result of Reno's scout. He became extremely upset about what he regarded as Reno's flagrant disobedience of Terry's orders. At first, he chastised Reno for possibly alerting the Sioux to the troops' presence and again for not determining the number of Indians in his (Reno's) front, and then implied Reno's cowardice in not locating and attacking the Sioux. Custer's anger at Reno probably stemmed from his jealousy of Reno having struck a large Indian trail and his irritation at the man for having abandoned it. Custer broadly hinted at a possible court-martial for Reno. Reno had made a sincere effort to gather intelligence and resented Custer's tongue-lashing. Terry intervened before the two men came to blows. (On June 23, in the presence of other officers, Custer stated, "Here's where Reno made the mistake of his life . . . He'd made a name for himself if he'd pushed on after them. . . .")[3]

He said, "Few officers have ever had so fine an opportunity to make a successful and telling strike, and few have ever so completely failed to improve their opportunity."[4]

Company I Private Francis Johnson (born Francis J. Kennedy), who was on Reno's reconnaissance, stated that Reno wanted to push on in pursuit of the Indians, but was persuaded not to, presumably by his fellow officers on the reconnaissance (manuscript, Fred Dustin Collection, CBNM).

The question of Reno's disobedience is still hotly debated, but he *had* located the Indians—somewhere farther up the Rosebud. Crook knew as much on the seventeenth when he had been attacked by the Sioux there. Terry, on the other hand, was elated at the valuable intelligence Reno had gathered.

22

2. The *Far West* Conference
June 21

On June 21, near the mouth of the Rosebud at its confluence with the Yellowstone, Terry, Gibbon, Custer, Reno, and Major James S. "Grasshopper Jim" Brisbin, Second U.S. Cavalry, Gibbon's chin-whiskered cavalry commander, held a prebattle conference aboard the *Far West*. Meeting in the cramped conference room on the boiler deck of Captain Grant P. Marsh's wooden stern-wheeler, the officers discussed the whereabouts of the Sioux encampment. The consensus was that the Sioux probably were somewhere in Montana's valley of the Little Bighorn. While the *Far West* conference was in progress, the Indian encampment was nearly opposite the mouth of Sundance (now Reno) Creek on the west bank of the Little Bighorn. Three days later, the encampment changed locations to eight miles farther downriver. The snows of the Bighorn Mountains had melted, flooding the local streams, which made the Bighorn River nearly impassable. The Indian encampment was, therefore, approachable only from the north and east. Since Terry was emphatic that he would "not leave the infantry out of the fight," Gibbon's command, made up mostly of infantry, was assigned the northern route. To Gibbon's disappointment, Custer's Seventh Cavalry was to have the point of honor; that is, the first strike. Since Custer admitted to Terry that his regiment intended to trek thirty miles per day to reach the Little Bighorn Valley, a logistical problem existed in coordinating Gibbon's slower-paced infantry with that of Custer's cavalry. To solve this problem, according to Brisbin, Custer was to move his regiment up the Rosebud near the Wolf (or Little Chetish) Mountains, then move westward and come down the valley of the Little Bighorn to strike the Sioux village.[5]

Gibbon was to bring his column of troops within cooperating distance of Custer's anticipated scene of action by the evening of June 26 by marching to the mouth of the Bighorn River, sixty-plus miles away, ferry across the Yellowstone River to the mouth, and march south to the valley of the Little Bighorn.[6] Writing in his diary, June 20, 1876, Gibbon's supervisor of scouts, First Lieutenant Bradley, noted, "It is understood that if Custer arrives first, he is at liberty to attack at once if he deems prudent." The initial strike was left to Custer's discretion.

At the conference, Gibbon later recalled, "We . . . impressed upon

23

[Custer] that he should keep constantly feeling to his left . . . even should the trail turn toward the Little Bighorn . . . he should continue his march southward along the headwaters of the Tongue and strike westward toward the Little Big Horn. . . ."[7]

The maps which Terry used at the *Far West* conference were the 1859–1860 maps of Captain William F. Raynolds and First Lieutenant Henry E. Maynadier.[8] These maps plainly indicated topography of the region and on which the Rosebud, Little Bighorn and a major portion of the Tongue were accurately depicted, including tributaries. The Raynolds-Maynadier maps also depicted the roads of the region and compared favorably to modern mappings. The long-hidden (by the Army) Raynolds-Maynadier maps were not the falsified, missing-topographical-features maps submitted as Terry's 1876 campaign maps at the Reno Court of Inquiry in 1879. These same maps were presented in a journal article in 1896 for public view by Colonel (later Major General) Robert P. Hughes, Terry's brother-in-law and former chief of staff. Interestingly, all maps used on the Sioux campaign held by the chief engineering officers of the Departments of the Platte and Dakota were ordered returned to the Chief of Engineers in Washington, D.C., (War Department order dated November 20, 1876) to "furnish considerable material in correcting existing maps, gathered . . . during the recent operations against the Hostile Sioux Indians." The "corrected" maps show far less accurate topographical features than the older Raynolds-Maynadier maps.[9]

The conference adjourned after dark. Before it broke up, Terry informed Custer that he (Terry) would personally accompany Gibbon's command in the movement against the Sioux, which left Custer with an independent command. Custer was delighted that Terry had chosen to accompany Gibbon's column. Terry was a desk soldier (since the Civil War) on his first field campaign, cautious by nature, due in part to his legal background, and an impediment to an officer such as Custer who believed in the old cavalry tradition of "riding to the sound of the guns." Custer, however, was not to be completely free of Terry.

Terry offered Custer a platoon of three Gatling guns, which were part of Gibbon's command, but Custer declined the offer as he felt that the Seventh had enough firepower. Far too much has been made of

Custer's refusal to take the ponderous trio of .50-caliber Gatling guns, which collectively weighed 1,878 pounds and would have impeded the march. Each Gatling gun, together with its carriage and empty limber, weighed 626 pounds. A fully loaded limber with its 3,750 rounds of ammunition, spare parts, and servicing tools added even more weight to each gun. The Gatling was a hand-cranked gun with six rotating barrels which was nearly stationary and capable of firing 200 rounds per minute. A drawback of the weapon was that its upright cartridge feeder was exposed to enemy gunfire and, if struck, exploded the cartridges that were unfired in the feeder. The Gatling also was not conducive to the mobile warfare necessary to combat the Plains Indians. The weapon's major drawback was that it overheated and jammed after several continuous minutes of firing. It then required a cooling-down period of several minutes. On Reno's reconnaissance, one of the Gatling guns had overturned and injured three troopers. The reconnaissance had been delayed until the Gatling was righted and repaired. The gun also couldn't keep pace with Reno's moving column and was cached. Custer's decision in not taking the Gatling guns was a sound one.

***

Brisbin, who confessed his lack of faith in Custer to Terry, was no admirer of the erstwhile "Boy General." When Terry questioned Brisbin's confidence in Custer, the latter replied frankly, "[I have] none in the world [in him]. I have no use for him." [10] Brisbin believed Custer an "insufferable ass" [11] with little common sense. Brisbin privately asked Terry aboard the *Far West* if he would detach his (Brisbin's) four-company battalion of Second Cavalry from Gibbon's command and assign it to Custer's regiment; he also asked Terry to take personal command of Custer's troops. Brisbin believed that the large encampment of Sioux discovered by Gibbon's scouts on May 27 indicated that Custer would need as much firepower as he could muster. Terry, a reluctant field commander, declined to command Custer's column of troops, but told Brisbin, if he wished, he could ask Custer's permission to accompany the Seventh Cavalry. Brisbin did so, but Custer declined the former's offer by saying, "The Seventh can handle anything it meets." Later, Custer confided to a fellow officer that "this is to be a

25

Seventh Cavalry battle and I want all the glory for the Seventh Cavalry there is." [12] It seems that Brisbin was willing to put aside his intense dislike of Custer for a better chance of success in the campaign.

Custer certainly had his detractors. His regimental commander, General Sturgis, thought Custer selfish and that he was "insanely ambitious for glory and the phrase 'Custer's luck' [was] a good clue to his ruling passion." [13]

3. Custer Takes the Advance
June 22

While Terry did not accompany Custer's command, he did issue the following written instructions to Custer:

Camp at Mouth of Rosebud River [*sic*], although Terry thought Rosebud was a river, it was a creek;

Montana Territory
June 22, 1876
Lieutenant-Colonel Custer, 7th Cavalry.

Colonel:

The Brigadier General Commanding directs that as soon as your regiment can be made ready for the march, you will proceed up the Rosebud in pursuit of the Indians whose trail was discovered by Major Reno a few days since. It is, of course, impossible to give you any definite instructions in regard to this movement, and were it not impossible to do so the Department Commander places too much confidence in your zeal, energy and ability to wish to impose upon you precise orders which might hamper your action when nearly in contact with the enemy. He will, however, indicate to you his own views of what your action should be, and he desires that you should conform to them unless you shall see sufficient reasons for departing from them. He thinks that you should proceed up the Rosebud until you ascertain definitely the direction in which the trail above spoken leads. Should it be found (as it appears almost certain that it will be found) to turn toward the Little [Big] Horn, he thinks that you should still proceed southward, perhaps as far as the headwaters of the Tongue, and then turn towards the Little [Big] Horn, feeling constantly, however, to your left, so as to preclude the possibility of the escape of Indians to the south or southeast by passing around your left flank. The column of Colonel Gibbon is now in motion for the mouth of the Big Horn. As soon as it reaches that point it will cross the Yellowstone and move up at least as far as the forks of the Big and Little [Big] Horn. Of course its future movements must be controlled by circumstances as they arise, but it is hoped that the Indians, if upon the Little [Big] Horn, may be so nearly enclosed by the two columns that their escape will be impossible.

The Department Commander desires that on your way up the Rosebud you should thoroughly examine the upper part of Tullock's Creek and that you should endeavor to send a scout through to Colonel Gibbon's column with information of the result of your examination. The lower part of the creek will be examined by a detachment from Colonel Gibbon's command. The supply steamer, *Far West,* will be pushed up the Big Horn as far as the forks if the river is found to be navigable for that distance, and the Department Commander, who will accompany the column of Colonel Gibbon, desires you to report to him there not later than the expiration of the time for which your troops are rationed [15 days but the soldiers packed only twelve days' supply of bacon], unless in the meantime you receive further orders.

> *Very respectfully, your obedient servant,*
> *E. W. Smith,*
> *Captain Eighteenth Infantry,*
> *Acting Assistant Adjutant General*

Prior to leaving the stern-wheeler *Far West,* or Custer's tent in the early morning hours of June 22, Terry was overheard by Custer's black cook, Mary Adams—a preponderance of evidence supports Mary's presence on the campaign—telling Custer, "Use your own judgment and do what you think best . . . and whatever you do, Custer, hold onto your wounded." [14] This latter statement makes the century-plus-long debate over whether or not Custer disobeyed Terry's written orders a moot point. Terry had given Custer his head.

Much also has been made of a proposed three-pronged attack against the Indians by the commands of Terry, Crook, and Gibbon to trap them somewhere among the three. This was utter nonsense as far as reality was concerned. Crook's command was out first and fought the Indians in March. The second time Crook's command went out, it never coordinated anything with the other two commands. Nor did Crook try to do so. Judging from the *Far West* conference, Custer was to strike the Sioux first with Gibbon functioning in support.

***

Shortly before noon, the Seventh Cavalry's German-born Chief Trumpeter Henry Voss sounded "Boots and Saddles," and several minutes later the regiment began its march. The column, consisting of

581 enlisted men—136 of whom were recent recruits (those who had joined the regiment a year or less prior to the battle) and only one of whom claimed prior military service; 29 officers (including an attached infantry officer and one surgical officer); 33 full-blooded Indian scouts; 17–22 (depending on the number of civilian packers accompanying the regiment) attached civilian personnel (including two civilian surgeons contracted by the Army—acting assistant surgeons by title); and two private citizens marched en masse toward the mouth of the Rosebud. Each enlisted man carried 100 rounds for his single-shot .45-55 Springfield carbine (Model 1873)—the so-called "Trapdoor" Springfield—and 24 rounds for his breechloading single-action .45 Colt revolver (Model 1873). (The .45–55 designation meant that it used a .45-caliber carbine cartridge fixed with 55 grains of dense musket black powder.) One first sergeant carried a Sharps rifle. Officers, some scouts, and civilians carried various weapons and additional cartridges. Except for two foreign-born officers, the regiment marched saberless.[15] Each horse carried thirteen pounds of oats. Additional oats were carried on the pack mules.

First Lieutenant (later Brigadier General) Edward S. Godfrey, the 32-year-old, enormously mustachioed acting commanding officer of the white canvass-trousered Company K, watched some of the 175 mules toting supplies, spare cartridges (packed by twelve of the mules), and equipment break formation and throw their loosely tied sacks before the regiment was even out of camp. (The carelessness of the packers in securing the packs later had a profound effect on the fate of the regiment.) This was the only black mark, Godfrey thought, as the proud Seventh paraded past the reviewing generals, Terry, Gibbon, and Custer. Godfrey was particularly irritated at the condition of the 90-odd mules which had been on Reno's reconnaissance. "[These mules] were badly used up," Godfrey later wrote, "and promised to seriously embarrass the expedition." Godfrey was one of only two West Point graduates (class of 1867) among the regiment's first lieutenants who were on duty on the campaign.

Reno had his mind on horseflesh as the regiment marched away. The major noted to himself that the "horses of the regiment were in the best of condition." Some troopers had to ride mules because of the shortage of available, serviceable cavalry mounts. Private Dennis

Lynch, Company F, was left aboard the *Far West* with Custer's luggage so scout George B. Herendeen could ride his horse.

The long column of soldiers, riding with the rattle and clink of a cavalry on the move, and the pack mules plodded slowly from the camp. The hooves of the animals kicked up clods of sodden turf soaked from the previous day's violent hail and rain storm. The temperature had fallen and the afternoon had turned cold and windy.

Terry sat stiffbacked in his saddle—even a little saddle time made his gouty hip ache—and crisply returned the salute of each passing officer. Godfrey recalled that the good-natured Terry had a pleasant word for each officer as he returned the salute. Finally, Custer took leave of Terry and Gibbon, and spurred his mount after his troops.

"Now, don't be greedy, Custer. Save some Indians for us," Gibbon shouted in a half joke.

"No, I will not!" Custer called as he galloped away.

***

The regiment trekked to the narrow, shallow-depth mouth of the Rosebud. At this site, Custer briefly halted and had his men regirt their horses. Crossing to the left bank of the stream, the regiment pushed ten saddle-weary miles up the valley of the Rosebud. In the movement, the column trekked through deep ravines and across hills spotted with sparse grass, prickly pear cacti, and sagebrush. Camp was made for the day at 4:00 P.M. in a verdant valley of lush grass and numerous cottonwood trees.

Day's March: 12 miles in 4:03:30

The regiment ungirted and Custer held "Officers' Call," briefly outlining his orders to his officers, who had gathered around the general's headquarters tent: trumpet calls were suspended except in emergency; the day's march would begin each morning at five o'clock; troop commanders were responsible for their respective companies and everything, except when to strike the camp and where to halt for the day, was to be left to their discretion; initially, the marches would be short and then gradually increase in distance; the present day's march probably would be the shortest as General Terry had been informed that he (Custer) intended to march thirty miles per day; and that he (Custer) intended to follow the

29

hostiles all the way to their reservations, if necessary. He informed his officers that he had declined Terry's offer of four companies (two squadrons) of Second Cavalry and the trio of Gatling guns because he believed that the Seventh Cavalry was more than enough to handle the Sioux and that the Gatlings would only slow down the regiment. Before the council ended, Custer offered to entertain any suggestions, even from the newest "shavetail." Then Custer dropped "a bombshell" on his officers: he admitted that he was angry because some of the regimental captains had been openly critical on the march.

Forty-one-year-old Captain Frederick William Benteen, the regiment's clean-shaven senior captain and the commanding officer of Company H, looking somewhat older with his lion's mane of long, white, wavy hair, was a self-proclaimed Custer hater (and proud of it) since joining the regiment in 1866. But then, the dark-sided, moody Benteen, a petty, jealous man by nature who was plagued by periodic bouts of drunkenness, liked few of his fellow officers. Benteen's dark moods, in part, might have stemmed from the tragic fact that he and his wife had lost four children in their infancy to spinal meningitis. Benteen, himself, suffered a curved spine. (Judging from the penises he drew on his letters to his wife, Benteen also suffered from an overactive libido.) While Benteen shared Reno's attitude toward Custer, the senior captain's dislike of Reno precluded their friendship—or a dark alliance against Custer. Still, Benteen was a competent and able officer and he was the only officer of the Seventh Cavalry on the campaign with a brevet (a colonelcy) for Indian fighting.

Benteen felt a personal indictment at Custer's stinging remarks about the regiment's disgruntled captains and asked Custer to specifically name the offending officers. Custer replied that his remarks were not personally directed to Benteen as he had not heard the senior captain utter any derogatory remarks on the campaign. But, "I want the saddle to go where it fits," Custer told Benteen. Custer undoubtedly was placating Benteen, an adversary who often was critical of Custer. Custer could not help but remember that a letter of Benteen's, which had found its way to the newspapers, had criticized Custer for the Washita fight (1868) and falsely accused Custer of abandoning Major Joel H. Elliott, Benteen's friend, to his death. While in camp on the night of June 20, Benteen had recalled his lack of support in the

30

Washita fight, in front of several officers. Custer was present and resented Benteen's remark. He goaded Benteen about his killing of a Cheyenne boy (actually a 21-year-old warrior) at the Washita. Benteen became chafed at Custer's remark.

***

The officers' council had ended on a somber note. Some of the officers felt that Custer seemed less elated than usual on the eve of a major campaign. Godfrey, Canadian-born First Lieutenant Donald McIntosh, a 37-year-old half-Indian of the Six Nations who was the acting commanding officer of Company G, and Second Lieutenant George D. "Nick" Wallace, only a week from his twenty-seventh birthday, walked together after the conference toward their tents. Wallace, a West Point graduate (class of 1872) who had been detached from G Company to keep the official itinerary of Custer's march, saw ill omens everywhere.

"Godfrey, Custer is going to be killed on this trip," Wallace remarked.

When Godfrey asked the superstitious Wallace why he thought so, Wallace replied, "Because I have never heard Custer talk in that way before. He acts, talks and looks like it. Mark my words; he will be killed."

Godfrey pooh-poohed the thought.[16] But when Godfrey reached the area where the Indian scouts were bivouacked, he was confronted by Mitch Boyer, the 39-year-old offspring of a French father and a Santee Sioux mother and one-time protégé of the legendary fur trapper and mountain man Jim Bridger. Boyer's face and features were that of an Indian, although he dressed as a white man. The multilingual Boyer—he was married to a Crow Indian woman—had been detached from Gibbon's command with six Crow scouts to serve Custer. He spoke to Godfrey in deliberate English (as was his custom when speaking to a white man).

"Have you ever fought the Sioux [Lakota]?"

A somewhat startled Godfrey replied, "Yes."

"Well," Boyer continued, "how many do you expect to find?"

"It is said we may find between 1,000 to 1,500," Godfrey replied. Choosing his words carefully and looking straight at Godfrey with

31

his dark eyes, Boyer said, "Well, I can tell you we are going to have a goddamn big fight."[17]

But not everyone in camp was as pessimistic as the dour-faced Boyer. After Custer's council, Reno and several other officers gathered and sang songs for an hour. And at least one person even felt that the regiment was on a wild goose chase for the summer. Dr. James M. DeWolf, a 33-year-old Harvard Medical School graduate and one of the two acting assistant surgeons with Custer's command—he had been on Reno's reconnaissance—had penned his wife only the previous night, "I think it is very clear that we shall not see an Indian this summer . . . it is believed that the Indians have scattered and gone back to their reservations."[18]

Even as DeWolf penned these lines, the Sioux were camped in great numbers on the west bank of the Greasy Grass (Little Bighorn), a few days' march away.

4. Hard Day's March
June 23

The camp came alive at 3:00 A.M. and a hard march up the Rosebud began at 5:00 A.M. The morning sun brought clear skies and extremely warm temperatures. The extreme heat became more intense throughout the day, and together with the rugged terrain, the men and horses of Custer's command suffered terribly. The regiment plodded through deep ravines lined with sparse grass and up steep, rocky, tree-dotted hills. Thirty-year-old assistant surgeon (First Lieutenant) George E. Lord, the frail, bespectacled—he wore pince-nez which hid deep-set eyes—acting regimental surgeon and a former Massachusetts high school principal, felt terribly ill and weak from exhaustion. Lord halted along the trail and rested after receiving Custer's permission to fall behind the column of troops. The gaunt surgeon hadn't the physical constitution for such rigorous marching. Custer even had offered to relieve Lord of his medical duties, but the proud surgeon declined the kind offer.

During the day—perhaps it was on the twenty-fourth; Godfrey could not recall—Godfrey and others thought they had seen rising smoke in the direction of Tullock's Creek. They informed Custer, but he dismissed it because the scouts had not reported any signs in that direction.

Five times during the first three miles of the march the regiment crossed and recrossed the gravel-bottomed Rosebud, crossing for the fifth time to the stream's right bank. A halt was made at the ten-mile point to allow the slow-moving pack mules to close the gap between them and the main column. The regiment then recrossed to the Rosebud's left bank and moved fifteen miles farther up the stream. The terrain the regiment passed was broken, low-lying hills clustered with juniper trees and rugged buttes, all hued in soils of pink, red, and yellow. Three old Indian campsites were passed along the route, including one which Reno had discovered on his reconnaissance. The area around each campsite was strewn with bleached bones and strips of bison (buffalo) hides and was nearly denuded of grass, a sign that a large pony herd had grazed at each site recently. Godfrey later wrote, "Everybody was busy studying the age of [the] pony droppings and tracks and lodge trails, and endeavoring to determine the number lodges."

A final halt for the day was made at 4:30 P.M. on the right bank (after still another crossing) of the Rosebud. The last of the pack mules, however, had not yet caught up. Although the water was brackish, there was plenty of grass for grazing the command's livestock. It was nearly sunset before Benteen and three companies escorted the last of the pack mules into camp. Benteen fished the Rosebud for his supper, caught nothing, and begrudgingly settled for a repast of "sonofabitch stew" (which might contain anything and everything edible that was available to a company cook) and a bedtime pipe.

An hour after sundown, a frantic Dr. Lord galloped his well-lathered mount into camp. The surgeon was surprised to learn that he had not been farther back on the trail than he thought. Weak and exhausted, Lord declined nourishment except for a cup of tea before he collapsed in his bedroll. After sundown, Custer's six Crow scouts were sent out on a night reconnaissance.

Day's March: 33 miles in 11:30:00

On the night of the twenty-third, the Sioux and their Cheyenne allies were camped near the mouth of Sundance (Reno) Creek—also called Ash Creek by the Crows—on the west bank of the Little Bighorn River. On the twenty-fourth, they moved their villages eight miles down the Greasy

Grass (what the Sioux called Little Bighorn). Custer's scouts had not detected the presence of the Cheyenne who were then in the Sioux camp. But even without the Cheyenne, the Seventh Cavalry was marching against what often has been described as the largest encampment of hostile Indians ever assembled on the North American continent in the post–Civil War West.

3
Following the War Trail
June 24

The Seventh Cavalry was up and marching at 5:00 A.M. Custer's June 23 campsite had been slightly south by due west of the headwaters of Tullock's Creek, so before marching too far, Custer told George Herendeen, a 29-year-old Montana resident, that he and scout Charles A. "Lonesome Charley" Reynolds should ready themselves for a reconnaissance of the upper Tullock's as per Terry's orders. Herendeen had been detached from Gibbon's command for the specific purpose of reconnoitering the Tullock's, for which he was to be paid an additional $200 to his regular pay.

Herendeen later recalled, "I told the General it was not time yet as we were traveling in the direction of the head of Tullock's and I could only follow his trail [until then]."

Boyer, at Herendeen's asking, reinforced the latter's statement: "Yes, farther up on the Rosebud we'll come opposite a gap; then we can cut across and strike the Tullock's in about a fifteen-mile ride." [1]

"All right. I could wait," Custer replied.

By the time the regiment neared the cutoff to Tullock's Creek, Custer would be on a fresh trail that had been trekked by enough Indians to occupy his entire command for two days. At that point, scouting the Tullock's for Indians would have been redundant. Custer said as much to Herendeen at the time. "The time for getting [the Tullock's] information to Terry in time to be acted on is too late." [2]

After an hour's hard ride, the column met four of the Crow scouts returning from their night reconnaissance. The Crows reported a fresh trail of pony tracks which became fresher ten miles ahead somewhere in the vicinity of the mouth of present Lame Deer Creek. The troop was halted and Custer held a brief officers' meeting. A short time later, Custer led two companies out at a trot, leaving the remainder of the command to follow at a half-mile interval. As the morning sun climbed higher in the sky, gray cloudlets of mist hung over the valley, convincing Second Lieutenant (later Brigadier General) Winfield S. Edgerly, who strained his squinting eyes at the distant horizon, that he was seeing the smoke fires of the Indians. Edgerly was a handsome 30-year-old West Point graduate (class of 1870) with a lion's mane of wavy hair. (During World War I, Edgerly was recalled to, and commanded, a mobilization camp.) Interestingly, Edgerly later served as the Seventh Cavalry's lieutenant colonel, from 1901 to 1903—Custer's rank and position, the only Little Bighorn officer to hold such distinction.

The valley was heavily marked with lodgepole trails and pony tracks. Dung littered the trail. The regiment passed several abandoned campsites of similar size along the trail. Godfrey recalled that one of the campsites was larger than the others "where the grass for a considerable distance around it had been cropped close, indicating that large herds had been grazed there." Godfrey also noted that "they were the continuous camps of several bands" which were "of nearly the same age." A halt was made at one campsite which contained the remnants of a few lodges, including a Sundance lodge. (From June 6 to 11, the Sioux had held the sacred Sundance at this site.) The sacred Sundance (or sun-gazing-dance)—*wiwanyag wachipi* (in the Lakota tongue) was the predominant religious ceremony among the North American Plains Indians. Its functional justification varied from tribe to tribe. The ceremony began with an individual's vision (or vow) of a personal sacrifice for the good of his people. A shaman managed the ordeal in which the principal dancer—the one of the vision or vow— had his skin cut and skewers passed through his chest and attached to a center pole by leather thongs. He then pulled and tugged until he passed into unconsciousness or the thongs tore loose from his flesh. Other members of the tribe danced with the principal dancer. All abstained from food and water during the sacred four-day ordeal.

A fresh scalp of a white man dangled from the Sundance lodgepole. Custer's friendly Sioux scouts discovered pictographs drawn in the dust inside two of the lodges. The scouts interpreted these as meaning the Sioux knew of the soldiers' presence and that their medicine was strong enough to defeat the bluecoats.

Sergeant Robert H. Hughes, K Company, a goateed, Irish-born veteran of Custer's 1868 Washita campaign and who carried the colors, stuck the staff of the flag in the ground near the Sundance lodge. A strong swirl of breeze blew the flag to the ground with its staff pointing to the rear of the column of troops. Godfrey picked up the flag and stuck its staff back into the ground. Again, the colors fell, and again its staff pointed to the rear of the troops. Godfrey then stuck the staff in the ground where it had the support of a clump of sagebrush, Nick Wallace, as superstitious as ever, witnessed the flag-falling incident and remarked that it was an ill omen for Custer.

***

The command splashed across two flowing tributaries of the Rosebud (Lame Deer and Muddy creeks), the first running streams encountered since leaving the camp at the mouth of the Rosebud, and some of the troopers had difficulty spurring their thirsty mounts through the waters. At the mouth of Muddy Creek, Godfrey noticed that a travois trail veered to the left of the main trail and cut up a dry channel of the creek. Both Godfrey and Herendeen reported the presence of this second trail to Custer. The General became peeved at Second Lieutenant Charles A. Varnum, who had been detached from Company A to serve as Custer's supervisor of scouts, for not reconnoitering this second trail. Varnum, a large-nosed, prematurely balding officer—the Arikara (Ree) Indian scouts called him "Peaked-Face"—had graduated from West Point (where he had roomed with Wallace) in 1872 and had just celebrated his twenty-seventh birthday only three days before. Prior to entering the United States Military Academy, Varnum had entertained a career in the U.S. Navy, where he served briefly as a paymaster clerk from August 18, 1866, to March 31, 1867. (Dying in 1936, Varnum survived all officers present at the Little Bighorn after being on retired officer's duty for the Army as late as 1918–1919.)

Custer, after Varnum's long scout, was willing to send out another officer in charge of a night reconnaissance to the divide, but proud Varnum would have none of it. "The General knew damn well I'd go," Varnum later recalled. Tired and hungry, Varnum halted long enough to secure a fresh mount, and with a detail of Arikaras, rode ten miles back to where the travois trail cut from the main trail. Varnum and his party reconnoitered the east Muddy Creek trail far enough to see that it eventually swung back onto the main trail.

The regiment made a second halt at 1:00 P.M. at a deserted camp-site to await Varnum's reconnaissance. The men of the Seventh brewed coffee and engaged in soldier talk. It was a long wait. Three hours later, Varnum and his party returned and Varnum reported to Custer that the travois trail was only a tangential one, although he told Custer that he was impressed with the immensity of the trail. Later that evening, Custer detached Second Lieutenant Luther R. Hare, the clean-shaven, stoic-faced, 24-year-old junior officer of K Company and 1874 West Point graduate, as Varnum's assistant. Hare's detachment left Godfrey as the only officer on duty with K Company. Companies B, C, G, and (later) M also had only one officer per each company on duty. (Hare was the third officer present at the Little Bighorn who saw—albeit it as a retired officer—some kind of military service during World War I: teaching military science in 1918–1919 at a Texas college.)

At 5:00 P.M., the column resumed its march toward the forks of the Rosebud where the scouts reported a fresh campsite. During the march, the regiment crossed an Indian trail running from the south. The trail was a mile wide, a telltale sign that the command was trekking after an enormous group of Indians. The troops passed several abandoned campsites. Judging from the moistness of the trail droppings, the Indians were no more than thirty to thirty-five miles to the front.

At 7:45 P.M. a third halt was made, near a scattering of ash and elder trees on the south bank of the Rosebud near the site of the present town of Busby, Montana. At least three of the Crow scouts, White-Man-Runs-Him, Goes Ahead, and Hairy Moccasin, now were sent ahead to reconnoiter. The three Crows followed the hostile trail until it crossed the divide into the valley of the Little Bighorn. They returned about nine o'clock that night and reported their findings to Custer. In the meantime, Frederic F. Gerard, who was accompanying the regiment as the official interpreter for the Rees, told Custer, upon the latter's inquiry, that his regiment would have to fight upward of 2,000 Indians. (Thirty-three years later, Gerard upped this figure to 4,000 for Walter M. Camp and came to believe in retrospect that the regiment was going to face that many warriors even before it had left Fort Lincoln.)

At 9:30 P.M., Custer sounded Officers' Call and then issued orders for a night march beginning at eleven o'clock. By now, Custer had decided to move the regiment across the Wolf (Little Chetish) Mountains—actually only rugged, elevated terrain—which straddled the divide, in pursuit of the hostiles. Custer also had been informed by the Crows of a good observation point a few miles south of the divide between the valleys of the Rosebud and the Little Bighorn.

A half hour before the Officers' Call, Custer had dispatched Varnum (who had eagerly volunteered for the assignment despite his lack of sleep) and a detachment of scouts to reconnoiter the Crows' lookout point. Varnum's detail consisted of: Charley Reynolds, known to the Arikara scouts as "Lucky Man," a 34-year-old, shy, taciturn man who had been in the West since 1859; Michel "Mitch" Boyer; six Arikaras, Bull, Black Fox, Strikes-the-Lodge, and Forked Horn; and five of the six Crow scouts, White Swan, White-Man-Runs-Him, Goes Ahead, Hairy Moccasin, and Curley.

One of the Crows, Paints-His-Face-Half-Yellow, was left behind to guide the regiment's night march over the unfamiliar terrain.

Reynolds was suffering from an abscess on his hand. It had been lanced to relieve the pain. Reynolds was emotionally shaken by a premonition of his own death on the campaign and had given away his personal effects before riding out with Varnum's scouting detail. Twice, without success, Reynolds had asked General Terry to relieve him of his duties, so strong was his premonition. Captain Grant Marsh, skipper of the *Far West,* had offered Reynolds the shelter of his boat, but the scout had indicated that he didn't want to miss the action for the proverbial world. Reynolds's only solace was an occasional drink of whiskey to bolster his faltering courage. There were those who wondered whether Reynolds would have any sand left in his craw when the time came.

***

Custer's tentative plan, as outlined to his officers, was to move the regiment across the divide where they would conceal their presence in the Little Bighorn valley throughout the twenty-fifth while his scouts checked out the hostile encampment. They would attack at dawn on the twenty-sixth.[3] This strategy had worked successfully at the Washita eight years before; it was not the judgment of a rash mind.

While the Seventh Cavalry made preparation for its night march, 43-year-old, side-whiskered Mark H. Kellogg, the bespectacled, Canadian-born "stringer" of the Bismarck (Dakota Territory) *Tribune* and St. Paul (Minnesota) *Pioneer,* feverishly wrote by a dim light past midnight on what proved to be his last known dispatch. Penning a last line, Kellogg prophetically wrote, "I go with Custer and will be at the death."[4] Clement A. Lounsberry, the 33-year-old editor and publisher of the Bismarck *Tribune*, later wrote that Kellogg was a last-hour replacement for him [Lounsberry] on the campaign. There is some doubt that a permanently lame Lounsberry, a man with a family and with pressing business and editorial concerns, was in a position to be away from Bismarck all summer on an Indian campaign.[5] Kellogg was Lounsberry's editorial assistance.

The regiment, once saddled, began its march across a muddy stream a half hour late at 11:30 P.M. The moonless night made the crossing slow and difficult. The stream first was crossed by eleven companies of the regiment. On the opposite bank, they halted to wait for the pack mules to trudge across with the assistance of the twelfth Company. The unenviable task of coaxing the unruly pack mules across the mud-caked creek fell to Company I and its 34-year-old Captain Myles Walter Keogh, a handsome, goateed, Irish-born soldier of fortune. It took the heavy-drinking Keogh, amid every Irish oath repeated several times, and his troop more than an hour to prod the last of the stubborn mules across the stream. Wallace, the itinerary officer, noted that it was nearly 1:00 A.M. before the regiment finally got under way.

There are those who have written that Custer pushed his regiment at such a punishing pace that he exhausted the horses of his command; but the slowpoking pack mules somehow managed to keep pace with the rest of the regiment.

Day's March: 28 miles in 10:45:00

4
Journey Into Battle
June 25

The march of the Seventh Cavalry was a tedious one because of the moonless night and the heavy dust raised by the column, so that the troopers could not see their hands in front of their faces. The Italian-born Private Augustus L. DeVoto of Company B wrote historian Walter Mason Camp in 1917 (Camp Papers—CBNM) how he was able to grope his way through the darkness. There was a mule in front of him, with some camp equipment strapped on its pack saddle. "I followed the noise made by the kettles hitting against the saddles," DeVoto recalled. Half-Yellow-Face guided the column through the darkness.

A controversy continues as to which route the command took to the divide—Davis Creek or Thompson's Creek; the latter stream was 2.5 miles south of Davis Creek. Davis Creek is the more probable route used, for several reasons: its proximity to the divide; it was a less rugged trail than Thompson's; a hat lost by "chief scout" Varnum was found by Half-Yellow-Face on Davis Creek trail, which he later returned to Varnum; the Indian trail followed Davis Creek; and Dr. Norman V. Lincoln, M.D., has found U.S. Cavalry artifacts in the Davis Creek Valley. (Lincoln, talk, June 25, 1991, at Sheridan, Wyoming.)

Custer called a halt at 2:00 A.M. in a hollow a short distance east of the divide to await news from Varnum's scouting detail. Up to this point, the regiment had marched about eight miles, as estimated by Lieutenant Wallace, the itinerary officer. The site where the halt was made was poor and the nearby water had a strong brackish taste of alkaline.

Reno, Benteen, and Second Lieutenant Benjamin H. "Benny" Hodgson, the regimental favorite and 1870 West Point graduate who had been detached from Company B to serve as Reno's acting assistant adjutant general, took advantage of the halt to wolf down an early

41

breakfast of fat bacon, hardtack, and brackish-tasting coffee. Frederic Gerard, the interpreter for the Ree scouts, for one, was too exhausted to eat. The 46-year-old, bearded Gerard slipped bone-weary from his saddle, lay down, and instantly fell into sleep. Gerard, an ex-trader, had been in the upper Missouri River country since 1848 and had married a Ree woman. Despite his extensive service to the Army, Gerard, surprisingly, was on his first field campaign.

Sometime during the early morning, Herendeen, anxious to earn his additional $200, approached Custer about scouting Tullock's Creek. It was at this time that Custer told Herendeen that it was now too late to get information to Terry.[1]

The Crow's Nest

About 2:30 A.M., Varnum's scouting party had reached a juniper tree–dotted promontory called the Crow's Nest east of the divide of the valleys of the Rosebud and Little Bighorn on the south side of Davis Creek about eight miles in front of the regiment. Varnum's route to the Crow's Nest had been up the right bank of Davis Creek and across and up this stream to a line of broken hills to the lookout point.[2] This promontory was a marked elevation on the western side of the Wolf Mountains. These "mountains" actually were rutted terrain marked by Juniper tree–dotted, deep, narrow gullies and ravines. The Crows traditionally had used this particular promontory as a lookout point.

The Crow's Nest was not the highest promontory in the proximity of the divide, but it offered an unobstructed view of the valley of the Little Bighorn (Greasy Grass) without blockage from the intervening ridges and trees. The promontory was located approximately one-half mile or less east of the divide's summit near the present divide marker. The Crows' observation point actually was well below the crest of the peak. Here the scouts waited for the faint grayness of dawn to break over the valley. In the meantime, an exhausted and hatless Varnum, now without sleep for nearly twenty-four hours, dropped to the ground, and went to sleep. The others also lay down until first light.

***

As a dull, yellow glow rose on the eastern horizon about 4:30 A.M., and the valley gradually opened clear and bright, the Crow scouts climbed to the lookout point where they viewed many tepee tops and an enormous pony herd grazing on the brown-hued flats across the serpentine Little Bighorn River. White-Man-Runs-Him even distinguished some white horses in the Sioux herd. Hairy Moccasin saw the bleached skin lodges of the village where faint wisps of smoke curled skyward. On the brown-hued hills beyond the village, Hairy Moccasin also saw hundreds of Indian horses. Boyer awakened Varnum and told him that the village had been sighted. Rubbing the sleep from his eyes, Varnum strained to see the encampment. Varnum's tired and irritated eyes (from the alkaline trail dust) saw nothing save for two deserted tepees standing on the north side of Sundance (Reno) Creek some distance from the Crow's Nest. Even with the aid of a spyglass given him by the Crow scouts, Varnum saw no village. Intervening, ash-gray bluffs rising above green cottonwoods along the Little Bighorn blocked Varnum's view of the camp. The two tepees seen by Varnum were eight miles down the north bank of Reno Creek opposite some white-hued buttes.

Reynolds strained his eyes through field glasses, but he, too, failed to see any village. The Crows insisted that the large, dark blanket on the low, grassy slopes and benchland on the west side of the Little Bighorn was the grazing Sioux pony herd. Boyer's faith in the eyesight of his wife's people was unshakable. Look for "crawling worms," Boyer told Varnum, because horses resemble worms from great distances. The village lay 14.5 miles (as the crow flies) in the distance. Three miles beyond the river, lay the Indian encampment. White-Man-Runs-Him hopelessly tried to show Varnum that the white-colored objects on some hills beyond the river were grazing horses. The Ree scout Red Star, then only twenty-one years old, pointed out a wisp of smoke curling in the valley. Again, Varnum saw nothing. A long line of bluffs hugged the east bank of the river and blocked sight of the village. At the east end of the valley, the river serpentined through thick groves of cottonwoods.

Far down the valley of the Greasy Grass, sitting 200 feet above the river on a plateau rising in the west, sat what has been called the largest encampment of hostile Indians ever gathered at one time on the North American continent (which may or may not be true). The subtribes assembled of the Teton (Plains) Sioux were the Oglala, the

Hunkpapa, Miniconjou, Blackfoot, Brulé, Sans Arc, and Two Kettle. Also present were the Santee (or Eastern) Sioux and the Yankton Sioux. With them were the Northern Cheyenne and a handful of Arapaho. The encampment, which had been in this location since June 23, stretched for more than two and one-half miles down the river. At the south end of the village stretched flat, open bottomland broken by sloughs.

The total strength of the Indian encampment at the Little Bighorn is one of the most baffling aspects of the battle. Many historians claim upward of 10,000 Indians in the village, of which about 3,000 to 3,500 were of warrior age. Agencies reported an inflated 35,800 Sioux population in 1875 compared to the reliable 1890 census which placed the total Sioux population at only 15,010. Since the Sioux wars had been over since 1877, that meant nearly 21,000 Sioux had been killed or had died off during the intervening thirteen years if the 1875 figure is accepted! Since no accurate census of the Indian village ever existed, each historian has his own estimation. The numbers in the accompanying table have been arrived at from Indian agency records, minus their inflations based on the 1890 census; the painstaking research of Dr. Charles A. Eastman, a three quarters-blooded Sioux physician who served his people; and the memory of the Cheyenne warrior Wooden Leg. My figure for the total number of people in the entire Indian encampment is near the 6,000 figure which Nicholas Ruleau, an interpreter for the Sioux who knew and talked with several of the Sioux participants over the years, gave to Judge Eli S. Ricker, an amateur Indian wars historian, in a 1906 interview.[3]

The fighting strength of the encampment (warriors at age 16 to 38) was somewhat more than Custer had expected (1,500), but considerably less than the number generally said to have been present (3,000–4,000) by some survivors of the regiment who grossly exaggerated the Indian numbers.

Except for the five Arapaho warriors, which were all of the Arapahos known to be present, five persons arbitrarily were figured to a lodge with an arbitrary multiplier of 1.5 warriors to a lodge.

***

At about 5:00 A.M.[4] (according to Varnum's recall) Ree scouts Red

TABLE I
NUMBER OF INDIANS

Tribe	Lodges	People	Warriors (ages 17–38)
Sioux (Lakota)			
Teton Division of subtribes			
Oglala	240	1,200	360
Hunkpapa	224	1,120	336
Miniconjou	190	950	285
Blackfoot	140	700	210
Brulé	140	700	210
Sans Arc	85	425	128
Two Kettle	18	90	27
Santee Division	15	75	23
Yankton Division	10	50	15
Subtotal:	1,062	5,310	1,594
Cheyenne			
Northern	91	455	137[*]
Southern	22	110	33
Subtotal:	113	565	170
Arapaho	1	5	5
Total:	1,176	5,880	1,769

[*] This total included one Ute warrior who lived with the Northern Cheyenne.

Star and the 19-year-old Bull were sent to Custer with a message that the Indian village had been sighted by the scouts. The two scouts rode back on the trail as streaks of flaming light from a just-gleaming orb broke over the valley. Bull was poorly mounted and he soon fell behind Red Star and would not arrive at Custer's camp until sometime after Red Star.

After the departure of Red Star and Bull, those at the Crow's Nest saw six mounted warriors a mile and a half to the west. Varnum also saw an Indian leading a pony with a lariat, followed by a mounted Indian boy. Varnum, Reynolds, Boyer, and two of the Crows started after the pair, but soon became lost in an entanglement of intersecting ravines. After a time, Varnum's party heard the calls of Crow Indians coming from a nearby hill. The two Crows with Varnum answered the calls. Soon reunited, the entire scouting party returned to the Crow's Nest. Later in the morning, Varnum saw seven mounted warriors riding along the crest of a ridge north of the divide and parallel to Custer's advance. These Indians were nearly two miles away. Two of these Indians were sighted galloping down a dry coulee. These two Indians were the Sans Arc father and son, Brown Back and Deeds. The other five Indians were seen disappearing into some timber at the base of a hill. Varnum feared that these Indians knew of the presence of the troops and he informed Custer of that when the general later arrived at the Crow's Nest.

***

At the point near the divide where the regiment had halted, Bloody Knife, a half-Ree and half-Hunkpapa Sioux who had been in government service since 1868, and Custer's great favorite, had become irritable and apprehensive about the growing number of Indians in the command's front. Bloody Knife approached Custer with much reluctance and told Son-of-the-Morning-Star (the name the Crows called Custer) that his soldiers would meet enough Sioux to keep them busy for two or three suns. The 36-year-old Bloody Knife, his raven hair already streaked with gray, spoke through the interpreter Gerard. Bloody Knife chose his words carefully and hoped that Son-of-the-Morning-Star would not think that Bloody Knife's heart was that of a woman's. Son-of-the-Morning-Star had befriended Bloody Knife and had given him a blue bandanna dotted with huge white stars which he proudly wore around his forehead as proof that he was Son-of-the-Morning-Star's favorite Indian. This morning, Bloody Knife had not nipped at the white man's whiskey, of which he had become inordinately fond. It was Bloody Knife's one failing in his long association with the white man. But a Ree warrior had no need for false courage, and if he spoke from the heart without the smell of the white man's liquor on his breath, Son-of-the-Morning-Star could not misjudge his true meaning. Bloody Knife told Custer that there were more Sioux in the regiment's front than there were cartridges in the belts of his soldiers.

When Bloody Knife had finished speaking, Custer asked Gerard, "What's that? What's that he says?" The squawman gave Custer an honest interpretation of Bloody Knife's words. Custer replied, "I guess we can get through with them in one day."[5] Bloody Knife now felt a great sadness in his heart.

***

Red Star brought in his dispatch about 7:30 A.M. and an hour and a quarter later the regiment was back in the saddle and marching up the left side of the Rosebud. At Custer's orders, issued previously and on the contingency of having sighted the Indian camp, First Lieutenant William Winer Cooke, the 30-year-old, thinning-haired, Canadian-born regimental adjutant, magnificently bewhiskered in the style of Lord Dundreary, galloped back on the trail and ordered the civilian packers to march the pack mules off the main trail to avoid raising too much dust. This would lessen the chance of the mass of swirling dust clouds kicked up by the column of troops alerting the village of the regiment's presence. Cooke, a brevet lieutenant colonel, perhaps the regiment's most intelligent officer, had a doglike loyalty to his close friend Custer and was affectionately known as "The Queen's Own" to his fellow officers and as "Lord Dundreary" to the Custer family. (Lord Dundreary was a character with long, flowing sideburns in the 1858 play *Our American Cousin*.)

The troops trekked through a dry ravine toward the divide. After moving four miles, the regiment was halted at 10:07 A.M. in a woody ravine about four miles from the Crow's Nest. They unsaddled their mounts and the company cooks brewed coffee in the hope of washing down the morning's trail dust. Herendeen desired sleep and not coffee. He hunted up another ravine and took a nap during the halt. Custer, Gerard, Chief Trumpeter Henry Voss, and Ree scouts Bloody Knife, Bobtailed Bull, and Little Brave, even before the regiment had resumed its march toward the divide, had hurried ahead to the Crow's Nest with a freshly mounted Red Star as guide. Custer was so anxious to receive such intelligence that he didn't stop to saddle his horse or take his field glasses before galloping off for the Crow's Nest.

Captain Thomas Ward Custer, the General's 31-year-old brother who was serving as a member of his staff, and the Custers' brother-in-law, First Lieutenant James "Jimmi" Calhoun, the acting commanding officer of Company L on detached service from Company C where he was executive officer, had followed Custer, Gerard and the others to the Crow's Nest without permission. Both officers were ordered back to the command by an angry Custer. Tom Custer also committed a

47

second blunder when he failed to pass on his brother's order to Adjutant Cooke not to resume the march until the regimental commander had returned from the lookout point. Custer, as a manner of courtesy, spoke to the Crow scouts (through Mitch Boyer): "These people [the Sioux] are very troublesome and bother the Crows and white people. I am going to teach them a lesson today. I will whip them and will build a fort at the junction where the Little [Big] Horn flows into the Big Horn and you Crows may then live in peace."[6]

From the Crow's Nest, Custer had a good view of the valley of Tullock's Creek, and saw no Indian trail leading in that direction. But Custer saw no Indian village anywhere.

At the base of the Crow's Nest, Custer greeted a red-eyed Varnum. "Well, you've had a night of it," he said. Custer, as was his character, had forgiven Varnum's indiscretion of the previous day. "Yes, sir! But I can still sit up and see things," Varnum replied.[7] Custer then climbed to the lookout point.

Seeing nothing from the lookout point that resembled a village, Custer decided that he wanted another look at the alleged camp from the crest of a nearby peak south of the Crow's Nest, so he and Reynolds moved away to this second promontory.[8] From this second juniper tree-dotted hilltop, Reynolds motioned in the direction of the village, but Custer saw nothing. The two men were joined by Gerard. Reynolds handed Custer his field glasses and Custer scanned the river and beyond, but again saw no sign of any village. A disappointed Custer pointed out that there was no visible smoke rising above the treetops and said he doubted that the Crows had seen anything but some white buttes down what is now Reno Creek. He expressed this doubt to Boyer, who told Custer that down in the valley was the largest encampment of Indians that he had ever seen in all of his years on the plains. Reynolds, whom Custer deeply respected, agreed with Boyer, but admitted that he had not seen anything himself. Gerard, who had been scanning the terrain beyond the river with field glasses, spied a large, dark mass on some distant hills or table land and said that it looked as if the Sioux pony herd was on the move.

"Well, I've got about as good eyes as anybody and I can't see any village," Custer told those within earshot.

Boyer flushed with anger. He felt that Custer had insulted the

Crows, Boyer's tribe by marriage. Anger overcame the proud Boyer as he spoke in his deliberate English, "Well, General, if you don't find more Indians in that valley than you ever saw together, you can hang me."

Custer stammered (as was his custom when excited), "It would do a damn good sight to hang you, wouldn't it?"[9] Custer's language was above reproach and Varnum was surprised to hear him utter the word "damn."

White-Man-Runs-Him stepped forward and told Custer—Boyer translated—of the Sioux warriors sighted earlier in the valley. He urged Custer to attack at once because the Sioux knew of the soldiers' presence. "This camp has not seen our Army," Custer replied. "None of their scouts have seen us."

"They have seen the smoke of our camp," White-Man-Runs-Him persisted. (From the Crow's Nest the Crows had seen the smoke-fires of the regiment back on the trail.) Boyer translated the scouts words for Custer.

Custer, with just a hint of anger in his voice, coldly replied, "I say again we have not been seen. That camp has not seen us."

White-Man-Runs-Him was adamant in his belief that the Sioux had seen Custer's camp and argued that Custer should not delay the attack which he had planned for dawn of the twenty-sixth. "That plan is bad! It should not be carried out," White-Man-Runs-Him, warned Custer.[10] Evidently, White-Man-Runs-Him, who was only eighteen years old and a man of extreme physical courage, did not have his friend Boyer's nagging doubts about "taking on" so many Lakota.

Custer broke off the conversation and galloped back to the regiment unconvinced that the Crows had seen the Sioux camp. Sometime after Custer's departure—with the sun now up for better viewing—Varnum sighted a group of Indians moving their sixty lodges from the mouth of what is now Reno Creek at a point where it formed a junction with the Little Bighorn, about eleven and half miles away. This movement by the Indians raised swirling dust clouds which caused Varnum to believe that the village had seen the command and was fleeing and promptly sent word of this to Custer. But Varnum's Indians were not a part of the much larger encampment of Indians farther down the valley. Gerard, in retrospect, explained that this smaller village, which was on the move to the larger encampment, led to the false belief that the Sioux were stampeding.[11]

On returning to the regiment, Custer told his officers that the Crows claimed to have sighted the Indian encampment and that they "say that the ponies down there are as thick as grass, but I cannot see them. . . ."[12]

Little things began happening which led Custer to alter his battle plans. The Rees informed Gerard that the Sioux had seen the command's morning coffee fires and Gerard so informed Custer. Herendeen reported to Custer that he had spotted an Indian (or Indians) watching the regiment from several hundred yards away. Custer also was told that a pack of hardtack had fallen from one of the pack mules and when a sergeant and two privates were sent back for the pack, they had seen three Cheyenne trying to open a tin of hardtack from a dropped pack. The Cheyenne had then spotted the soldiers and scurried away. The Cheyenne who discovered Custer's lost hardtack were from the seven-lodge camp of Cheyenne Chief Little Wolf en route to the Little Bighorn camp. This band of Indians had been trailing Custer's regiment since the Powder River. Surprisingly, Little Wolf's band reached the camp after the battle. When Charley Reynolds learned of this incident, he bemoaned, "I knew well enough they [the Indians] had scouts ahead of us, but I didn't think that others would be trailing along to pick up stuff dropped by our careless packers."

Custer weighed these reports and decided to strike the village at once. Custer knew all too well—as did every other officer in the Indian-fighting Army—that if Indians were surprised in their camp they would try to run rather than fight. History is replete with little things which have determined destiny and fate.

Custer readied the Seventh for pursuit of the Indians and ordered "sound to horse." The regiment stirred with excitement.

The Rees began singing their death chants and "making their medicine." Earlier that morning, Custer had seen that the Rees were "spooked" and had attempted to bolster their sagging courage through a ruse. Speaking through Gerard, Custer had told Bloody Knife that his brother, Captain Tom, was so scared of the Sioux that his heart was in his throat. "When we defeat the Sioux, he will become a man," Custer reassured them. Tom only smiled at his brother's remarks. Tom was a recipient of two Medals of Honor for Civil War heroics and he carried a facial scar for one such medal.

In the meantime, Adjutant Cooke had sought out the high-powered, Austrian-made field glasses of First Lieutenant Charles C. DeRudio, a swarthy-complected Italian-born officer with waxed mustache tips and a long, narrow goatee, who had been detached as the executive officer from Company E for duty with Company A because Custer believed him incompetent to command E Company while the company commander, Captain Charles S. Ilsley, was on permanent detached service. Just two months from his forty-fourth birthday, DeRudio was the oldest officer on duty with Custer. DeRudio—born Carlo C. di Rudio—was called "Count No Account" by his fellow officers because of his aristocratic Italian birth[13] and his many lurid stories. Benteen, in retrospect, stated that DeRudio "was always a fearful liar." DeRudio, a father of several children, was a self-proclaimed graduate of the Royal Austrian Military Academy.[14] He carried a knife scar on his face and other scars on his body from an 1856 political argument. DeRudio was an escapee from the Cayenne (French Guiana) penal colony, where he had been banished for his part in the January 14, 1858, assassination attempt on the life of French Emperor Louis Napoleon. Eight innocent people had been killed and countless others injured in the bombing of the imperial carriage. DeRudio had been sentenced to the guillotine for murder, but miraculously his execution had been called of as he ascended the steps to the guillotine. Louis Napoleon had generously commuted DeRudio's sentence to life imprisonment at Cayenne.[15] Several years after his escape from Cayenne, DeRudio joined the Union Army during the Civil War as an infantry private and as a paid substitute for another man.

DeRudio reluctantly gave Cooke the prized field glasses. On a second trip to the Crow's Nest, Custer scanned the valley with the field glasses. He saw only wisps of smoke curling above the treeline in the valley.

Boyer and Reynolds again cautioned Custer about the great number of Indians before the regiment. Their words fell on deaf ears. Retreat and caution were not in George Armstrong Custer's psychological makeup. The dashing "Beau Saber" of the U.S. Army had won too many victories and had earned too many laurels to practice cau-

51

tion. Attack and victory were synonymous to Custer. He was an ego-tistical, vain, glory-hunting martinet who also was one of the finest cavalry commanders the U.S. Army ever produced. Neither Confeder-ate soldier nor Indian warrior had ever posed a serious threat in the mind of Autie Custer.

"None of your soldiers will come back alive if you attack," Boyer warned Custer.

Custer by now was exasperated with the prophets of doom around him. "If you are afraid, stay behind," Custer stammered at Boyer.

"I can go anywhere you can," Boyer angrily retorted, but if we go in there we will never come out alive." [16] Pride was a stubborn (and often fatal) taskmaster for most men on the frontier and especially for a man such as Boyer, who had one foot in the white man's world and the other in that of the Indian. Boyer would ride to hell to prove his bravery to Custer. His pride saw to that.

***

Dr. Lord, with his gaunt physique, was suffering terribly from the rigors of the march. Custer generously offered to let him remain with the slower moving pack train, but the gallant doctor had declined and fallen in line with the general's headquarters staff.

The order for the advance was sounded and the regiment moved toward the divide. It was about 11:45 A.M. As the command started forward, an uneasy Bloody Knife twisted in his saddle and gazed toward the sun. He felt only sadness as he spoke. "I shall not see you old friend go down behind the hills tonight."

***

The unenvied task of escorting the stubborn pack mules and their handful of civilian packers fell to 31-year-old, goateed Captain Thomas M. McDougall, a son of a former Army doctor and the com-manding officer of Company B, because his troop had been last in reporting ready for the march. However, it is interesting to note that B Company had the highest number of recruits in the regiment; 41 percent of McDougall's troop were recruits.

The Regiment Moves Across the Divide

The regiment straddled the divide in a halt at 12:07 P.M. Custer and Cooke went off to the side of the trail and divided the command into three battalions. One noncommissioned officer and six privates from each of the regiment's twelve companies were detached and assigned to the pack train as additional packers. Thirty-eight-year-old First Lieutenant Edward G. Mathey, a French-born officer with an imperial (a small beard below the lower lip) and a vinegar tongue, was detached from Company M to become acting CO of the pack train. Mathey's assignment left only one officer on duty with Company M. Mathey, ironically, had been in charge of Custer's pack train at the Washita in 1868. An officer who once had studied for the Roman Catholic priesthood, Mathey's extensive use of profanity had jokingly earned him the moniker "The Bible Thumper" among his fellow officers. Whatever his faults, Mathey was a good man with packs.

TABLE 2
PACK TRAIN AND ITS ESCORT

Officers:	2	
Enlisted Men:	8	soldier-packers (Cos. A–M)
	56	escort (Co. B)
		Private John Burkman, (Co. L), Custer's "striker"
		Private Edwin F. Pickard, (Co. F), Captain Yates' orderly
Civilians:		Chief Packer John C. Wagoner˙
		Teamster-Packer R. C. Churchill˙
		John Frett˙
		Frank C. Mann˙
		Moses E. Flint˙
		E. L. Modre˙
Also (perhaps):		
		William Alexander
		Teamster-Packer George Edwards
		John Lainplough
		William Lawless
		Chris Loeser
		Harry McBratney
		Boston Custer˙˙ (forage master)
		Scout Pretty Face [also known as Good Face] (Ree)

˙The first six men are *known* to have been at the Little Bighorn.
˙˙Boston Custer, a former forage master at Fort Abrahams Lincoln, was the younger brother of General and Captain Custer. He was employed as a civilian guide on the campaign.

53

The remainder of the regiment had been divided into three striking battalions. Reno was given command of Companies A, G, and M, the Ree scouts and the attached civilian personnel save for Boyer. Benteen, as senior captain, took command of Companies D, H, and K. Custer kept Companies C, E, F, I, and L under his personal command. (The U.S. Army had no companies designated with the letter "J." [17]) Boyer and the Crow scouts were assigned to Custer. Kellogg, the correspondent, ultimately accompanied Custer's battalion, as did Harry A. "Autie" Reed, the Custers' 18-year-old nephew, who was a guest on the expedition. The general told his young nephew to remain with the pack train, but the boy would have none of it and told his uncle that if there was any excitement, he wanted to see it. [18] Benteen was ordered to strike to the left of the main trail and scout a line of broken hills a mile away.

Reynolds was telling Custer that the Indian camp was the largest he had ever seen when Benteen asked, "Hadn't we better keep the regiment together, General? If this is as big a camp as they say, we'll need every man."

"Colonel Benteen, you have your orders," Custer replied curtly. [19]

Over among the Indian scouts, Stabbed was exhorting his fellow Rees to be brave. He rubbed some clay he had carried from Fort Lincoln between his hands and then rubbed a little on the body of each Arikara for "good medicine."

At 12:12 P.M. the battalions of Custer and Reno crossed the divide separating the valleys of the Rosebud and the Little Bighorn and entered the latter valley—en route to their rendezvous with destiny. As the regiment moved across the divide, several of the troopers now discarded their extra bags of oats. The battalions of Custer and Reno began the trot down Reno Creek, a narrow, meandering stream infested with numerous rattlesnakes. At 12:12 P.M., Benteen's battalion also crossed the divide, but veered on an oblique scout to the left of the trail. Dragging the column, the advancing pack mules and their one-company escort struck the divide at 12:32 P.M.

After the regiment had moved some distance across the divide, Adjutant Cooke galloped back on the trail with Custer's orders for Mathey to march the pack mules off the main trail as the animals were kicking up huge dust clouds which might alert the Sioux of the command's exact presence. Still later, Custer again sent Cooke to the pack train to check on Mathey's success at keeping the mules off the main trail.[20]

Unbeknown to the regiment, a small band of Oglala warriors out of the Red Cloud Agency, led by Black Bear, which was en route to the larger encampment of Indians, secretly viewed the Seventh Cavalry as it moved across the divide.

***

Custer's regiment had trekked 105 miles in four days, averaging 26.25 miles per day. The horses of the regiment had made this march on only two pounds of oats per day for each horse and little grass. This forage seems to have been sufficient since the troopers discarded spare feed at the divide. Much has been made of Custer's "played-out" mounts, which in itself is a moot point, since the horses of the command had nothing to do with the result of the battle. Custer neither chased nor attempted to flee from the Indians. The horses of the command accomplished their sole purpose, that of transporting the regiment into action against the Sioux and Cheyenne.

Testimony to the overall good condition of Custer's horses includes:

Godfrey: "General condition of the horses were good."

Dr. Henry R. Porter: "The horses generally were in good condition . . . [and] high spirited. . . ."

Private Edward Davern: "The horses of the command were in tolerable condition."

Gerard: "The horses of the command did not seem fatigued. They were on the bit . . . and comparatively fresh. . . ."

John Frett, civilian packer: "Horses and mules were in average condition." (Actually, the mules were not in good condition.)

Day's March: 32 miles in 9:30:00[*]

---

[*] In fact, during that day, Custer had rested his command from 2:00 A.M. to 9:45 A.M. and again from 10:07 A.M. until 12:10 P.M., when the regiment started across the divide.

55

5

Benteen's Scout

12:12–2:20 P.M. (actual scout)

TABLE 3
BENTEEN'S BATTALION

Officers	5	
Enlisted Men	109	(Cos. D, H, K)
Scouts	0	
Civilians	0	

The reason for Benteen's scouting detour to the left of the trail was left to speculation, due to a large part, because Benteen, himself, alleged that Custer did not give him a specific reason for the scout. Custer, it is certain, did not order the scout in compliance with Terry's June 22 orders, which had instructed Custer to feel "constantly . . . to your left so as to preclude the possibility of the escape of the Indians to the south or southeast. . . ." since Custer was not bound by said orders while in the proximity of the Indians.

While Benteen later proclaimed that his scout was a "senseless" trek of "valley hunting ad infinitum," he privately admitted in letters to his wife shortly after the battle and to a former Seventh Cavalry trooper, Theodore W. Goldin, that Custer *had* sent him in search of the valley.[1] The valley was that of the Sioux-infested Little Bighorn. Benteen knew that Custer had really sent him in search of Indians.[2] The officers of Benteen's battalion were aware, too, that the true purpose of the scout was a hunt in the valley of the Little Bighorn for Indians.[3] Benteen's actions throughout the twenty-fifth can be termed rank indifference in the opinion of one Seventh Cavalry trooper.[4]

Custer had instructed Benteen to scout the line of bluffs to the left and front of the command and to "pitch into anything he came across"—and to notify him of said action at once. If no Indians were seen, Benteen was instructed, return to the main trail and rapidly

56

follow the regiment's line of march.[5] Before his battalion had trekked much distance, Benteen was notified of Custer's additional instructions, first through the regimental Chief Trumpeter Henry Voss, and then through Sergeant Major William H. Sharrow, to continue his line of march beyond the second line of bluffs into the next two valleys, if necessary. About a mile into his scout, Benteen was instructed specifically by Custer through Voss to proceed to the second line of bluffs, if he found nothing at the first line of bluffs. Custer later instructed Benteen through Sharrow to move into the next valleys beyond the second line of bluffs. During the scout, German-born Private Charles Windolph of Company H noted the rough terrain over which the battalion was passing and thought, "we are on a wild goose chase."[6] Edgerly later recalled, "We kept skirting along the hills [on the trek] . . ." The rugged, broken terrain was extremely hard on the battalion's horses. Regardless of the fatigue of his mounts, Benteen was bound to his scout.

Benteen, per Custer's instructions, kept a scout point out. Riding this point was the Company H's executive officer, the moon-faced First Lieutenant Francis M. "Frank" Gibson, and a detail of six troopers, who rode 200 to 300 yards (183–275 meters) in front of the battalion. Gibson, a brother-in-law of McIntosh, the acting commanding officer of Company G, was a 28-year-old nondescript officer with little initiative who had no military service or West Point education prior to his commission as a 20-year-old from civilian life. The men of Company H disliked Gibson, an officer who cursed his men when in garrison, and when in the field; they lacked faith that Gibson would "do anything."[7] From a ridge beyond the second line of bluffs, Gibson recalled in 1910, he had seen far enough "to look down on the valley of the south fork of Reno Creek." In 1908, however, Gibson had written Godfrey that he clearly had seen a long distance down the valley of the Little Bighorn with the aid of field glasses.[8] At any rate, Gibson saw no Indians through his field glasses.

At this point, after receiving Gibson's report, and after trekking two valleys and rugged, low, rolling bluffs, plus two ridges, Benteen swung his battalion to the right, skirting some hills, after a scout of only three and a quarter miles. Benteen later—at the Reno Court of Inquiry—tempered his deliberate disobedience of Custer's orders by describing his scout as "a wild goose chase" and stating that if he had carried out the orders, "I would have been at least 25 miles away . . . certainly too far to cooperate with Custer when he wanted me." But less than hour into the scout, Benteen's men had occasional glimpses of Custer's battalion, distinguished by the gray-hued horses of Company E. Benteen's battalion also heard distinctly the loud cheering of Custer's men [See Chapter 9] and the scattering gunshots of the Ree scouts riding toward the Little Bighorn River. All of this proves Benteen was within earshot of Custer and the remainder of the regiment. Benteen claimed he had a premonition that Custer would "strike a snag" and need him. Earlier, a more truthful Benteen had written the New York *Herald* (of August 8, 1876) that "as I was anxious to rejoin the command, as there was no sign of Indians, [only] then decided to rejoin the main trail. . . ." It was another 4.25 miles back to the regiment's main trail, which was struck about 2:20 P.M. It is not known with any degree of preciseness just where Benteen's battalion cut back on the regiment's trail. It is only known that Benteen struck the main trail somewhere along the south bank of Reno Creek about one mile below a morass or seepage of alkaline water. The precise location of the morass also is in doubt, although modern scholars of the battle believe its location was one to one and a half miles east of where the south branch of Reno Creek forms its junction with the middle branch of Reno Creek.

As Benteen's battalion approached the morass, Boston Custer, the gaunt, 27-year-old brother of General Custer and Captain Custer, who had been left on duty with the pack train, now hurried past Benteen in an effort to catch up with his brother's command. Boston was eager to fight Indians. He rode by Benteen's battalion with a smile and shouted a cheery greeting to Company D's acting executive officer, Lieutenant Edgerly, a Custer family favorite. Boston later reached the Custer battalion and certainly must have told the general that Benteen was back on the regiment's main trail.

Benteen's battalion had reached the morass about 2:35 P.M. Despite Custer's orders to return rapidly after swinging back on the main trail, the slowpoking Benteen kept his battalion dawdling at the morass for twenty minutes watering its horses. The animals had not been watered since the evening of the twenty-fourth. While at the water hole, a few scattered shots were heard in the distance. It was 2:45 P.M.

Thirty-seven-year-old Captain Thomas B. Weir, the hard-drinking commanding officer of Company D, an 1861 graduate of the University of Michigan, and brevet lieutenant colonel, became impatient at Benteen's dawdling. Even the more patient Edgerly openly questioned why the battalion was wasting so much time at the morass. A frustrated Weir asked Godfrey to accompany him to urge Benteen to move out at once. Godfrey declined with the comment that as a lieutenant he (Godfrey) would be told by the regiment's senior captain to mind his own business. Finally, about 2:55 P.M., an agitated Weir led his troop away from the morass at a trot without Benteen's permission. Benteen and Weir, a Custer favorite since the Civil War and a former lieutenant colonel of volunteers in the Union Army, never were friendly. Several weeks later, Benteen and Weir nearly came to gunplay in a dispute concerning the battle.[9]

Benteen took the disobedient Weir's obvious hint and moved the remainder of the battalion from the morass—at a *walk*. Benteen's initial snail's pace movement from the morass indicated one of three possible psychological motives: Benteen simply did not believe that any Indians would be found in the valley of the Little Bighorn (despite the fact of several fresh campsites and dung droppings on the main trail) and, therefore, he had no sense of urgency; or that Benteen was pouting for not having been assigned to the attack; or that Benteen's virulent hatred of Custer was so deep-seated that it had warped his sense of military duty, which to Benteen's credit, was usually excellent.

As his battalion moved away from the morass, Benteen stood in his stirrups and shaded his eyes from the bright sun with his straw planter's hat and scanned the back trail. There he saw the lead mules of the pack train through the hazy heat vapors on the horizon.

The Pack Train

Approximately twenty minutes after Benteen's battalion had left the morass, the lead mules of the pack train reached the watering hole. Five or six of the parched mules plunged into the morass of alkaline seepage and became mired in the thick mud. McDougall dismounted his troop and his men assisted the packers in extracting the mules from the quagmire. By McDougall's own estimation, thirty minutes were spent in pulling the mules from the mire. The time delay at the morass is another reason why the pack train could not have averaged three miles per hour at a continuous pace as some students of the battle have suggested.

Since leaving the mouth of the Rosebud on June 22, the slowpoking pack train had managed to stay within striking distance of the main column. It would continue to do so throughout the remainder of the afternoon. The mules, however, were a little worse for wear despite the movement having been downgrade all the way from the divide. The mules, in Mathey's words, were scattered "two or three miles from front to rear." They were whipped to prod them along and were very tired. Many of them had festering sores on their backs because of the sloppiness in the technique of packing. Cargo often came loose from the mules' backs and this required frequent repacking.

While McDougall's troop extricated the handful of mules from the morass, Mathey kept the rest of the animals in motion and marched them past the waterhole. McDougall and Mathey certainly were unsung heroes this day.

6
Reno Gallops to the Advance
2:15–3:00 P.M.

The battalions of Custer and Reno continued their trot down opposite sides of the thickly wooded middle branch of Reno Creek. Custer's battalion rode on the north side of the stream while Reno's battalion advanced along the south side. A portion of Custer's battalion moved off to the right to lessen the dust clouds. About a mile from the site of the so-called "Lone Tepee"—a decorated lodge containing the body of a Sans Arc warrior fatally wounded in the Rosebud fight—Custer swung his campaign hat in the air, motioning Reno to cross his battalion to the north side of the stream. It was 2:15 P.M. as Wallace remembered it. Wallace's timepiece was on Chicago time, Chicago being the headquarters of the Division of the Missouri.

Custer halted his battalion while the battalion of Reno cut down the thickly wooded stream bank, crossed the creek, and scrambled up the opposite bank to the other side. Considering the terrain, this crossing was no easy feat on horseback. The two battalions then continued their advance toward this "Lone Tepee," with Custer in the lead. The burial tepee sat at a deserted campsite some distance below the divide. While the precise location of the Lone Tepee is in much dispute, it sat on the north side of the middle fork of Reno Creek. The burial lodge was at the site of what recently had been a large encampment of Indians. Lone Tepee, however, was a misnomer because at the site was a second tepee, partially wrecked. These were the two tepees seen by Varnum from the Crow's Nest.

The site of such a large camp made two C Company troopers uneasy. Farrier John Fitzgerald, an English-born trooper, and Irish-born Private John Brennan, a recruit, whispered to each other about deserting Custer's battalion before riding into combat. Fitzgerald and Brennan were among the four troopers dragging the rear of C Company.

61

Herendeen stopped to help Young Hawk, a Ree scout, slit open the tepee. Some of Custer's soldiers set the tepee ablaze before riding away. In the meantime, Custer ordered Reno (through the regimental adjutant, Cooke) to move his battalion to the front at a trot. Reno began a gallop as he called to his battalion, "Keep your horses well in hand."

As Custer did not halt the command at the burial tepee, but kept it moving, Hare, who had been scouting Custer's advance, reported on the move to Custer that he had seen forty to fifty Sioux from a knoll some two hundred yards away. Custer, by this time, had been anxiously awaiting any intelligence his scouts had of the Sioux ahead of his command. Meanwhile, atop a white rocky bluff—still plainly visible today—opposite the Lone Tepee, Boyer and the Crow scouts viewed through field glasses some Sioux galloping along the hills beyond Reno Creek. From atop these white bluffs, the sightline of the village was still obscured by the river bluffs along the east bank of the stream. The ever-vigilant Herendeen had viewed heavy dust and running stock in the valley and a few Indians on some distant hills across the Little Bighorn River.

Custer ordered the Ree scouts in hot pursuit of those few Sioux, the Rees' natural enemy, but they refused to move. Custer became angry and reprimanded them through Gerard and threatened to take away their horses and weapons.

"If any of you are cowards, I will take away his weapons and make a woman of him," Custer told them.

One Arikara sarcastically told Gerard that if Son-of-the-Morning-Star took away the weapons of all of his soldiers who feared the Sioux, it would take a long time to complete the task. A disgusted Custer ordered the Rees to the side of the trail to make room for the soldiers to pass. The Rees mounted their horses and galloped down Reno Creek.

When the Rees galloped forward, correspondent Kellogg—he had been trailing the command on a slow mule—rode after them with a pair of spurs, borrowed from Gerard, which he hoped would prod the mule into a faster gait. Kellogg soon learned that the Rees were not riding to the advance with Custer's battalion and he turned back in Custer's direction.

In the meantime, Gerard rode to a knoll forty to fifty yards to the right of the trail about one to one and a half miles from the Little Bighorn River and gazed down the far slopes. Gerard waved his hat in the air and gestured toward the valley below. "There are your Indians running like devils," Gerard bellowed to Custer. Gerard galloped back to Custer and reported that the Indians were on the move.

Custer observed a huge dust cloud swirling farther down the valley (probably the Sioux pony herd being herded to the village) and asked Half-Yellow-Face (through Boyer) its meaning. "The Sioux must be running away," the Crow replied matter-of-factly. In fact, these clouds were raised by a smaller, dismantled village on the move from the mouth of Reno Creek. They were the same Indians that Gerard had seen when he made his "running like devils" remark.

The belief that the Sioux would run upon seeing the soldiers was universal within the regiment. In countless fights with the Army, the Plains Indians *invariably* attempted to flee rather than stand and fight when they came under surprise attack. Only if cornered would they stand and fight.

On a flat about a mile to a mile and a quarter above the Little Bighorn ford, Adjutant Cooke rode up to Reno and gave him what proved to be Custer's final orders to his vice commander: "The Indians are two and a half to three miles ahead. They are on the jump. You are to move forward as fast as you can and charge everything before you and you will be supported by the whole outfit. Benteen will be on your left and will have the same instructions. Take the scouts with you." [1]

Reno, somewhat perplexed, asked Cooke for a clarification of the orders.

"Will I be supported by Custer?" an obviously worried Reno asked.

"Yes!" came Cooke's curt reply.

The Irish-born John F. Donahue of Company K, while holding the reins of Lieutenant Hare's horse, allegedly overheard—Donahue claimed to have heard a lot that day—Custer tell his officers, "Major Reno, you will charge down the valley and sweep everything that will come before you. Captain Benteen will take the extreme right. . . .[and] I will strike them [the Indians] on the opposite point and we will crush them between us."[2] Surviving officers of the regiment recalled no such detailed statement by Custer.

Reno might have misunderstood the difference between "support" and "reinforce." They are not one and the same in military definition. One unit can be *supported* by one or more units in combat against a common enemy without actually being "reinforced;" for example, Custer striking the Sioux at one point while Reno was fighting them at another point constitutes *support* in the military definition. Surely, Reno knew as much, for in a letter to Terry's acting assistant adjutant general, he wrote in part, "It was evident that Custer intended to support me by moving down the stream and attacking the village in the flank."[3]

***

Reno motioned his battalion forward at a trot at 2:20 P.M. by Wallace's watch. A short distance later, Reno forked left away from

TABLE 4
RENO'S BATTALION

Officers	9	
Enlisted Men	125	(Cos. A, G, and M)
	3	(Co. I)
	1	(Co. K)
	1	(Co. B)
	1	(Co. F)
Indian scouts	22	Ree
	4	Sioux
	2	Crow
Civilians	9	

James M. DeWolf, M.D.
Henry R. Porter, M.D.
Charles A. Reynolds, scout
Frederic F. Gerard, interpreter
George B. Herendeen, scout
Isaiah "Teat" Dorman, interpreter
William "Billy" Jackson, scout (1/4 Blackfoot)*
William Baker, scout (1/2 Arikara)*
William "Billy" Cross, scout (1/2 Sioux)*

* Jackson, Baker, and Cross, technically had enlisted with the Indian scouts. Since Jackson was three-quarters white and Baker and Cross were half-white, I have arbitrarily listed them as civilians.

64

Reno Creek in his ride to the ford. As Reno's battalion moved out, Boyer (on Custer's instructions) ordered the Crow scouts Half-Yellow-Face and White Swan to a nearby bluff for another look at the Little Bighorn valley. Through a misunderstanding and the excitement of the moment, both scouts hurried after Reno's command. Boyer and the other Crows then took to higher ground.

For some unexplained reason, both Captain Keogh of I Company and Adjutant Cooke accompanied Reno's battalion for some distance after it started for the ford east of the mouth of Reno Creek. Keogh was a troop commander in Custer's battalion and was that battalion's second-in-command; he should have been on duty there. Keogh rode to a point close to the ford before turning back. He shouted to Reno's stragglers to close ranks. Cooke might have been sent with Reno to assist the major's crossing of the river, but for what reason it is not known. Riding near Reno, Cooke jokingly told the regiment's junior major, "We are all going with the advance and Myles Keogh is coming, too." The adjutant's jovial mood only underscored the festive air of the regiment's officer corps as it galloped closer to an expected big victory.

In the meantime, Varnum, minus his Rees, galloped back to Custer on the flat above the mouth of Reno Creek. He had been scouting some low hills ahead. Eager to please a commanding officer he liked, Varnum had been reconnoitering on his own. He reported to Custer that he had seen some Indians and several tepees in the valley. (Actually, Varnum probably had seen the smaller, dismantled village on the move at the mouth of Reno Creek.) "The whole valley is full of Indians and you can see them when you take that rise [to the front]," Varnum told Custer.

Varnum then spied Reno's three companies descending to the flat and asked Custer where they were heading. "To begin the attack," Custer replied.[4] Varnum then asked for instructions. "You go where you please. You know your business," Custer told him.[5]

Joy and excitement of the moment overcame Varnum and he swung his straw planter's hat in the air as he shouted to Custer's troops, "Thirty days' leave for the man who gets the first scalp!" Varnum's excitement again underscored the whole regiment's anticipation of a big victory over the Indians. Varnum soon spotted Gerard riding after Reno. Varnum then spied Nick Wallace and called to him, "Nick, come on with the fighting men. Don't stay back with the coffee coolers." This impetuous action wound up saving Wallace's life. (Wallace was killed at the battle of Wounded Knee, South Dakota, December 29, 1890.) Varnum and Wallace then galloped after the rear of Reno's battalion. Before riding away, some of the soldiers set the Lone Tepee ablaze.

Although Reno had been ordered to the attack, Custer, surprisingly, was in no hurry himself. He trailed Reno's battalion along the north side of Reno Creek for about one and a half or two miles before he abruptly struck to the right of Reno Creek's middle branch, which he had been trekking. Later, Custer halted for several minutes and watered the thirsty horses of the battalion in the north fork or branch of Reno Creek. Custer moved his battalion away from the stream's north branch at a gallop about 2:35 P.M.

Two miles beyond the Lone Tepee, Privates John Fitzgerald and John Brennan feigned trouble with their horses and dropped back on the trail.[6] They remained clear of the action and hours later joined Reno's battalion. This cowardly action saved their lives.

***

On the ride toward the river ford, Reno's battalion saw two score of mounted warriors scurrying across the Little Bighorn ahead of them. On the ride down Reno Creek, too, some of the Ree scouts came across two Sans Arc Sioux, Brown Back and his young son Deeds, who had been out chasing some lost horses since early morning. The Rees riddled the young Deeds with several bullets and the lad toppled lifeless from his pony. He was the first casualty of the Battle at the Little Bighorn. One of the Rees jumped from his horse and lifted the dead boy's scalp. Brown Back galloped down the creek in a hail of bullets. He reached the village only minutes before Reno's charging battalion was sighted by those in the encampment.

In the ride to the crossing, Reno offered his rifle or carbine to Dr. Henry R. Porter, the 28-year-old acting assistant surgeon and Georgetown University Medical School graduate. Porter declined the weapon and reminded Reno of a surgeon's status as a noncombatant. The

Sioux, however, knew of no such formality. Later, the good doctor, abandoned his non-combat status.

The grim-faced Lieutenant Hare—he never seemed to smile— Gerard, and 21 of the Indian scouts, plus Billy Jackson, William Baker, and Billy Cross forded the Little Bighorn a half mile in front of Reno's advancing battalion. The scouts plunged into the river, crossed to the opposite bank, and galloped away from the river even before Reno's first trooper reached the crossing.

Billy Cross, the young half-Sioux, crossed the Little Bighorn but cut out from the other scouts and went off on his own. Cross rejoined Reno's battalion on the high bluffs on the east side of the river later in the afternoon.[7]

2:30–2:45 P.M.

At 2:30 P.M., Reno's battalion started across the serpentine Little Bighorn about one and a half miles south by west of where Reno Creek empties into the river (according to the 1988 *Official National Park Handbook, Custer Battlefield*). The ford was a natural one; about 10 yards in width and at a point where the river was horse-belly deep. The water was swift and many of the battalion's mounts sank to the sandy river bottom. Company M led the advance, followed by A and G.

At the ford, Adjutant Cooke rode into the river a short distance from the bank and observed the crossing of Reno's troops. There was much confusion and bunching at the ford when thirsty horses stopped in the stream. The troopers had a difficult time in prodding their thirsty mounts across to the opposite bank. Troopers' shouts and oaths filled the air. Some of the horses insisted on stopping to drink. Some of the troopers leaned down from their saddles and refilled their canteens. Others filled their campaign hats with water and then doused themselves with it before moving to the opposite bank. Cooke saw some M Company troopers riding their mounts too fast at the ford and he admonished them not to run their horses at such a pace for "you will need them in a few minutes," the adjutant called to them.

Private Roman Rutten of Company M, a German-born soldier, was one of the first troopers of Reno's command across the stream. Rutten's horse had become skittish at the ford and he'd had extreme difficulty in controlling the animal. The average cavalryman received slapdash training in horsemanship. (Any training was left to the discretion of the regiment's company commanders.) Across the river, Rutten continued to have difficulty with his mount. The animal and its rider kept circling Reno's battalion all the way down the valley. Many of Reno's men laughed at Rutten's plight.

Cooke finally turned away from the river and galloped back to rejoin Custer. Passing some of Reno's straggling troopers, the adjutant shouted to them to close ranks.

In the meantime, an apprehensive Gerard galloped back across to the Reno Creek side of the river and reported to Reno. Reno was at the ford sitting atop his mount and sipping whiskey from a flask. Gerard told Reno that the Rees had seen the Sioux coming upriver to meet the battalion. Herendeen also sought Reno out at the ford and reported the same thing. Reno completely ignored Gerard's report since he disliked the squawman and considered him a person of doubtful veracity.[8] The previous May 6, Reno had dismissed Gerard as interpreter in Custer's absence for allegedly stealing government property. Four days later, upon his return to Fort Lincoln, Custer had reinstated Gerard, who was doggedly loyal to Custer.

The Indians reported by Gerard's Rees probably were the same ones that had been seen earlier by Varnum, and which he had reported to Custer on the flat above the Reno Creek ford. These Indians also might have been the immense Sioux-Cheyenne pony herd on the move. Accurate intelligence as to who was viewing what at what point was difficult. Speculation abounds among historians of the battle on this topic. But it is safe to say that the command knew that Indians were on the other side of the river.

Gerard's loyalty to Custer was just as intense as his hatred of Reno. Receiving no response from Reno, Gerard rode back on the trail seeking Cooke. Gerard overtook the adjutant about 75 yards from the ford. "Well, Gerard, what is the matter now?" Cooke asked. Gerard told Cooke that the Indians were coming up the valley to meet Reno and showing fight. "All right, Gerard, you go ahead and I will go back and report," Cooke told the squawman.[9] The loyal Gerard then turned back toward the river and galloped after Reno's battalion. It is assumed Cooke reported same to Custer.

***

One of the last members of Reno's battalions to ford the river was DeRudio. DeRudio had stopped shortly after passing the Lone Tepee to answer nature's call and then had hurried to catch up with his troop. At the ford, DeRudio splashed water on Reno as he galloped by the major. Reno, who was still sipping whiskey from a bottle, jokingly called to DeRudio, "What are you trying to do? Drown me before I am killed?"

2:45–3:00 P.M.

Despite the difficulty at the ford, Reno had his battalion across the river in ten to fifteen minutes. On the west side of the stream, Reno halted his command in a wide grove of cottonwoods to regirt and reform his ranks. [Since every survivor of Reno's battalion almost always referred to these trees and those box elders as "timber," I have kept this terminology, for the most part, for *historical* ambiance.— author] The spot where Reno halted was about three and a quarter miles from the southernmost edge of the Indian village (the Hunkpapa tepees).

While Reno's command was in the timber, French-born Sergeant Stanislaus (or Stanislas) Roy of Company A heard some of the troopers shout excitedly, "There goes Custer!" Roy glanced across the river and had a fleeting look at Custer's battalion moving along the high bluffs east of the river.

Reno must have felt anxious about his front, for before riding from the timber, he dispatched Private Archibald McIlhargey of Company I, his Irish-born "striker," or personal servant, to Custer with the message that the Sioux were reported in strong numbers in his (Reno's) front. This was a meaningless message since Custer already knew that the Sioux were in the regiment's front in large numbers. Varnum had also reported this same fact to Custer. And Gerard had said as much to Cooke.

McIlhargey hurried back across to the east side of the river where he met Gerard coming in the opposite direction in an effort to catch Reno after having reported to Cooke. McIlhargey had no difficulty in picking up Custer's trail and overtaking the latter's battalion. In fact, his proximity to Gerard on the trail suggests that McIlhargey overtook Cooke a short distance from the river and that the two of them rode back to Custer together.

The stocky Reno was sweating profusely in the warm afternoon heat. The major's dark, blue military blouse had been soaked with perspiration since midmorning. At the river crossing, Reno had tied a handkerchief—variously reported as red or white—around his forehead to keep the rivulets of salt-stinging sweat from dripping into his eyes.

At 2:45 P.M., Reno moved his battalion from the timber. Companies M and A moved out on a left-to-right line with Company G to the rear. Company A hugged the timber as it galloped forward.

Reno and his acting assistant adjutant general, Second Lieutenant "Benny" Hodgson—he was called "Jack of Clubs" by the enlisted men of the regiment, and just five days from his twenty-eighth birthday—rode several yards to the rear of Company A. Reno's throat was parched by the heat and the thick, ash-white dust swirling about the battalion. Reno took a long swallow from his whiskey bottle and passed it to Hodgson. Benny swallowed from the bottle and passed it back to Reno. Neither officer broke gallop-stride during their drinking and bottle passing. This bottle-passing incident was seen by A Company Private William O. Taylor, who had glanced back at Reno and Hodgson from his position several yards to the front of the two officers.[10]

Benny Hodgson was extremely popular with his fellow officers, which was no easy task in the clique-plagued officer corps of the Seventh Cavalry. But Hodgson was beset with his own private demons. Hodgson admittedly had had carnal knowledge of a fellow officer's wife and feared that he had impregnated the woman.[11] Hodgson had tendered his resignation from the Army only to withdraw it when he learned that his regiment had been ordered against the Sioux. Hodgson also had attempted to shoot an enlisted man of his troop the previous April, but had been prevented from doing so by McIntosh, the acting commanding officer of G Company. An angry Hodgson shoved and cursed McIntosh, a superior officer, who had Hodgson placed under temporary arrest.[12] Nothing to date had been done about the incident, since Hodgson and McIntosh, a promotion-hungry, petty-minded officer, had been close friends. Hodgson might have suspected a court-martial in the near future. Benny Hodgson knew that his Army days were numbered. He had no idea just how numbered.

***

Varnum and Hare and the Ree scouts galloped forward to the extreme left of Reno's command. The battalion rode at a trot and increased to a fast gallop as it moved closer to the village. Some of the recruits were having difficulty controlling their mounts at such a rapid gait. Reno's more eager troopers began yelling and shouting in antici- pation of the battle. Reno cautioned them, "Hold your horses, boys, there's plenty down there for all of us!" Reno called to one wild-eyed trooper that there would be enough fighting before they were through for the day. The major, his sweat-drenched uniform caked with ash- gray dust, saw a mounted warrior scurry away farther down the valley.

***

The valley quickly opened before Reno's battalion and the troops could see a large dust cloud swirling downriver. This dust cloud was raised by the Indian herders driving the village stock downriver. Be- low, the column saw the serpentine Little Bighorn with its banks lined with clusters of cottonwood trees, felled logs, and dense woods. Reno, at this point, brought G Company up to the right of his advancing column parallel with the other two companies without breaking the battalion's gait; a skillful maneuver for a cavalry unit.

The battalion kicked up enormous clouds of dust, which were seen by the Indians in the village. These dust clouds were the first real knowledge that the village had that the soldiers were in the immediate vicinity, although some of the Indians had been aware of the regi- ment's presence in the area since observing its dust clouds at the Lone Tepee. Some of the Indians in the village later admitted that they actually had seen Custer's battalion on the high bluffs east of the river before they were even aware of Reno's presence in the valley. While there is some Cheyenne tradition that the Indians knew of Custer's presence as early as the Rosebud—see interview with John Stands-in- Timber by CBNM historian Don Rickey, Jr., August, 1956, CBNM— the evidence is overwhelming that the village was not expecting an

71

attack. Besides, knowledge of troops in the field is not necessarily translated into knowledge of an imminent attack. (Lack of a communication network among Indians was one serious drawback to their logistical, combat strategy.) The village as a whole, however, was unaware of the immediate presence of the soldiers until Reno's battalion charged across the flats of the Little Bighorn valley at which time the village warriors hurried up the valley to meet Reno in numbers that are disputed. Custer, indeed, had caught the village by surprise.

7
The Indian village
Midafternoon

Kate Bighead, a 29-year-old Southern Cheyenne, frolicked nude in the river with some Lakota (Sioux) women near the Hunkpapa lodges at the southernmost end of the huge camp. Suddenly, Kate heard the startled cry, "The soldiers are coming!" Kate's doeskin dress was several yards away on the river bank so she swam into some brush while several Sioux horsemen galloped by her hiding place. Several minutes after the horsemen had passed, Kate left the water, retrieved her dress, and ran toward her village at the northern end of the camp.

Kate had known the fear of being attacked by the bluecoats. She had been in the Washita River village of Chief Black Kettle in present Oklahoma when Custer and his Seventh Cavalry attacked at dawn on November 27, 1868. She was among the Cheyennes captured by Custer's bluecoats that frigid morning and had witnessed some of Long Hair's (Custer's) bluecoat chiefs (officers) sexually molest some of the Cheyenne women during her long winter of captivity.

***

In the Oglala camp, Low Dog, a war chief of his tribe, was sleeping late in his tepee when he was awakened by the cries that the bluecoats were nearing the village. (Many of the camp's warriors were asleep or resting in their tepees because tribal dances and celebrations had been held late into the early morning hours of the twenty-fifth.) A sleepy Low Dog refused to believe his ears. Surely, it was a childish prank, Low Dog thought, for the Sioux camp was much too strong in numbers to be at risk of such an attack.

***

Turtle Rib, a 28-year-old Miniconjou warrior, also was asleep in his lodge when he was awakened by loud cries that many soldiers were coming. He grabbed his rifle and ran naked (save for breechcloth) from his lodge, mounted his pony, and galloped out to meet the advancing Ree scouts, still in Reno's front.

***

Miniconjou Chief Red Horse was with four women a mile from the village digging wild turnips when he stopped to observe Reno's dust clouds rising toward the village. (While the Plains Indians were hunters, their women gathered and dug for wild edibles to supplement their diet. Red Horse, who admitted that he was with the women, in separate interviews in 1877 and 1881, probably accompanied the women as a protector.)

***

Wooden Leg (1858–1940), a young Cheyenne, and his older brother Yellow Hair, earlier had taken a late morning bath in the river with several other Indians. Wooden Leg and Yellow Hair, after bathing, had sought the cool shade of some cottonwoods near the river and had fallen asleep. They were suddenly awakened by a great commotion in the village. Wooden Leg heard someone shout, "The soldiers are coming!"

***

Two Moons,[1] a Northern Cheyenne chief, who had been at the northern end of the village washing his horses in the river, is known to have given contradictory figures for his age on at least two separate occasions, projecting his birth year back to 1842 and 1844 respectively. According to his official government death certificate, he was born in 1847 and died in 1917. On returning to his lodge on the day of the attack, Two Moons saw rising dust clouds swirling like a giant whirlwind up the Greasy Grass. He had been told on June 24 of the soldiers' coming by the blind prophet Box Elder. By the time Two Moons returned to his tepee, the sound of guns [Reno's] echoed from up the valley near the Hunkpapa tepees.

***

74

One Bull, the 23-year-old Hunkpapa nephew of Sitting Bull, was combing his hair in his tepee when the cry of alarm was sounded.

***

White Cow Bull, an Oglala, was in the Cheyenne camp when he observed the dust clouds and heard gunshots from the Hunkpapa village.

***

Red Feather, an Oglala and the brother-in-law of the renowned Crazy Horse, first knew of the soldiers' presence when fellow tribesman Magpie warned him that "the white men [Reno] are charging!"

***

Iron Hawk, a 14-year-old Hunkpapa, was eating a late breakfast when he heard someone sound the alarm that the soldiers were approaching.

***

Hunkpapa Chief Gall (1840–1894) was also in the Cheyenne camp when Reno's battalion came within sight of the village. Since the Hunkpapa lodges were the nearest to the charging bluecoats, Gall knew that he must hurry to his camp.

***

Thunder Hawk, a Brulé was in his tepee suffering in great pain from a wound in his left hip, which he had received in the Rosebud fight, when he heard scattered gunfire from the southern end of the village.

***

Dewey Beard (Iron Hail), a 14-year-old Oglala, and White Bull, the 26-year-old Miniconjou nephew of Sitting Bull (the Cheyenne chief), were with their respective pony herds when Dewey Beard heard warning shouts about the soldiers and White Bull heard gunfire. Dewey Beard died in 1955, the last surviving warrior of the Little Bighorn battle.

***

Iron Thunder, a 28-year-old Miniconjou and younger brother of War Chief Hump (which transcribes literally from the Dakota tongue as High Back Bone), had not seen Reno's dust clouds, nor had he heard any warning shouts, and knew nothing of the soldiers' presence until the first sporadic gunshots.

***

The great Hunkpapa Sitting Bull lay in his tepee, his thickset flesh still weakened from his torturous Sundance ordeal of June 6–11. Suddenly, some young Hunkpapa warriors entered Sitting Bull's lodge and shouted, "The soldiers are in the camp! Get up! The soldiers are firing into the camp!" Sitting Bull—at age 45 he was too old for active combat and would not fight this great day—was "big medicine" to his people and they looked to him for inspirational leadership. Sitting Bull's squaw was so panic-stricken at the news of Reno's approaching battalion that she fled to some nearby hills with only one of her infant twins. When she realized that she had left the other twin in her tepee, she returned to the village and rescued the infant from harm's way.

***

Crazy Horse, the great Oglala war chief, did not rush into battle at the signal that the bluecoats were charging the village. He would miss the initial action with Reno's bluecoats altogether as he took meticulous time to consult the tribal shaman and invoke the Great Spirit.

***

Hunkpapa Chief Crow King did not think there was any danger of battle until a runner to the village reported Reno's presence. This was the first that Crow King knew of the bluecoats.

***

Indian males were normally late risers—that is, afternoon—but, as noted, on the night before (June 24) many warriors were up until the early hours of the morning for various reasons, including a social dance; hence, the Seventh Cavalry caught the camp "napping."

76

Soon the camp was alive with shouts of "Hurry!" Utmost confusion reigned in the village. Many of the women and children fled in panic to the dry channel of Squaw Creek, north of the village, to hide. Women and old men wailed their death chants.

Through a now-and-then break in the swirling dust, the men of Reno's battalion could see the thick clusters of the tepees in the valley. Both Hare and Dr. Porter saw few Indians, and these were herding the camp's immense pony herd downstream toward the village. The troops were yelling and shouting as the battalion rode across the powdery, thin-soiled flats of the valley floor. Reno admonished the troops to "stop that noise!" The hooves of the command's horses kicked up the loose, ashen soil, almost barren of vegetation, on to the charging troops, coating man and horse with a thick, gray film.

Reno—he wore a straw U.S. Navy hat in place of the regulation Army campaign hat because it was cooler—and Benny Hodgson rode stirrup-to-stirrup. Suddenly, Reno bellowed above the din, "Charge!" The battalion trumpeters blared their bugles (but not the now familiar tune of countless cavalry motion pictures).

In the battalion's front, a few Sioux were setting fire to the prairie as a first line of defense. The grass of the nearly barren prairie was too sparse and it failed to produce a conflagration. Sporadic gunfire echoed in the valley. A few overly eager troopers in the vanguard of the charging battalion were recklessly firing random shots. The vanguard, First Sergeant John M. Ryan and ten M Company troopers, rode well in advance of the rest of the battalion. Ryan was a battle-tested Civil War soldier and a veteran of Custer's Washita fight.

Several hundred yards (or meters) to Reno's immediate front, the flat prairie opened into a horse-belly-deep, thirty-foot-wide ravine, the mouth of which curved into a bend or loop in the river. An uneasiness quickly came over Reno as his command galloped toward the ravine. Abruptly, Reno broke off his advance and halted his battalion, about a third of a mile from the coulee.

"Fight on foot!" came the cries of the battalion's first sergeants. It was 3:15 P.M. Troopers dismounted and grabbed their carbines. The company horse holders—veteran privates—each held the laced-together reins of four mounts.

In halting his battalion, Reno was unequivocally in disobedience of Custer's orders "to charge everything before him." Reno claimed at his 1879 Court of Inquiry that he halted his command because "the very earth seemed to grow Indians" and that "they were running toward me in swarms and from all directions." Reno further defended his decision by stating he "soon saw I was . . . into some trap . . . [and] I saw I must defend myself and give up the attack. . . ."

Hare later admitted he did not know why the halt was made. He thought that the battalion had halted before any Indians had appeared from the ravine.[2] Hare also stated that "if there were any [Indians in the command's immediate front], they were very few."

Herendeen, who was at the left and front of the battalion during the aborted charge, stated that he "did not see any [Indians] and I was in the front. . . . There were no Indians near enough to shoot at. . . ." Herendeen's position gave him a good view of the Indian village. Herendeen later told historian Walter Mason Camp that when the battalion dismounted, the nearest Indians were some mounted ones on the bluffs off to the left.

Gerard, admittedly anti-Reno, said that he saw only fifty to seventy-five warriors a thousand yards down the valley.[3]

Dr. Porter agreed with Gerard. Porter, who had been on Apache campaigns and in battles with the Army in the Arizona Territory prior to his service on the Great Plains, said that he saw no more than fifty Indians some eight hundred to nine hundred yards down the valley.[4]

Varnum said that he saw no Indians shooting at the time the battalion halted and that there were only scattered gunshots at that time.

Captain James Myles "Michie" Moylan, the 37-year-old commanding officer of Company A and a former sergeant major of the regiment (1866), a nineteen-year veteran of the Army, placed the number of warriors in and around the battalion front and left flank at a grossly exaggerated seven hundred.[5] Moylan was a veteran Indian fighter who had been cashiered as a second lieutenant from the Fifth U.S. Cavalry in 1863. At the 1879 Reno Court of Inquiry into the battle, Moylan stated that had the battalion gone 500 yards, it would have been "butchered."

Sergeant Ferdinand A. Culbertson of Company A, a veteran of the Seventh Cavalry and one of the few enlisted men to testify at the Reno Court of Inquiry, substantiated Herendeen's report of no Indians near. Culbertson had seen huge dust clouds in the ride down the valley, however, and recalled thinking that there were between 100 and 150 warriors in the battalion's front.[6]

After the battalion halted, Varnum said later, at least 300 to 400 Indians appeared in its front.[7] Hare agreed. After the command halted, he saw several hundred warriors pour from the ravine which had so troubled Reno.[8] Wallace estimated the warrior force at or near the ravine between 200 and 300 and that these numbers increased steadily with each passing minute.[9] The skeptical Herendeen believed the total number of warriors confronting Reno's battalion in the valley fight was less than 200.[10]

Soon after dismounting his command, Reno dispatched his Irish-born cook, Private John Mitchell of Company I, to Custer with the message that the Indians were swarming in great numbers against him (Reno). Reno believed that his command was facing between 500 and 600 hostiles.[11] Later he wrote that he was fighting against "all the Sioux Nation and . . . all the desperados, renegades, half-breeds, and squawmen between the Missouri and the Arkansas and east of the Rocky Mountains and they must have numbered at least 2,500 warriors."[12]

Reno displayed some confusion, perhaps anxiety, and obvious "nervous timidity"—the latter were Godfrey's words—in halting his battalion. It was Reno's first real taste of Indian fighting, as he had never been in an actual battle against hostile Indians prior to the Little Bighorn.[13] Godfrey recalled in later years that he doubted if Reno had ever before seen a hostile Indian.[14] Godfrey was wrong. Reno had served in the Northwest a few years before the Civil War where he rescued survivors of an Indian attack. He had even captured some Indians there and had chased Indians on the Great Plains. But Reno's list of career battles and skirmishes, compiled by the Adjutant General's office, failed to list a single battle against Indians prior to the Little Bighorn. Reno's lack of Indian fighting experience was precisely why Custer had requested the Seventh Cavalry's Major Lewis Merrill, a veteran of frontier service which predated the Civil War, as his vice commander on the campaign in place of the inexperienced Reno. But Merrill had been on detached service with the Centennial Exposition in Philadelphia and President Grant had revoked Merrill's orders to rejoin his regiment. Merrill, like Reno, was no great admirer of Custer.

Reno's error was that he had halted his battalion about two and a quarter miles after crossing the river. The southern end of the Indian encampment was approximately another two and a half miles down the valley. Reno's actions had eliminated the "Pivot" maneuver in Custer's mode of attack. (Custer's battle plan is explained in Chapter 14.)

In the meantime, Private Mitchell galloped back on Custer's trail and soon overtook the General's battalion. It was about 3:20 P.M.

8

The Indian scouts
Mid to Late Afternoon

When Custer left Terry's bivouac on the afternoon of June 21, he had thirty-three full-blooded Indian scouts: twenty-three Arikara (Ree), six Crows, and four friendly Sioux who were scouting for the Army because they had married Ree women. On the afternoon of the twenty-fifth, Pretty (or Good) Face had been detailed with the pack train while four of the Crows rode north with custer's battalion. The rest of the Indian scouts rode with Reno's battalion.

Being poorly mounted, seven of the cavalry's Indian scouts straggled far back on the trail and never did cross the Little Bighorn. These scouts were the Rees Bull, Charging Bull, Red Wolf (a nephew of Bloody Knife), Soldier, Stabbed, Strikes-the-Lodge, and White Eagle. Stabbed, who had been on a detailed scouting mission off to the left of the main trail while the regiment crossed the divide, finally caught up with fellow scout Soldier at the Lone Tepee. Farther on, the two scouts overtook Bull and White Eagle, who were struggling on fatigued mounts to catch up with those scouts who earlier had crossed the Little Bighorn ahead of Reno's battalion. Stabbed desperately prodded his played-out mount ahead of his three companions in an effort to reach the river ford. Soldier, Bull, and White Eagle struck Custer's trail and turned off to the right in Custer's direction. The three scouts soon saw Private McIlhargey joining Custer's battalion a short distance ahead. They kicked their mounts after Custer's battalion.

In their attempt to overtake Custer's battalion after he had struck northward from the middle branch of Reno Creek, the trio of scouts came across Private Peter Thompson, a Scottish-born trooper of C Company, who was cursing and kicking his collapsed horse. Thompson soon left his horse and hopelessly trailed after Custer's battalion on foot. He eventually became lost and turned back on the

TABLE 5
THE POSITIONING OF THE INDIAN SCOUTS

A STRAGGLERS	B RECONNOITERED FOR SIOUX PONIES
Bull	Black Fox
Charging Bull	Boy Chief
Red Wolf	Buffalo Ancestor
Soldier	Bull-Stands-in-Water
Stabbed	Little Sioux
Strikes-the-Lodge	One Feather
White Eagle	Red Star
	Strikes Two
TOTAL: 7	TOTAL: 8

	C VALLEY FIGHTERS
	Bloody Knife (killed)
	Bobtailed Bull (killed)
	Bear-Running-in-the-Timber
WITH CUSTER	Bear Waiting
White-Man-Runs-Him	Forked Horn
Goes Ahead	Goose (wounded)
Hairy Moccasin	Little Brave (killed)
Curley	Paints-His-Face-Half-Yellow
Michel "Mitch" Boyer (1/2 Sioux)	(Half-Yellow-Face)
	Red Bear (Good or Handsome Elk)
	Red Foolish Bear
	White Cloud
	White Swan (wounded)
	Young Hawk
TOTAL: 5	TOTAL: 13

D DETAILED TO PACK TRAIN	E MISCELLANEOUS
Pretty (or Good) Face	Billy Jackson (with Reno)
	Billy Cross (somewhere in valley)
	Billy Baker, (somewhere in valley)
TOTAL: 1	TOTAL: 3

trail. Several hours later, Thompson joined Reno's battalion, by then on the high bluffs east of the river.[1]

Soldier, Bull, and White Eagle soon came across another C Company trooper, Private James Watson, whose mount also was down for the second time. Earlier, Watson's horse had collapsed, but with some difficulty, he'd managed to get the animal back on its feet under the watchful eye of his first sergeant, German-born August Finckle. Finckle had remained mounted and had watched Watson struggle with his exhausted mount. Once Watson had the horse on its feet, Finckle galloped after Custer's battalion. In the meantime, Soldier, Bull, and White Eagle gave up hope of catching Custer's battalion and turned back toward the middle branch of Reno Creek.

Watson and Thompson later encountered each other. Watson later joined Reno's battalion on the bluffs. Two other C Company troopers, Fitzgerald and Brennan, who had deliberately dropped their horses behind Custer's battalion,[2] also later joined Reno on the bluffs, sometime after the arrival of the pack train. Fitzgerald, Brennan, Watson, and Thompson all survived. Brennan was dishonorably discharged from the Army in 1879 for another offense. Coincidentally, all four men had been the last troopers in Custer's column. Had Finckle suspected duplicity when he'd earlier watched Watson struggling with his mount? Both Watson and Thompson, however, seem to have made concerted efforts to catch up with Custer.

***

Red Wolf and Strikes-the-Lodge came over a ridge and met the returning Soldier, Bull, and White Eagle. By this time, Stabbed also had realized the hopelessness of trying to overtake those scouts who had earlier forded the river with Reno. He then joined Soldier's group. These scouts also were joined by Charging Bull.

***

Twenty-one full-blooded Indian scouts crossed the Little Bighorn ahead of Reno's battalion: Rees—Bobtailed Bull, the 45-year-old leader of the Ree scouts; Bloody Knife; Bull-Stands-in-Water; Forked Horn, who at age 61 was the oldest of the scouts, even though he'd lied, stating he was only 45 years old, for his enlistment; Goose; Little Brave, a brother of Bobtailed Bull; Red Bear (also known as Good or Handsome Elk); Red Foolish Bear; Young Hawk, the 17-year-old grandson of Forked Horn; Boy Chief; Red Star, a nephew of Soldier;

83

Strikes Two; One Feather; Little Sioux, the brother of Red Wolf and nephew of Bloody Knife; and Black Fox; Crows—Half-Yellow-Face and White Swan; and the four Sioux: White Cloud, Buffalo Ancestor, Bear-Running-in-the-Timber, and Bear Waiting. Three "breeds," whom I have classified as civilians, also rode with this group of "blooded" scouts: William "Billy" Jackson, the quarter-Blackfoot; William "Billy" Cross, the half-Sioux, and William "Billy" Baker, half-Arikara.

After fording the river with Reno's battalion, Boy Chief, Red Star, Strikes Two, Little Sioux, One Feather, Black Fox, Bull-Stands-in-Water, and Buffalo Ancestor, diverged away in search of Sioux horses. One Feather and Buffalo Ancestor soon separated from the other five scouts and rode off on their own, chasing a pair of Sioux horses. Buffalo Ancestor also reconnoitered for ponies on his own. Black Fox did the same thing. Black Fox seems to have advanced with Reno's battalion for some distance before reconnoitering for Indian ponies, however.

Boy Chief, Red Star, Strikes Two, and Little Sioux succeeded in capturing some Sioux livestock after first chasing three squaws and two young boys who had fled the village. These mounts were driven across the flats of the valley and up some hills with some trailing Sioux in pursuit. One Feather and Buffalo Ancestor became separated during their pony hunt. Both managed to capture some horses, but the Sioux herders succeeded in recapturing the livestock. Late in the afternoon—after Reno's battalion had been driven from the valley—Boy Chief's group managed to get its twenty-seven captured horses and two mules back on the Reno Creek side of the river. One Feather recrossed the river about the same time as Boy Chief. Buffalo Ancestor did not recross the river until much later.

Black Fox, too, was successful in capturing some Sioux horses before he returned across to the east side of the river and up the bluffs, where he came across White-Man-Runs-Him, Goes Ahead, and Hairy Moccasin returning from downriver with Custer. Still later, Black Fox hooked up with Curley, who, by that late in the day, had left Custer's battlefield in search of some hardtack dropped back on the regiment's trail. The two scouts separated on Reno Creek and Black Fox headed for the Rosebud. When Black Fox came across the Crows White-Man-

Runs-Him, Hairy Moccasin, and Goes Ahead, after these scouts had left Custer, the three Crows had a string of five Sioux horses which they had rounded up somewhere. Goes Ahead gave one of the horses to Black Fox.

***

A small group of full-blooded Indian scouts rode into battle with Reno's battalion despite the popular belief that these scouts had deserted the regiment in the face of the Sioux. Those thirteen Indian scouts who fought with Reno in the valley were: Bobtailed Bull; Bloody Knife; Forked Horn; Goose; Little Brave; Red Bear (Good or Handsome Elk); Red Foolish Bear; Young Hawk; Half-Yellow-Face; White Swan; Bear-Running-in-the-Timber; Bear Waiting; and White Cloud. These scouts were thirteen additional carbines for Reno's battalion.

In riding across the flats of the valley, Bloody Knife had broken away from the other scouts and captured three Sioux ponies. He herded the animals in the direction of his nephew, Little Sioux. Bloody Knife ordered his young kinsman to take possession of the horses, but Little Sioux was much too excited to heed his uncle's command. Bloody Knife let the captured mounts loose and galloped forward to catch up with the other scouts advancing with Reno's command.

Bobtailed Bull's group of scouts rode several yards to the left and in the advance of Reno's troops. This position proved to be the most vulnerable in fighting the Sioux and Cheyenne. Bobtailed Bull, trying to set an example for the younger Rees, rode well in the advance of the other scouts shouting encouragement. Herendeen, Billy Jackson, a young quarter-Blackfoot, and Isaiah "Teat" Dorman, a black interpreter out of Fort Rice, also advanced with Bobtailed Bull's group. Charley Reynolds and Gerard, however, wisely took little chance by riding at the rear of Reno's battalion.[3] The precise whereabouts and actions of the scouts William Baker and Billy Cross in the valley are not known, although presumably they were with Reno's battalion.

***

After Reno halted his command, the thirteen Indian scouts who remained with the battalion formed their own irregular skirmish line

85

several yards west of the soldiers. The veteran Bobtailed Bull was the farthest on the line by several more yards, a most vulnerable position should the line change positions. Unlike the soldiers who employed horse holders, the Indian scout simply used a slipknot to fasten his horse's reins to his cartridge belt. In this manner, a horse could be recovered and mounted in a few seconds.

Young Hawk, who was eager to prove his mettle, swung into action almost immediately. He shot and killed one Hunkpapa warrior. The teenaged Ree spied a galloping Sioux pony dragging its hapless rider. Young Hawk squeezed off a shot with his carbine and brought down the horse. Another Hunkpapa warrior galloped close to Young Hawk only to be shot dead by the young Ree. The two warriors the young Ree killed were White Bull (not to be confused with Sitting Bull's nephew or White Bull the Cheyenne chief) and Swift Bear.[4] Young Hawk this day proved to be one of the most gallant warriors fighting under Reno.

9

Custer Rides to the Attack

2:00–3:30 P.M.

A determined Mark Kellogg still trailed Custer's battalion. The correspondent was having a difficult time prodding his slowpoking mule. Gerard's spurs, borrowed earlier, had had minimum effect on the animal's stubbornness, but Kellogg continued doggedly on Custer's trail down Reno Creek.

After leaving the north fork of Reno Creek, Custer turned his battalion on a route which led it several hundred yards to the east of what is now Reno Hill. Sergeant Daniel A. Kanipe (not Knipe) of Company C stated in 1903[1] and in 1908 (to historian Walter M. Camp) that Custer's battalion at this time could see Reno's troops and the Indian scouts charging down the valley toward the Indian village. Many historians of the battle long have believed that Custer rode across or near Reno Hill, but Hare later found no shod-horse trail on or near Reno Hill.[2]

Several hundred yards to the north the battalion spotted sixty to seventy-five Indians on a high ridge (now called Sharpshooter's Ridge) some 500 yards to the north of Reno Hill. Sergeant Kanipe had first spotted these Indians and so reported to his first sergeant who reported this fact up the chain of command. Custer reached the ridge— by then the Indians had disappeared—and halted his command for about ten minutes. From this vantage point, Kanipe recalled that Custer and his staff officers viewed the Indian encampment for the first time through field glasses.[3]

The southernmost lodges of the village sat off a wide loop in the river about a mile and a half downstream. Even though the main portion of the village was still hidden from Custer's view, he now saw that it was a much larger village than he had anticipated. When Custer's troops saw the many tepees in the valley, they began yelling and hollering. While on Sharpshooter's Ridge, Custer and others heard

87

gunfire ripple in the valley. Custer had been visible (albeit momentarily) from the valley. (Four enlisted men [Sergeant Stanislaus Roy, Private Daniel Newell, Private Henry Petring, and Private Thomas F. O'Neill], plus Gerard, DeRudio, and Varnum all saw Custer's battalion on the bluffs and ridges at various times.) When Reno had dismounted his battalion, Varnum had a glimpse of the white and gray horses (Company E) of Custer's battalion moving along Sharpshooter's Ridge. Even Godfrey, while scouting with Benteen, claimed to have occasionally glimpsed Custer's horses. Where Custer's battalion was at these various sightings is open to speculation and debate.

Custer's battalion moved forward along the ridge at a trot. Some of the troopers wildly kicked their mounts forward in helter-skelter order. Custer called to them, "Hold your horses, boys, there's plenty of them down there for all of us."[4]

Custer now ordered Tom Custer, who rode alongside him as a staff officer, to dispatch a courier to McDougall to hurry along the pack train. Tom Custer galloped back to C Company and ordered Sergeant Kanipe, "[Tell McDougall] to bring the pack train straight across to high ground. [Tell him] don't stop to fix them, cut them off. [Tell him] to come quick; big Indian village."[5] Kanipe also was instructed to tell Benteen, if he happened across him, "to come quick; a big Indian camp."[6] The 23-year-old Kanipe galloped back over the battalion's trail searching for the pack train. Along the route, off to his right, Kanipe saw a band of yelling Indians herding a pony herd at a gallop. The herd kicked up a huge dust cloud and, as it passed Kanipe, he readied his carbine. But he soon saw the Indians were Ree scouts.

About this time, Kanipe saw Benteen's dust cloud off to his right. Kanipe forked right and galloped over to the senior captain and his battalion. Kanipe met Benteen about a mile west of the site of the Lone Tepee. Kanipe reported to Benteen, who, merely replied that the pack train was not his responsibility and that the packs were farther back on the trail with McDougall. Kanipe then moved on to the pack train. As he galloped by Benteen's battalion, Kanipe jubilantly called, "We've got them, boys! They're lickin' 'em!"[7]

(This was an erroneous assumption by Kanipe since he had left Custer's battalion before it had become engaged.) Kanipe's words touched off cheering by some of Benteen's battalion.

Kanipe came across the head of the pack train about a mile east of the Lone Tepee site. The pack mules at this time were spread out over several hundred yards. Both McDougall and Mathey later denied that Kanipe ever reported to them individually, although McDougall later was of the opinion that Kanipe had reported to Mathey. Kanipe recalled nearly a half century later that he had reported to McDougall, the senior officer. Private Augustus DeVoto, a Company B packer, stated that a messenger from Custer *had* arrived at the pack train seeking Reno.[8] After reporting to the pack train, Kanipe remained on duty there.[9]

***

Custer now moved his battalion forward, veering to the left, in columns of fours. Previous to this, the battalion rode all five companies abreast. The movement now was to a high ridge one-half mile beyond (northwest of) Sharpshooter's Ridge. Custer halted his battalion in a swale below this second ridge, which is now called Weir Point (or Weir Peak or Weir Ridge). Here Custer told Boyer to dismiss the Crow scouts. This was just prior (according to what Goes Ahead told Walter M. Camp in 1909) to Custer's battalion reaching what is now Cedar Coulee. "You go back to the pack train and let the soldiers fight," Boyer told the Crows. White-Man-Runs-Him, Goes Ahead, and Hairy Moccasin soon cut out and headed back over the trail which Custer had just trekked. Curley, however, remained with Boyer and did not leave at this time.

From Weir Point, Custer and his staff officers, Tom Custer and Adjutant Cooke, scanned the more than two-and-one-half-mile encampment with field glasses. Some revisionist historians of the battle now believe that Custer bypassed Weir Point altogether. Custer, however, badly needed any intelligence as to the true size of the village and its exact location. Weir Point offered Custer his "best look" at the Indian encampment. Weir Point was much higher and closer to the edge of the bluffs in 1876 before the present service road was cut through the ridge to what has become known as the Reno-Benteen Defense Perimeter. It was also only a few minutes later, in nearby Cedar Coulee, that Custer dispatched what proved to be his final messenger (Martin) to Benteen. The "complete look" of the size of the village (as afforded by Weir Ridge) also prompted the urgency of Custer's famous final message to Benteen (see Chapter 11). Lieutenant Edgerly of D Company, later stated that he and Weir saw no sign of Custer's shod-horse trail on Weir Point. That is because Custer *did not take his whole battalion to the ridge.* There was no need for that when Custer was only seeking an observation point. The Custers and Cooke, together with the General's orderly, Trumpeter John Martin of Company H, took a side trip, galloping up and using the ridge summit for an observation point.

Custer was not deterred by the enormous size of the village, which attests to the fact that it was not a village the size of 3,000 to 4,000 warriors as many have claimed. No warriors were then in sight. Only a few of the camp's women, a few children and dogs were seen milling about. "We've got them this time!" Custer exclaimed as he scanned the village with DeRudio's field glasses. (Custer had failed to return them to DeRudio.) Cooke or Tom Custer suggested that most of the warriors were out hunting buffalo.[10] "We've caught them napping!" Custer exclaimed. He waved his wide-brimmed, whitish-gray hat in the air and called to his battalion, bunched below him, "Hurrah, boys! We've got them! We'll go down and make a crossing; finish them up and then go home to our station."[11] At Custer's words, the men of the battalion removed their campaign hats and waved them over their heads in a loud cheer.[12] This cheer was loud enough for the partially-deaf Godfrey and others in Benteen's battalion, some distance up Reno Creek, to have heard. Custer swung his hat in the air as a signal for his battalion to move forward. Custer soon noticed a moving dust cloud in the valley—probably the camp's pony herd—and exclaimed, "They are skedaddling!"

***

A short distance below and to the east of Weir Ridge, Custer's battalion cut into a coulee 1,600 yards long which was shrouded in juniper trees. This coulee, called Cedar Coulee by Walter Camp, angled northeast into a meandering coulee called Medicine Tail Coulee, which, about one and three-quarter miles away (as the crow flies), emptied into the Little Bighorn. From the east side of the river, while in Medicine Tail Coulee collecting grazing horses, Standing Bear, a

17-year-old Miniconjou, spotted Custer's dust clouds rising above Cedar Coulee.[13] Other Indians also saw Custer's dust clouds, but surmised them to be a herd of moving buffalo (bison).

***

A short distance northeast of Weir Ridge, Boyer and the Crow scout Curley witnessed the fighting of Reno's battalion on the valley floor. Carried away by the excitement of the moment, Boyer waved his hat several times in the air while shouting encouragement to Reno's troops. From the valley, some members of Reno's command mistook Boyer for Custer. Boyer's cheery mood quickly passed because he and Curley then saw Reno's battalion fleeing the valley.

A few minutes later, a more somber Boyer told Curley to go back and stay out of the soldiers' fight. "Custer and his men are going to get all cleaned out," Boyer told Curley. Making Curley a gift of his field glasses, Boyer told the young Crow that Custer was seeking high ground to await the arrival of reinforcements before attacking. "I am going with Custer," Boyer told Curley. Boyer then galloped away to head off Custer's battalion.[14]

The 20-year-old Curley meandered to a high ridge northeast where he viewed the initial action of Custer's battalion with Boyer's field glasses before turning back on the trail from which Custer had trekked. He later met Black Fox, who, by that time, had come up from the valley. The two scouts later separated, after searching for some lost hardtack. Curley, after happening across the pack train, departed for the Yellowstone River via Tullock's Creek forks where he hoped to rejoin the other Crow scouts under Gibbon.

The other three Crow scouts, White-Man-Runs-Him, 23-year-old Goes Ahead, and 22-year-old Hairy Moccasin, also witnessed Reno's flight from the valley as they rode along the edge of the bluffs. The three Crows moved for some distance along a ridge until they reached a bluff which overlooked a circle of tepees in the valley. The scouts could barely see the tops of the tepees because of the intervening trees. Here they stopped long enough to fire three or four rounds apiece at the tepee tops. They then rode back on the trail looking for other soldiers. At one point, they came across the dismounted Watson. Later, about a third of a mile north of the mouth of Reno Creek, they met

Benteen's battalion. The three Crows eventually headed for the Yellowstone seeking Gibbon's column so they could rejoin the other Crow scouts.

***

Just prior to entering Medicine Tail Coulee, Custer briefly halted his battalion, long enough to dispatch Trumpeter John Martin (born Giovanni Martini), his Italian-born orderly, who had been detached from Company H, to find and hurry along Benteen. Custer must have known that Benteen was back on the main trail by observing (through field glasses) the large dust clouds raised by Benteen's battalion. The 23-year-old Martin—he had been a drummer boy for the Italian patriot Giuseppe Garibaldi in 1866—was instructed to tell Benteen that there was "a big village" and to "come on and be quick and bring the packs."[15]

Martin started to leave, but was quickly called back by Cooke. The quick-thinking adjutant was aware that Martin was a recent immigrant with a poor command of English. Cooke hurriedly penciled a message on a leaf of notebook paper. Tearing the leaf from the notebook, Cooke handed the note to Martin and instructed him to ride as fast as he could over the high ground the command had just trekked, find Benteen, and give him the message. Cooke also instructed Martin to return to Custer's battalion if at all possible, otherwise to remain on duty with company in Benteen's battalion. Martin saluted and galloped back up Cedar Coulee.[16] Custer's battalion passed into history at this point.

It was about 3:30 P.M.

***

Probably in the vicinity of Sharpshooter's Ridge, whose western side Cedar Coulee skirted, Martin came across a hard-riding Boston Custer, fresh from duty with the pack train. Boston yelled to Martin as he came alongside him, "Where's the General?"

"Right behind the next ridge you'll find him," replied Martin.

"Is he under attack?" Boston inquired.

"Yes," Martin replied.[17] Martin warned Boston about the Indians, but the youngest Custer brother (at age 27) merely replied, "I am going to join the command anyway."

Before riding on, Boston called Martin's attention to the fact that the orderly's horse was limping. Prior to meeting Boston, Martin's horse had been hit by a stray bullet fired by an Indian. When the horse was hit, its blood splattered on the back of Martin's blouse. The wound suffered by Martin's horse pointed out that warriors were on the east (Custer) side of the river. Martin then moved on seeking the elusive Benteen as Boston waved goodbye, and galloped away to catch the action.

Within a short distance, Martin met Troopers Fitzgerald and Brennan, who sheepishly asked Martin the whereabouts of Custer's battalion.[18] Martin told them Custer was "over there behind the next bluff" and then galloped away on his limping horse.

***

Custer exited Cedar Coulee, angled to the left and dropped his battalion down into the extremely wide Medicine Tail Coulee at a point one and three-quarter miles (as the crow flies) from the river. Medicine Tail Coulee is a sagebrush-shrouded ravine whose bed eventually sloped abruptly to a fifteen-foot dropoff at the river's floodplain. Boyer had cut across from his vantage point near Weir Ridge and caught up with Custer in Medicine Tail Coulee after taking leave of Curley. Boyer conferred with Custer in an animated discussion for several minutes. Boyer undoubtedly told Custer of Reno's fight and the fact that the major's troops were fleeing from the valley.

Destiny would soon close on Custer's battalion.

10
Shoot-out in the Valley
3:15–4:00 P.M.

Reno's halting of his battalion before reaching his objective—the village—allowed the camp's warriors time to secure their weapons and to get to their respective pony herds, mount up, and ride out to meet the enemy. With each passing minute, the warriors grew more numerous in Reno's immediate front.

When Reno halted his battalion, Private George E. Smith of Company M, another soldier who had had difficulty with his skittish horse in the ride down the valley, lost control of his mount and the frenzied animal bolted near some timber and was never seen again.[1] His head might have been one of the three charred heads found hanging by wire from a lodgepole on the site of the abandoned village on June 27,[2] or one of several others found at the campsite.

Three of Smith's fellow M Company troopers were more fortunate. The skittish horse of Private Roman Rutten plunged far ahead of the battalion and carried him through the Indians coming from the village to meet Reno. Rutten's horse galloped wildly into the Hunkpapa camp, the tepees nearest to Reno's charging battalion. The frenzied animal circled to the right into a clump of cottonwoods, with Rutten desperately holding on. In the trees, Rutten managed to control his mount and he galloped back to Reno unscathed.[3]

German-born Private John H. "Snopsy" Meier also was carried into the Hunkpapa camp by his frenzied mount.[4] Meier pulled his revolver[5] and began shooting at the Indians.[6] Meier finally gained control of his mount and cut a wide circle around the hostiles and returned to Reno's lines.[7]

Ten years after the battle, Hunkpapa War Chief Gall revealed that his two squaws and three children tragically were killed when Reno's battalion neared the Hunkpapa lodges.[8] Meier, in his frenzied escape

94

from the Hunkpapa village, must have killed most, if not all, of Gall's family.

Private Henry Turley also had trouble controlling his horse when Reno halted his battalion. (Several of the Seventh Cavalry mounts were new and had never before been in combat or around Indians.) Turley fortunately got his "spooked" mount under control before it carried him into the Indian ranks. Some historians of the battle report that Turley was killed at that time, on the basis of what First Sergeant Ryan said, years later, "That was the last I saw of him."[9] Ryan had been riding in advance of the battalion just after the crossing of the Little Bighorn, and should have been in a position to have seen the runaway horses. Turley did survive that incident—however briefly. After some frantic riding, he rejoined Reno. But he was killed a short time later in Reno's retreat from the river bottoms.

First Skirmish Line

Upon dismounting, Reno's battalion had quickly deployed in skirmish order at five- to seven-yard intervals. At this time—according to a sighting by Gerard reported at Reno's 1879 Court of Inquiry—"Custer's column . . . [was] going at a fast trot . . . [on the bluffs] and raising dust." What warriors initially confronted Reno poured from the ravine in the command's front. A short time later, more warriors rode up the present Shoulder Blade Creek to pressure Reno's left flank. Reno had only ninety-three troopers (if we counted orderlies but not the horse holders) on the skirmish line as thirty-one others were needed as horse holders. One of the most vexing problems concerning Reno's fight in the valley has been the location of the battalion's first skirmish line. The late Fred Dustin, one of the ablest students of the battle despite his extreme anti-Custer bias, spent nearly a half century in an effort to accurately locate this skirmish line.[10] Dustin, unfortunately, did not have the benefit of modern metal detectors and archaeological artifacts. The discovery of several spent .45-55 Springfield carbine cartridge cases by modern historians and local citizenry pinpoints Reno's first skirmish line.

The line began about 500 feet west of the southwest corner of the present GarryOwen Loop of the Little Bighorn (it was not there in 1876)—about 100 feet west of (across) present U.S. Interstate Highway 90, and just a few yards east of the Burlington Northern Railroad tracks which run parallel to the highway[11] for about 475 yards[12] on an east-to-west line. The 475 yards is an estimation, taken from the belief that the ninety-three troopers (minus thirty-one horse holders) were spaced at regular five-yard intervals. The Indian scouts were still farther to the left of the line. The line formed at a prairie dog village and some of the troopers used the mounds as breastworks. Company G occupied the line near a dry, thickly wooded creek channel; A Company held the center of the line while M Company held this line's left flank.

Company M was under the command of the fleshy 33-year-old Captain Thomas H. "Tucker" French, a former U.S. State Department clerk. Despite his affinity for whiskey and whores, French was a most able officer, and according to his first sergeant, John Ryan, was as brave an officer as ever served in the Seventh Cavalry. On his own initiative, French sent Ryan and a detail of ten troopers to form a mini skirmish line in a wide batch of thick woods clustered with waist-high cottonwood saplings some fifty yards east of the main skirmish line, near the west bank of the little Bighorn. Ryan's detail failed to find any Indians lurking in the woods and returned and reported this fact to French. French, or Reno, upon hearing the report, ordered the battalion's mounts taken to the woods.

Moving Robe Woman, a 23-year-old Hunkpapa who had observed Custer's rising dust above Cedar Coulee behind Weir Ridge while digging turnips with Red Horse's group, was in her village by the time Reno had deployed his men in skirmish order. She heard a terrific volley from Reno's carbines which shattered the lodgepoles of the Hunkpapa tepees. She saw one warrior running from his tepee for his horse when he was struck by one of the bullets and was killed.[13]

Most of the troops on the main skirmish line fired from a prone position as mounted warriors pressed the line from the center and the left. Reno stood on the line coolly firing his revolver at the half-circling warriors. French, a deadly marksman, was on the line firing his single-shot .50-caliber, long-barreled Springfield rifle (commonly called a "Long Tom")—each cartridge packed with 70 grains of powder—and dropped several warriors from their ponies. French, a former infantry private, gloated over his lethal marksmanship. To a few nearby troopers, French gleefully exclaimed in his falsetto voice,

96

"There goes another sonofabitch," as each shot dropped a warrior. French notched the stock of the rifle every time he shot an Indian.[14]

The troops on the skirmish line fired at will at the circling, horse-backed warriors. Reno, French, and Hodgson also walked up and down the line cautioning the men to lie low, keep cool, and fire low. None of the other officers or first sergeants attempted to regulate the firepower of the command. Too many cartridges were needlessly used up. Several troopers dropped off the line and scurried to their mounts to secure the reserve carbine cartridges in their saddlebags. Reno's skirmish line advanced about 100 yards despite the swarming cordon of screaming warriors.

The Indian scouts on the extreme (and very precarious) left of the line bravely held their ground with their limited firepower as mounted warriors flanked their position from the west. Fighting on the line with the Rees and Crows were Isaiah Dorman and the 19-year-old scout Billy Jackson and possibly Billy Cross and William Baker. Dorman, reportedly a former runaway slave from the Deep South,[15] had been in the upper Missouri River country since about 1851. He was married to a Sioux woman and had been employed steadily in U.S. Army service since 1865. He had accompanied the regiment, so he said, to see the Sioux country once more before he died.

Gerard and Reynolds, however, did not fight. Gerard, for one, believed that his duty was to interpret, not to fight. The bearded Gerard was heard to vow that he would never again accompany the regiment on a field campaign. The once plucky Reynolds was in such severe pain from the abscess on his right hand that it made discharging his rifle difficult. Gerard and Reynolds had tied their horses in the woods near those of the battalion and had gone to the rear of the extreme right of the line, next to G Company, where they observed the action.

Herendeen, who found his position in a swale on the left of the skirmish line much too dangerous, soon went to the edge of the woods and tied his horse. He then went to the right of the skirmish line.

***

While positioned near A Company, Reno received a report that the Sioux were swimming a loop in the river and were infiltrating the timber northeast of the skirmish line. Reno left Hodgson in charge of the skirmish line and went to the woods with the first platoon of G Company under McIntosh. The woods trailed along and down a steep, old cut bank of the river to a dry, gravel-bottomed channel bed. The densely thicketed woods were several feet below the level of the surrounding prairie.

In the meantime, an apprehensive Moylan (Company A) had noticed that the battalion's horses were actually in an exposed position. "The Indians are circling around to our rear," Moylan yelled to Varnum, who had just reported for duty with his troop. "They'll get the horses with the ammunition."

"I'll attend to that," Varnum yelled back.

As he started for the Company A horses, he glanced at some distant bluffs near what is now the vicinity of the Reno-Benteen Defense Area (Reno Hill) and spied the gray and white horses of Company E in Custer's battalion.

Varnum then guided A Company's horses to a sheltered place in the timber to near the right of the skirmish line. The horse holders of G and M followed Varnum and the A Company horse holders, believing that all of the battalion's mounts had been ordered into the timber.

Excitement had permeated the troops when Reno and the first platoon of G Company left the skirmish line. Several troopers thought the movement signaled a charge on the Indians. Varnum went to check with Reno. Out on the prairie, warriors circled to the left of Reno's skirmish line and rode up and down some nearby foothills before charging the troops. The warriors' horses kicked up enormous clouds of alkaline dust, which allowed Reno's troops few clear shots at the enemy. Reno and Varnum conferred while in the woods, and then Reno sent Varnum to the skirmish line for a report. Before Varnum departed, Moylan came to the edge of the woods and shouted that the situation on the skirmish line was becoming desperate. En route to the line, Varnum met Hodgson and asked him how things were going. Hodgson replied that the battalion was in danger of suffering an enfilade. Hodgson reported the same to Reno, who, judging that the line now had become untenable, ordered the acting adjutant to bring the battalion to the woods.

Without orders, DeRudio led a half dozen troopers of Company A off to the northeast—away from the skirmish line to where the river over the years had cut away the bank to eight feet—to head off an attack on the right of the line. While there, DeRudio said later, he spotted Custer, Cooke, and another man waving their hats and cheering atop a high ridge. DeRudio even claimed to have seen Cooke's enormous beard—across the river more than 2,000 yards away! Custer's battalion soon disappeared down Cedar Coulee and out of DeRudio's abnormal eyesight. From atop the cut bank, DeRudio and his borrowed carbine and his six troopers kept up a continuous fire at the warriors. This movement to the cut bank DeRudio later came to regret, as it nearly cost the Italian soldier of fortune his life, a life he was determined to save, at any cost to his personal dignity.

Second Skirmish Line

The battalion had been on the line for about twenty-five minutes when it did a flank-right movement to the woods. In the fallback to the woods, Reno told his troops, "Retreat to your horses, men! Steady, men—fall back slowly! Face the enemy and continue your fire," Reno cautioned.[16] Company M covered the fallback of A and G. When the battalion gained the timber, the Reno-hating Gerard noticed the major empty the contents of a partially filled whiskey bottle.[17]

At the edge of the timber, a second skirmish line was formed, several yards south of the southern bank of the present GarryOwen Loop of the river. This second line stretched southward for about 160 yards along a former bed of the river.[18] Facing from the skirmish line, G Company was on the left of the line near a bend in the river; A held the center; M was on the right of the line. An old, dry river bed meandered to the rear of the line.

Private Edward Davern of Company F, Reno's Irish-born orderly, recalled at the 1879 Reno Court of Inquiry, that the Indians did not pursue the retreating troops to the timber, but remained 700 to 800 yards away and did not fire very much.

Despite the heavy shooting on the first skirmish line, Reno's only casualty prior to the flank right movement to the timber had been the missing-in-action Trooper George Smith. Yet Reno had only seventy-one or seventy-two troopers then on the second skirmish line, with orderlies but without the horse holders, the first platoon of McIntosh's

99

G Company—still reconnoitering in the woods—and minus three additional casualties. When the movement to the woods occurred, Reno suffered his three additional casualties.

M Company Sergeant Miles F. O'Hara, who recently had been promoted to sergeant and who was his company's guidon bearer, was struck down with a bullet in the chest. O'Hara sat up and screamed at fellow M Company trooper, Private Edward A. [or D.] Pigford, "For God's sake, don't leave me!" A badly "spooked" Pigford callously ignored O'Hara's screams, as did others of M Troop save for one trooper who picked up the falling colors before fleeing,[19] and O'Hara was cruelly abandoned to his fate, the Indians now about fifty yards from the timber. O'Hara's body was never found, although his charred head reportedly was found suspended by wire from a tripod inside a tepee in the abandoned village after the battle.[20]

William Heyn, the German-born first sergeant of A Company, took a bullet in his left knee. Heyn couldn't walk, but he was assisted to the timber by his fellow troopers. Another German-born sergeant, Charles White of M Company, stopped a bullet with his right elbow. White winced at the pain, cursed, and continued to the woods where his mind was on a coveted treat, a jar of jelly in his saddlebags.

All of the Indian scouts, despite their precarious position on the left of the skirmish line, gained the shelter of the woods. There they kept up a continuous gunfire at the swarming warriors near the timber. En route to the timber, Young Hawk even had time to capture a riderless Sioux pony and present it to Half-Yellow-Face as a gift.

The Indians' most prominent casualty fighting in the valley was the Oglala chief Knife Chief, who was struck and unhorsed by three bullets; one in the body and one in each arm, both of which were broken by the shots. Knife Chief was so severely wounded that he lay where he fell until after Reno had fled the valley. Only then could his family remove him via a horse-pulled travois. Knife Chief, nevertheless, survived his wounds.

***

Moylan's A Company had shot an inordinate number of cartridges on the skirmish lines because he had failed to regulate the fire of his men. Troop A exhausted its primary cartridge supply and each man of

100

the company who was on the line had to alternately drop off the line and return to his mount for reserve ammunition in the saddlebags.[21] Evidently, French regulated the fire of his own troop, M Company, for Private Pigford stated that he had fired only four or five rounds on Reno's first skirmish line.

French displayed his shooting skills on both skirmish lines. Eighteen times during the fight in the valley, French aimed his "Long Tom" and squeezed off a round and eighteen times a warrior toppled from his mount. Sergeant Ryan noticed that with each "kill," French notched the stock of his rifle with a penknife. Hare, who squatted on the right of the line with Wallace's .50-70 Springfield rifle, pumped round after round at the Indians. DeRudio, who had borrowed the wounded Sergeant White's carbine, squeezed off two shots to the left of the skirmish line at a pair of warriors on some distant hills. Both shots fell well short of their mark.

***

A band of Sioux warriors led by Sitting Bull's nephew, One Bull, and Black Moon, son of the Hunkpapa subchief of the same name, charged dangerously close to the timber. The troops fired on these Indians, unhorsing a trio of warriors and turning the warriors' charge. One of the latter trio, White Bull (not Sitting Bull's nephew of the same name) was killed. Young Black Moon, another of those unhorsed, escaped only to be killed later fighting against Custer shortly after crossing the river to meet the "Long Hair's" troops. The third unhorsed Hunkpapa, Good Bear Boy, had received crippling wounds in both hips and legs. Good Bear Boy made a feeble attempt to crawl out of range of the bluecoats. One Bull, in a supreme act of individual courage, rode through Reno's firepower to the fallen Good Bear Boy. Reaching his wounded comrade, One Bull dismounted, lifted Good Bear Boy onto his [One Bull's] mount, remounted, and galloped away in a shower of bullets.[22]

***

Meanwhile, a perplexed Reno, with the tide of uncertainty lapping about him, became more apprehensive with each passing minute. Custer's promised support was nowhere in sight and "the Goddamn Indians were everywhere." The befuddled Reno believed that his battalion was facing every renegade Indian west of the Missouri. Still, the battalion was not being pressed in the timber. DeRudio later testified that "the men in the timber were firing . . . only when they saw a good chance . . . and there was no chance of being shot. . . .

Reno's determination to hold his position was fast slipping away in the gloom-haunted valley. Even whiskey had failed to steady Reno's anxiety. Reno had seen no real combat since the Civil War. In the war, he'd had a horse shot from under him at Kelly's Ford in 1863, been promoted to colonel, and earned a brigadier general of volunteers brevet. But in the decade after the Civil War, a lack of combat had softened Reno.

11
Benteen: "Come On . . . Be Quick"
2:20–4:00 P.M.

Since leaving the morass, Benteen's battalion had picked up its gait at a gallop for most of the distance. Benteen, himself, rode 200 to 300 yards in advance of the battalion. At the still-smoldering Lone Tepee, Benteen faced what he called "the horns of a dilemma" as the Custer-Reno shod-horsed trail forked left and right where these two battalions separated. A hot debate ensued among the battalion's officers as to which of the two trails was Custer's. Most of the jawboning was between Benteen and Weir. Weir and his D Company peeled off and followed the left trail (Reno's) while Benteen and the rest of the battalion followed the right trail (Custer's). Benteen and his orderly rode the middle ground between the two trails. Eventually, the battalion was reformed before reaching the mouth of Reno Creek. Benteen's battalion then turned north on a line toward Reno Hill.

***

Trumpeter Martin's well-lathered and bleeding horse was nearly played out when he came across Benteen and his orderly shortly before 4:00 P.M., some two or two and one-half miles west of the Lone Tepee. Benteen and his orderly were more than 200 yards in front of the battalion at this point. Martin reined in alongside Benteen, saluted, and handed the senior captain Custer's message. Benteen read the message:

> Benteen—
> Come on. Big
> Village, be quick
> bring packs.
> *W. W. Cooke*
> *PS bring pacs.*[1] [sic]

"Where is the General?" Benteen asked Martin.

"About three miles from here," Martin replied.

"Is he being attacked or not?" asked Benteen.

"Yes, [he] is being attacked," Martin replied.[2]

Both Benteen and Godfrey, however, recalled that Martin had said the Indians had "skedaddled"[3] [an obvious error].

Benteen then asked Martin why his horse was limping and the trumpeter replied that the animal was tired. Benteen then pointed out to Martin that the horse had a bad wound in its right rump and that its blood had splattered Martin's back. Benteen told Martin that he was lucky the horse, and not he, had been hit. Benteen had little regard for Martin, of whom he later wrote, "was a thick headed, dull witted Italian, just about as much cut out for a cavalryman as he was for a King . . ."[4]

Weir galloped forward and Benteen handed him Custer's message. Weir read the note and returned it to Benteen without comment. Edgerly, acting executive officer of Company B, on loan to Benteen's battalion, also read the note and commented that Custer did not mean for Benteen to return for the packs as McDougall was bringing them along. First Lieutenant Gibson, executive officer of Company H, later offered, "We didn't wait for the packs as we felt pretty sure no Indians had passed our rear."

Benteen later claimed that he was perplexed as to how he could "come on" and "be quick" and still ride back to "bring the packs" forward. The pack mules then were spread out for the better part of two miles and the "slowpoking" McDougall (Benteen's accusation) could bring the packs along just as quickly as he (Benteen). To justify his gross disinterest in the packs, Benteen made the absurd statement at the Reno Court of Inquiry: "Before the last order reached me . . . I believed that General Custer and his whole command were dead." Benteen had no such evidence to support such an irresponsible statement.

The truth is that Benteen had questioned Martin as to whether Custer was under attack and Martin had replied, "Yes, being attacked."[5] Even this statement was erroneous, as Martin had been dispatched to Benteen before Custer's battalion was engaged, but it shows Benteen lied when he stated that he then thought Custer's command was wiped out. Martin further volunteered the erroneous belief that Custer was killing Indians "right and left."[6] Benteen, therefore, could not possibly have believed that Custer's command was dead either before or after he received Custer's message via Martin. Benteen, perhaps, was more perceptive than he afterward led others to believe. Despite his snide comment to fellow officers of how could he "be quick" and still return to the pack train, Benteen might have realized that Custer had wanted the twelve mules, each of which carried two boxes of cartridges with 1,000 rounds per box, and not the whole pack train. A detail of men could have been sent back to cut out the dozen mules and hurry them forward to Custer in some thirty-five to forty minutes. Benteen, instead, chose to ignore his commanding officer's final orders in the field of combat.[7] He simply tucked the note into his pocket and told Martin to fall in with his company. Martin, in 1922, stated that Custer wanted the ammunition packs, something Martin had failed to mention in his testimony in 1879 at the inquiry into Reno's conduct at the Little Bighorn, or in his later discussions with Walter Camp. In his haste to scribble a message in a stressful moment, Cooke probably had left out the word ammunition. Cooke's oversight muddled Benteen's perception. It is also possible Custer merely wanted what the note said: Benteen and [all of] the packs.

During the first century after the battle, historians treated Benteen as "a sacred cow" and "a savior" of the remnants of the Seventh Cavalry in light of Reno's "timidity" in the valley fight and on the Reno-Benteen Defense Perimeter. This image of Benteen was further reinforced by Herendeen and a number of enlisted men of the regiment who volunteered such statements as "Benteen was the bravest man I ever saw," and "Benteen was the coolest man in the regiment."

While Benteen later took actual—but not official—command of the defense perimeter from a lethargic Reno and thus bolstered the regiment's sagging confidence by his open display of fearlessness, "Benteen the Savior" is a myth perpetrated, for the most part, by Benteen himself in the aftermath of Custer's annihilation and Reno's exposed "nervous timidity" (Godfrey's words).

***

Benteen's battalion pushed on with the senior captain always in advance of the column. Sometimes Weir and sometimes Godfrey rode the point with Benteen and his orderly. On the first rise north of the mouth of Reno Creek, Benteen and Godfrey met the three Crow scouts, White-Man-Runs-Him, Goes Ahead, and Hairy Moccasin.[8] Godfrey was unsuccessful in communicating with one of the Crows before they moved on to the Yellowstone. Some distance farther along the trail, Godfrey also happened across one of the Ree scouts herding a string of captured Sioux ponies.

12

Reno Disgraced: Panic and Rout

3:45–4:15 P.M.

Reno was uneasy and his anxiety must have been high. Reno, as he later wrote, believed Custer had been rash in riding away in one of his usual glory-seeking "hurrahs" while he (Reno) was left to fend for himself. Within a few minutes, a decision was made which haunted Reno to a premature grave thirteen years later.

***

Captain French of M Company came off the skirmish line and conferred with Reno in a parklike area in the woods. This "park" was a 500-foot squared area which previously had been the site of an Arapaho camp, but was now denuded of vegetation.

"What are we going to do, now?" French asked.

"To fight!" Reno replied.[1]

Sergeant Ryan of M Company overheard the two officers and commented, "There is nothing to do but mount your men and cut your way out. Another fifteen minutes and there won't be a man left."[2]

Reno and French stared at Ryan and said nothing.

Reno's stomach churned from indecision. He asked French what he would do. "Get the hell out of here!" French replied. Reno then queried French on a possible line of retreat. Afterward, he told French that the point of retreat was a line of bluffs on the east side of the river. Reno told French to "mount your horses and follow me." Reno, in his official report dated July 5, 1876, wrote that "I saw that I was fighting odds of at least five to one, and that my only hope was to get out of the woods . . . and gain some high ground." He never wavered from that belief. What Reno really felt was revealed in his letter of July 4, 1876, published in the Harrisburg (Pennyslvania) *Daily Telegraph* of August 7, 1876 ". . . I have never seen any Indian fight like it, and no one else ever will. . . . I never expected to get away alive. . . ."

Varnum, after having sequestered A Company's mounts in the woods, joined Reno in the park. When Reno inquired as to how things were going on the line, Varnum replied that he did not know. Reno ordered him to Moylan's sector to find out and report back. Varnum left the park and came across Hodgson, who was hurrying to Reno from the line. Varnum told him to report the situation to Reno. Hodgson's only comment was that he thought his horse was wounded.

Gerard and Reynolds also were "sweating it out," to the rear of Reno's skirmish line. Reynolds was visibly shaken and Gerard personally felt that he was in "the second tightest spot in his life." (In 1863, Gerard and seventeen other men had successfully fought off an attack by several hundred Yankton Sioux.) Gerard met Varnum, who asked how things were going. Gerard told him, "Mighty bad." Gerard suggested a drink, with the somber comment, "It may be our last." Reynolds admitted that he was depressed and needed a stimulant. He drank freely and Gerard cautioned Reynolds to keep a cool head and not drink too much. When Reynolds had drunk his fill, Gerard and Varnum slaked their thirst with long swallows of whiskey.

Captain Moylan of A Company had come off the skirmish line where minutes earlier he had asked Billy Jackson to carry a message to Custer. Jackson demurred and waved a hand in the direction of the swarming hostiles, "No man could get through that alive." Reno asked Moylan his preference for a line of retreat out of the valley. Reno clearly had the idea of retreat on his troubled mind.

Benny Hodgson now arrived at the park, reporting that things were hot on the skirmish line. Reno ordered Moylan and McIntosh to "saddle up" their companies. He sent Hodgson to give the same orders to French, who earlier had left the park. Reno had decided "to charge" — Reno's words—back across the river to the high bluffs to the east. If the major planned an orderly retreat, fate soon deemed otherwise.

The battalion had been on the second skirmish line for about twenty minutes when disaster struck. A band of Indian warriors collected below the high clay bank of the dry river channel just north (or downstream) of Reno's position at the edge of the woods. Moving Robe Woman, the Hunkpapa, was among this group of warriors. Mounted on a black horse and carrying a war staff, her heart was heavy for her young brother, One Hawk, who had been killed earlier.

Ryan saw this movement by these warriors and shouted above the din that the Sioux were circling the rear of the battalion.

"Oh, no, that's some of General Custer's men!" replied French.[3]

It was this action by the Indians that precipitated Reno's panicked rout from the valley, which eventually sealed Custer's doom. What if French had checked out Ryan's warning?

These warriors moved to within thirty yards of the right of Company M's position on the line. A few minutes later, they let loose a fusillade which ripped the woods. At that precise time, Crazy Horse, who was late entering the battle, made a charge with his warriors against Reno's line. One of the fusillade bullets struck Irish-born Private Daniel Newell of Company M in the left thigh as he stood holding his horse, and another bullet probably struck a kneeling Private Frank Braun, a Swiss-born trooper of Company M, in the left thigh.

"I am hit!" Newell yelled to his Irish-born sergeant, Patrick "Patsy" Carey, who replied, "Mount your horse and stick to him as long as you can. You are fighting Indians, not white men."

German-born Privates Henry Klotzbucher and George Lorentz of Company M—the latter was French's orderly—were just climbing into their saddles when bullets from the fusillade ripped their bodies. Klotzbucher, who was French's "striker," screamed as a slug tore into his stomach.[4] His fellow M Company Privates Frank Neely and William C. Slaper dragged Klotzbucher into a clump of thick brush.[5] The bullet which struck Lorentz tore through the back of his neck and exited in a cascade of blood from his mouth.[6] "Oh, my God! I have got it!" Lorentz screamed. Lorentz, who had just sat in the saddle when hit, slipped from his mount and onto the ground. M Company Private William E. Morris lifted and carried Lorentz to some brush and propped him up. (Morris had a half brother, Private Byron L. Tarbox of Company L, with Custer's battalion.) Morris at first refused to leave Lorentz. But Lorentz insisted, "Go on. You cannot do me any good." The white-coated Dr. Porter rushed to attend Lorentz, or Klotzbucher, as Indian bullets whined around him.[7] Reynolds called to Porter to watch the gunfire in his direction. Miraculously, the surgeon was not hit. Sergeant John Ryan, the virtual executive officer of M Company, quickly told French, "Captain, the best thing that we can do is cut right through them."

Bloody Knife was mounted a few feet from a horsebacked Reno. The Ree had been trying without success to communicate in sign language with Reno when the Sioux fusillade erupted. Bullets ripped into the face and head of Bloody Knife and he toppled backward off his mount a dead man. (The enemy warriors later found the Ree's body, decapitated it, and impaled the head on a pole.) When Bloody Knife was hit, his blood and brains splattered Reno's face and tunic. Bloody Knife's gore gagged a now-juiceless Reno and he nearly vomited. Reno, visibly unnerved to the point of being senseless, cried out incoherently, "Mount! Dismount! Mount!" Wild-eyed and dripping with gore, he galloped to the edge of the woods and shouted, above the din, "Any of you men who wish to make your escape, follow me!"[8] Someone—not Reno—then yelled, "Every man for himself!" Reno then rode out of the timber and into everlasting shame.

Someone called above the din, "Men, to your horses!" A puzzled Gerard asked Reynolds, "What damn fool move is this?" Gerard, like some of the troopers near Reno, thought the battalion was charging the Indians. Reynolds replied that he didn't know, but said they would have to go. "We will have to get out of this," Reynolds told Gerard. Both men then went in search of their horses. A confused Varnum jumped to his feet when the battalion began its movement from the timber and asked no one in particular, "What's that?"

Dr. Porter hurriedly administered a dose of laudanum to Lorentz and then quickly mounted his horse for what he, too, believed was a charge against the Indians. Both Lorentz and Klotzbucher were cruelly abandoned in the timber. Lorentz was found alive by the Indians and horribly killed. Klotzbucher was not discovered by the warriors in the woods, but he died of his wound anyway.[9]

Flight from the Timber

In the panicked rout from the timber, it was every man for himself. The result was a bloody disaster. The warriors, according to Red Feather, the Oglala, were glad that the soldiers bolted from the timber. Some of the Indians shouted to let the bluecoats pass out of the timber because "we

TABLE 6
RENO'S CASUALTIES PRIOR TO LEAVING THE TIMBER

Killed	Wounded	Missing In Action
O'Hara	Heyn	G. E. Smith
Bloody Knife	White	
	Klotzbucher	
	Lorentz	
	Newell	
	Braun [?]	

can't get at them in there." [10] This substantiates Frederic Gerard's later claim that the timber was a good place for a defense.

Reno's Retreat

Several of the men began shouting, "We are going to charge!" Moylan began to mount A Company to follow Reno out of the timber. A dumfounded Hodgson saw A leaving the woods and called to Moylan, "What is this, a retreat?" A stern-faced Moylan replied that the battalion was going to "charge." "It looks most damnably like a rout," Hodgson called. [11] Hare recalled that he, too, "first thought it was a charge."

A startled Varnum saw the movement from the timber and thought the men were deserting the line. When he heard the cries of "Charge!" Varnum jumped up, crying, "What's that?" Varnum saw the first platoon of G Company mounted and moving through the woods. Varnum called to Reno to ask where that company was going. Reno did not answer, but several troopers shouted, "They're going to charge." When Varnum realized the "charge" was going away from the Indians, he screamed, "For God's sake, men, don't leave the line! There are enough of us here to whip the whole Sioux nation!" No one heeded Varnum.

Sergeant Roy of Moylan's troop couldn't locate his horse in the confusion and turmoil which swirled about the woods. Roy happened across Lieutenant Wallace and told the itinerary officer of his problem. "Take any horse you can find and get out of here quick!" Wallace warned. Several minutes passed before Roy located his horse. He was among the last troopers to leave the timber. On the flats, Roy's horse took a slug through the jaws and went down, spilling its rider. Fortu-

111

nately, Roy and his horse both scrambled to their feet and Roy, re-mounted, was able to gallop away.

Private Francis M. Reeves of Company A was shot from his horse at the edge of the timber. Moylan later recalled that an A Company trooper—Moylan didn't give the man's name—had been killed before the command rode from the woods. Reeves was the only A trooper shot down before the battalion had cleared the timber and undoubtedly he was the trooper erroneously reported by Moylan as being killed in the woods. Reeves, however, was not killed. Bleeding from a body wound, he staggered to his feet, glanced around, and saw his horse, which fortunately had stopped only a few yards away. Reeves climbed back in the saddle and galloped after his troop.

Reno's pell-mell retreat from the timber forked into eastern and southern routes. Those troopers taking the eastern route—it was most of the battalion—rode across difficult terrain. First crossing a small brush-dotted slough, they crossed two separate loops of the serpentine Little Bighorn to reach the main crossing to the bluffs on the eastern side of the river. The last leg to the main ford was across 264 yards of charred timber.

A trio of A Company troopers are known to have taken the south-ern route across the open flats from which the battalion had charged before the opening of hostilities. One of these troopers, realizing that escape was futile via this route, turned his horse eastward and escaped into some timber, where he hid. The other two troopers were not as fortunate. One of these men turned his mount to the west and rode up to some benchland, where he was killed. The other soldier rode all the way to the west bank of the river, opposite to where Reno Creek empties into the Little Bighorn. There, this unfortunate trooper dis-mounted and darted into some woods, where he was cornered in some woods. After having given a good account of himself with his revolv-er, he was mortally wounded and his horse was killed.[12]

***

Varnum had thought the battalion was charging until he saw the troops retreating from the Indians. Varnum caught his horse, a blooded Kentucky colt, but had great difficulty in mounting the spirited ani-mal. The mount still was not under control when a now-mounted

Varnum broke from the timber. Shortly before the animal jumped a small ravine, Varnum gained control of him.

Private Edward Davern of Company F, Reno's Irish-born orderly, had just galloped past two dismounted troopers of G Company, when he was thrown over the head of his horse, just as some Indians to Davern's left ran their horses together and went down in a heap. This gave Davern a lifesaving opportunity to mount his own horse as it stood up and to gallop away.

The two unhorsed soldiers of G Company, who panicked and fled the woods on foot, tried to outrun several mounted warriors in pursuit of them. Wallace, who fled with the second platoon of G from the woods on the heels of Moylan's troop, tried to save one of these men. He gallantly rode back to pick up the unhorsed trooper, but the man was ridden down and killed before Wallace could reach him. The same fate befell the trooper's companion.[13]

Cheyenne warriors Wooden Leg and Little Bird pursued some soldiers. Wooden Leg fired four revolver shots at the fleeing soldiers. The two warriors closed on another G Company trooper, who was riding a flagging horse. The two warriors, their revolvers emptied, moved on either side of the hapless trooper and repeatedly struck him with their pony whips. The soldier fired his revolver at Little Bird, who fell from his pony with a thigh wound. Wooden Leg struck the trooper across the head with the elk-horn handle of his whip and then jerked the carbine strap slung across the soldier's back. Wooden Leg then pulled the carbine strap over the trooper's head and the soldier fell to the ground; he was undoubtedly killed by pursuing warriors.[14]

***

Varnum's thoroughbred had overtaken the head of Reno's retreating column. According to both Dr. Porter and Varnum in their testimony before the Reno Court of Inquiry, Varnum tried to quell the panicked rout of A Company by admonishing the troopers, "For God's sake, men, don't run! There is [sic] a good many officers and men killed and wounded and we have to go back and get them." Reno, riding a few yards away with Moylan, overhead Varnum's words and remarked, "I am in command here, sir!" A sheepish Varnum dropped back and said no more.

***

When Company A left the timber, DeRudio and his detail were still at the cut bank near what is now the GarryOwen Loop of the Little Bighorn. DeRudio and his men only learned of the battalion's movement from the woods when A Company Trumpeter David McVeigh brought DeRudio his horse with the report that the battalion was vacating the timber. DeRudio refused to believe the report. But the men with DeRudio panicked at McVeigh's report and fled to their horses. DeRudio called after German-born Sergeant Henry Fehler to retrieve the company guidon, planted near the top of the cut bank. Fehler replied sarcastically, "To hell with the guidon! Don't you see the Indians are coming?"

The guidon had been planted on a cut bank above a dry channel of the river. It was only fifteen yards from DeRudio, so he went back and scampered up to get the guidon. Just as DeRudio raised his head above the top of the bank, a band of warriors, some forty to fifty yards away, cut loose a volley of shots at the officer. The bullets ripped the soil on the top of the bank, sending flying dirt into DeRudio's face. DeRudio grabbed the guidon and dropped down the bank. DeRudio then led his horse up the cut bank to the edge of the woods and tried to mount it, but the already frightened animal jumped and bolted riderless from the woods when a deer—DeRudio's later story—shot from the woods and caused DeRudio to become stranded.

His near brush with death took the stomach out of DeRudio. He later admitted that he had "gone through too many dangers and too many sacrifices and had lived too long to die in so unjust and obscure manner."[15] DeRudio showed the "white feather" (a frontier expression meaning cowardice) and skulked in the river timber as the battalion deserted the valley. Custer believed he knew the full worthlessness of DeRudio as an officer. The previous May, Custer had written the Adjutant General that "Lieutenant DeRudio possesses neither the experience nor the ability . . . nor is he a fit person in my opinion to exercise the . . . command of . . . a cavalry company . . . he is . . . the inferior of every first lieutenant in this regiment as an efficient and subordinate officer." DeRudio, as the senior officer of Company E (present on the campaign), should have been CO of that troop, but

Custer had assigned him duty with Company A under Moylan. That transfer saved DeRudio's life.

***

When the battalion broke from the timber, the first platoon of G Company remained in the woods where McIntosh had left it when he had gone in search of Reno. Several troopers of his company failed to get out of the woods. Some troopers did, however briefly. Sergeant Martin Considine, G Company, an Irish immigrant, galloped from the timber and rode several yards out onto the prairie. But an Indian marksman squeezed off a shot which toppled Considine backward off his mount. If the bullet didn't kill Considine, he was soon dispatched by the Indians.

Another G trooper, the German-born Private Henry Petring, was among the last of his company to leave the woods. When Petring went to get his horse, he found that the animal had been killed. Petring took the horse of a fellow G trooper, Private Eldorado J. Robb, and rode from the timber, only to have his mount shot from under him a few yards from the woods. Petring quickly retraced his steps to the timber, located still another mount, and rode after his fellow troopers.[16]

Irish-born Private Thomas F. O'Neill, also of G Company—he had once deserted from the Seventh Cavalry—had been one of the men reconnoitering the brush with McIntosh. When McIntosh failed to return to his platoon, and with the battalion deserting the timber, the 30-year-old O'Neill went in search of his horse. Locating the animal, he started to mount when the horse was shot, so he let the animal go. O'Neill found another trooper's horse and mounted him, only to have Irish-born Corporal James Martin of G Company pull rank and claim the animal for his own use. It was, indeed, every man for himself. O'Neill then started out of the woods on foot after the retreating battalion, but the warriors were so numerous in O'Neill's front that he realized he would never get through alive. He started back to the timber. At the edge of the timber, a mounted warrior tried to ride him down, but O'Neill turned and shot the Indian dead with his carbine before darting into the woods. A dismounted G trooper, the German-born Private Henry Seafferman, was run down and killed beside O'Neill as Seafferman tried to hide in some brush.[17]

115

In the meantime, McIntosh had failed to locate his orderly, who had the officer's horse. Confusion seemed to reign in the timber. Panic-stricken troopers galloped past the buckskin-shirted McIntosh without stopping as he frantically tried to catch up on a passing trooper's mount. Finally, Private Samuel McCormick, an Irish-born member of McIntosh's G troop, gallantly stopped and offered the officer his horse with the comment that they were all dead anyway. The not-too-proud McIntosh accepted McCormick's generous offer of the horse. The half-Indian McIntosh was one of only four line officers present at the Little Bighorn who had received his officer's commission sans Civil War service or a West Point education.

O'Neill met his CO, McIntosh, mounted on McCormick's horse, in the woods, and inquired as to the whereabouts of the command. McIntosh then callously abandoned O'Neill in the woods and rode out after the battalion.[18]

After McIntosh left the timber, O'Neill met German-born Private John Rapp of his company. Rapp, McIntosh's "lost" orderly, still held the lieutenant's horse. Rapp inquired of O'Neill about the whereabouts of McIntosh. A few minutes later, Rapp's life was ended by Indian bullets as he walked about the timber.[19]

***

M Company was the last of the battalion's three companies to leave the timber; only G Company's stragglers remained. Private David "Sandy" Summers of M was killed as he rode to the edge of the timber.[20] His body later was horribly mutilated by squaws. Corporal Frederick Streing, also of M, galloped a few yards from the woods and was killed instantly.[21]

French attempted to steady his company on its break from the timber. "Don't turn your back to the enemy . . . you damned fools!" French screamed in his falsetto voice to the panic-stricken men of Company M.

Corporal Henry M. Cody of M Company—he had enlisted under the alias of Henry M. Scollen—was wounded upon leaving the timber and his played-out mount stumbled, throwing him into a marsh. When Cody's horse went down his fellow M Company trooper, William Morris, trailing close by, avoided disaster and leapt his horse over the downed Cody and his mount. Another fellow M Company trooper, Private Daniel Newell, bleeding from the wound in his left thigh, nonetheless stopped to try to give Cody a hand up in his [Newell's] saddle. But Cody was too seriously wounded to climb up on Newell's horse. "Good-bye, boys!" Cody shouted as Newell and others rode away.

Another M trooper, Private Rollins L. Thorpe, who was trailing the company, saw the wounded Cody and gallantly dismounted to assist the hapless Cody. Thorpe succeeded in raising Cody into the saddle, but the weight of both riders caused Thorpe's exhausted mount to stumble in the spongy terrain, throwing both men. Thorpe was quickly on his feet, managed to catch a riderless Indian pony, mounted, and rode on after the battalion, satisfied that he had done everything possible to aid the unfortunate Cody. With his two chances at rescue gone, Cody drew his revolver and calmly waited for death. Several charging warriors rode through the bog and over Cody, riddling his body with numerous bullets. How many warriors Cody managed to kill before he was killed is not known. Squaws later horribly mutilated Cody's body and cut off his right leg.[22]

Private William Morris, also of Company M, had been delayed in leaving the timber because he had aided the wounded Lorentz. Morris, therefore, was among the last of his troop to leave the woods. Morris had just stepped into a stirrup when the animal bolted. He quickly bellyflopped across the saddle as the horse loped through some thick brush and scrub trees, which cut and slashed Morris' face.

French, bringing up the rear of his retreating company, attempted to stem the panic rout of his men. In his falsetto voice, French called, ". . . Steady there men. Steady. Keep up a continual fire, you damned fools! Don't turn your back to the enemy. Steady, you damned fools!"

***

The befuddled McIntosh prodded Private McCormick's troublesome mount southward across the broad prairie over which Reno's battalion had trekked in its charge down the valley. The horse angled right, carrying McIntosh farther out on the prairie. The battalion, or at least most of it, had retreated eastward upon leaving the timber. Hordes of breechclothed, screaming warriors soon caught and sur-

117

rounded McIntosh. The officer fired his revolver repeatedly at the swarming warriors as they circled him. When McIntosh's revolver was empty, a warrior rode forward and knocked him from the saddle with a stone hammer. McIntosh's horse was dragging its lariat behind it. The lariat suddenly hooked a snag and jerked the animal, sending it tumbling to the ground. A warrior galloped near the stunned McIntosh and shot a round into his chest while the glassy-eyed officer lay on his back.[23] The bullet tore through a small memorandum notebook he carried in a breast pocket.[24] The copper-skinned McIntosh looked more Indian than white and the Indians were particularly unmerciful. Amid blood-curdling screams, frenzied warriors swarmed the body of the fallen officer and pounded his head with their war clubs. McIntosh's features were obliterated by the blows and his scalp was lifted from the top of his forehead to the nape of his neck. His body was later scorched when the Sioux set fire to the valley grass on the twenty-sixth.

Hare, on loan as second in command of the scouts, also among the last to leave the timber, was more fortunate. On duty in the South since his 1874 West Point graduation, Hare was on his first campaign. The command already had deserted the woods when Hare's orderly, Private Elihu F. Clear of K Company, brought the officer his horse and told him of the battalion's movement. (For more than a century, historians of the battle have erroneously passed off Clear as Dr. J. M. DeWolf's orderly. The fact that Clear had charge of Hare's horse in the timber [Hare to Walter M. Camp, February 7, 1910, BYU] proves that Clear was Hare's orderly.) This was the first that Hare knew of the battalion's leaving the timber. Hare and Clear galloped from the woods. Hare erroneously believed Clear was killed a short time after leaving the timber.[25] But Clear was not killed at that time as shall be seen later. A few warriors nearly caught Hare in a wild ride to the river, but he rode on and galloped passed Private Morris, who was riding hard to catch up with his company. Hare later wrote his father: "I am out of this fight without a scratch, but how it is I don't know. I ran the gauntlet of about 1,500 [sic] of them and they didn't touch me or my horse. To kill a man's horse was certain death to him."[26] Sergeant Ryan agreed with Hare. Ryan recalled (Hardin *Tribune*, June 22, 1923) that "as we cut through them [the Indians] the fighting was hand to hand, and it was death to any man who fell from his horse or was wounded and was not able to keep up with the command."

***

Teat Dorman, the black interpreter who was dressed in a soldier's uniform, rode from the woods on the extreme right of Reno's second skirmish line. The Negro did not get far. A band of warriors led by Runs-the-Enemy cut off Dorman's escape when he was fifty to sixty yards from the timber. Dorman killed one Indian before his horse crumpled under him in a shower of warriors' bullets. Dorman quickly rolled free of his dead mount, grabbed his carbine, raised himself on one knee, and began firing at the howling warriors circling him. Private Rutten galloped by without stopping and Dorman called above the din, "Goodbye, Rutten!"

The Sioux showed Dorman no mercy. Dorman sat up after evidently being struck by a bullet. A Hunkpapa woman named Her Eagle Robe came up to Dorman while he was sitting on the ground and pointed her rifle at him. He asked her not to kill him because, he said, he would be dead in a short time anyway. Her Eagle Robe scolded Dorman for fighting against the Sioux and then shot him.[27] Dorman's lower legs were riddled with numerous revolver bullets and several arrows were shot into his chest. Squaws horribly mutilated Dorman's body. He was stripped naked. A metal picket pin was driven through his testicles.[28] A squaw gutted the black man's stomach and collected his blood in a tin cup and coffee pot from Dorman's mess kit. Several squaws then pounded Dorman's face and head into wet pulp with stone-head hammers. A horrified Herendeen looked on at the grisly sight as he tried to break out of the ring of warriors. As a final indignity, Dorman's penis was severed and stuffed into his mouth. The women also decapitated Dorman.

Many Indian women followed their warriors into battle to encourage them and to emasculate and otherwise mutilate wounded or dead soldiers. Other Indian women, such as the Cheyenne Twin Woman, whose husband, Lame (Walking) White Man, was killed fighting Custer, were too afraid to go near the battlefield.

Herendeen, who also had been among the last to leave the timber, was some distance from the woods when his horse stumbled and threw

119

him. A band of about twenty mounted warriors nearly trampled Herendeen to death in a cloud of alkaline dust before he could scramble to his feet. After the warriors rode on, Herendeen was on his feet, retracing his steps back to the timber.

A winded Herendeen reached the timber just as scout Charley Reynolds was mounting to ride out. "You can't make it!" Herendeen called to Reynolds. Reynolds, moments before, had been plagued by indecision as to whether he should dart from the woods. Reynolds ignored Herendeen's warning and galloped from the timber. Within a short distance, a warrior's bullet tore into Lonesome Charley's chest. Reynolds screamed and dropped his rifle as he fell from his mount. As he fell, one of his feet became entangled in the stirrup and he was dragged for several yards before he succeeded in freeing himself. Somehow Reynolds had kept his hat on during his fall. Severely wounded, with hordes of screaming warriors swarming about him, Lonesome Charley, the Lucky Man, now resigned himself to certain death. The veteran scout coolly drew his revolver, and while kneeling on one knee, emptied his pistol at the frenzied warriors, who rushed over Reynolds's body and hacked and cut it. One warrior decapitated the scout with a battle ax and carried away his grisly trophy.

In the meantime, Fred Gerard and young Billy Jackson had ridden from the timber only to have their route blocked by hordes of screaming warriors. The two men turned their horses and rode back to the woods in a hail of Indian bullets. Years later, Gerard would tell historian Walter Camp that the "timber was a splendid place for defense."

***

Bobtailed Bull and the 26-year-old Little Brave, one of whom was wearing a warbonnet taken from a warrior he had probably killed, had become separated from the other Indian scouts during Reno's retreat from the valley. Both scouts—dressed in white shirts and blue Army trousers—fled on their played-out horses from a large band of Sioux and Cheyenne. Their pursuers were Oglala War Chief He Dog (1838/1840–1936 [he reported both years as his birth year]); Oglalas Red Feather, Kicking Bear, Running Eagle, and Eagle Elk, the 15-year-old cousin of the renowned Crazy Horse; Miniconjous High Horse and Turtle Rib; Elk Stands Above (High), a Sans Arc; the Sioux

Young Skunk, who was killed later fighting Custer, and Runs Fearless; and Cheyenne Crooked Nose, [Little] Whirlwind, a 16-year-old warrior, and the ever-busy Wooden Leg.

One of the Ree scouts fled across a timber-dotted bog before crossing a lower loop in the river. Although separated, both Little Brave, who had sustained a wound in his right shoulder, and Bobtailed Bull made it across to the east side of the river, some distance below Reno's retreat crossing. Red Feather had shot the horse from under one of the Rees (probably that of Little Brave for Bobtailed Bull's survived and returned with the Seventh Cavalry to Fort Lincoln). The teenaged Whirlwind closed on the Ree still mounted. Suddenly, this scout turned on Whirlwind and charged him. Both fired their long guns at the same time and both fell dead or dying.

The other Ree momentarily held off his pursuers from behind a sagebrush-shrouded knoll, from which he shot and killed Elk Stands Above. Wooden Leg and others circled around to rush this scout when he fell from a bullet fired by Running Eagle. Wooden Leg rushed forward; the scout raised to fire his carbine again but Wooden Leg and others rushed him. Wooden Leg struck him in the head with his captured carbine and Kicking Bear shot the hapless Ree twice. Red Feather finished the scout off with a knife.[29]

Little Brave was decapitated[30] and a pointed willow reed was driven into the chest of Bobtailed Bull by their frenzied killers.

(It is of interest to note that in 1890 Kicking Bear was an apostle of the religious Ghost Dance craze which swept the Plains tribes that year.)

Red Bear (also Good or Handsome Elk), another of the Ree scouts, was more fortunate. Red Bear became unhorsed when his mount stumbled and threw him on the ride to the river. Fortunately, Red Bear's horse stopped in some nearby thickets, but before the Ree could remount, a Sioux warrior galloped toward the scout. Red Bear grabbed his carbine and fired at the warrior, killing him. Red Bear quickly remounted and rode across the river and up the steep slopes east of the river.

***

Two more A Company men failed to reach the main retreat crossing of the river. One of these troopers became unhorsed and was killed near the middle of the large loop in the river below where Reno's command retreated across the Little Bighorn to the bluffs. This soldier's skeleton was discovered in 1926. Perhaps the trooper was the one seen with his foot caught in a stirrup and being dragged by his runaway horse across a creek. A little farther on, about a fifth of a mile short of the main retreat crossing, the second trooper and his horse were killed. The skeletons of this poor wretch and his horse were discovered in 1928.[31] This trooper might have been the one Wooden Leg spoke of (Marquis, *I Wooden Leg,* p. 221) who was shot in the back of the head and shoulder with two arrows by a Sioux warrior. The trooper's horse fell to the ground near him and was probably killed.

***

Private Petring was among the last of Reno's troopers still trying to ride out of the valley and who had not yet reached the crossing ford. (Several stragglers had taken haven in the timber.) Petring could only reach the first loop of the river before a handful of warriors blocked his route. One warrior took aim at Petring, but the trooper fired first. Petring's bullet struck the Indian who, along with his pony, tumbled down a cut bank into the river. The other warriors closed on Petring, who leaped from the back of his horse into the river. A shower of bullets ripped the water around Petring. Petring swam several yards downstream and hid beneath a rotted tree stump that was sticking out from the bank. Later he moved into some thick willows on the west bank of the river. After some time, Petring happened across Private Benjamin Johnson of Company G and other troopers in the woods who had been left behind in Reno's wild retreat from the valley.[32]

The Retreat Ford

The main ford used by Reno's battalion in its wild flight across the Little Bighorn was on a narrow buffalo trail which cut down a clay bank some five to six feet high on the west side of the river. The stream was horse-belly depth for its twenty- to twenty-five-yard width but provided the best available natural crossing opportunity to the high slopes on the east side of the river. Other "fords" used were meanders or loops of the river which frenzied troopers used in their desperate attempts to escape the valley. The retreating command reached the ford at 4:00 P.M. by Lieutenant Wallace's watch.

Those A Company men leading the retreat were forced to jump their horses into the stream from the top of the cut bank. The bank eventually caved in a few feet, from the hooves of the horses cutting away the clay at the top of the bank. Those troopers crossing after A Company found an easier ford to cross. On the opposite (eastern) side of the ford, the climb up the cut bank was some eight to ten feet.

Congestion and bedlam reigned at the ford in the mad scramble across the Little Bighorn. The scene there was one of shouting and bumping of panic-stricken troopers who were bunched on frenzied mounts. Some of the men escaped the logjam by crossing the stream several yards above or below the main ford. Since no officer had ordered any covering fire at the main crossing—a serious breach of military tactics—the warriors eventually (after crossing) lined both banks of the stream crossing and poured gunfire at the bunched blue-coats. Some of the warrior marksmen lined the bluffs above the ford. Two Moons recalled that "the air [at the ford] was full of smoke and dust. I saw soldiers fall back and drop into the riverbed like buffalo fleeing."[33]

The French-born Private Jean B. Gallenne of Company M was more fortunate. Gallenne's exhausted mount collapsed near the river, rose again and carried his rider across the river. Surprisingly, Gallenne had not lost hold of the reins of the riderless horse which raced aside his own mount. Across the river, he surrendered this second mount to fellow M Company trooper Daniel Newell.

The turkey shoot at the main ford took the lives of six soldiers. The skull, arm bone, and clavicle of one of these troopers were found at Reno's retreat crossing on the west bank of the Little Bighorn in 1989. A forensic study of the skull revealed that this man had met death when hit across the right side of the face with a sharp instrument or a war club, which had sheared off at least three teeth down to the roots. One of these six remains unidentified, although the others can be accounted for.

Five troopers of A and G Companies were bunched at the ford. Wooden Leg rode into these troopers and clubbed two of them from their mounts with his captured carbine.[34] Both men tumbled down the

123

west cut bank into the river[35] where they were killed by gunfire from the warriors lining the banks. One of the troopers was Private William Moody (or Moodie), Company A, a Scottish-born trooper [believed by Walter Camp to have been an English cavalryman], leaped his mount down the west bank of the river. A warrior on the east bank—warriors had crossed up and downstream of the main crossing to head off retreating troopers on the opposite bank—fired a shot which killed Moody.[36]

One Bull, Sitting Bull's nephew, killed two of the soldiers at the ford by cleaving them with his war club on the east riverbank. Jumping his horse into the water, he then caught another trooper and cleaved him.[37] Four of the A and G troopers killed at the ford, in addition to Moody, can be identified. One of them was German-born Edward Botzer, acting first sergeant of Company G. What is probably Botzer's skull was found opposite Reno's retreat crossing in May, 1989.[38] Only Botzer and Moody (Moodie) match the physical and age descriptions ascribed to the skull. The cutmarks on the skull indicates that its owner was violently bashed in the face and knocked from his horse with a sharp-edged weapon. Botzer might have been the soldier killed by a saber-wielding warrior.[39] Moody was shot from his horse. The other three men were A Company Corporal James Dalious; Corporal James Martin, the G company noncom who had commandeered Private O'Neill's horse in the timber; and Irish-born John Sullivan of Company A.[40]

Another of Reno's retreating troopers killed in the race to the river—but not among those killed at the ford—was Farrier Benjamin J. Wells of Company G. Wells was killed near a lower bend in the river below the main retreat crossing when his frenzied horse bolted into a crowd of pursuing Indians. Somehow Wells at first rode clear of these Indians, but he was killed when shot off his horse in the stream.[41] The Silesian-born Private Gustave Korn of Company I, who was on detached service with Reno's battalion, possibly as one of Reno's orderlies, had his horse killed near the river. Korn managed to hide out and rejoin Reno on the hilltops on the night of June 25. (Korn was killed in the battle at Wounded Knee, South Dakota, on December 29, 1890.)

French, Hodgson, and Company B Private George B. Mask, who earlier had been detached from Custer's headquarters staff (Richard

G. "Dutch" Hardorff, talk with author, June 25, 1991, Sheridan, Wyoming), but now was serving as Hodgson's orderly,[42] reached the ford and found it clogged with warriors on both banks. French, with a smoking revolver, galloped through a cordon of warriors, twenty yards on either side of him. Two howling warriors moved toward French as he crossed to the west bank of the river. French's revolver exploded twice and both warriors dropped from their ponies. French plunged his mount down into the river, rode up the opposite bank, and disappeared up the eastern slopes.[43]

Hodgson, the regimental "pet," and his orderly Mask plunged their mounts down into the stream just as the warriors on the opposite bank fired at them. Mask was shot from his horse. The river's current carried Mask's body downstream, never to be seen again, or at least never identified.[44] While riding near the wounded A Company Sergeant William Heyn, Hodgson was struck by a bullet which tore into his groin below his saber belt, exited a thigh, and entered and killed his horse. (It was once thought that Reno's acting assistant adjutant general had been struck by two different bullets and that a third had struck his horse.)[45] Benny floundered in waist-deep water streaked with his blood.

***

M Company was the last to reach the retreat crossing. One of its members, Private Frank Braun, had wounds in the face and left thigh as he neared the ford. Braun probably had been wounded in the timber before the battalion left there since the nature of his leg wound indicated that he was crouching when hit in the lower left leg. The bullet moved upward and lodged in the thigh. Despite these wounds, Braun made it across the river and up the bluffs to safety. He died on October 4, 1876, of his wounds.[46]

Private Slaper rode through a volley of Indian gunfire and a cordon of howling warriors at the ford. Slaper crossed the river and rode up the eastern slopes, unscathed with Indian gunfire directed at him all the way.

Snopsy Meier slumped in the saddle as a bullet tore into his back. Another bullet felled his horse a few yards from the west cut bank. Meier scampered to his feet, ran to the bank, and dove into the stream.

Meier managed to catch and mount a riderless cavalry horse mid-stream just seconds before the unhorsed Hodgson could reach the animal. Meier galloped to the east cut bank in a hail of Indian gunfire and on up the bluffs.[47]

Troopers splashed by the wild-eyed Hodgson, nearly riding over him, as the officer screamed, "For God's sake, don't abandoned me!" Sergeant Ferdinand A. Culbertson of Company A, trailing his troop's retreat by several minutes, rode by Hodgson, ignoring the officer's pleas. Charles "Bounce" Fischer, a German-born trumpeter of M Company, rode past Hodgson and thrust out a loose stirrup. Hodgson grabbed the stirrup with one hand and was pulled part way across the stream,[48] but he lost his grip before reaching the opposite bank. Fischer rode on.

Private Morris was riding directly behind Fischer. At the ford, Morris had emptied his revolver wildly at a group of warriors blocking his path to the river. A few of the warriors tried, unsuccessfully, to lasso Morris from his mount. From the ford, Morris saw Hodgson near the opposite bank.

"Don't abandoned me! I'm shot in both legs," Hodgson cried with the stark look of fear on his face. Morris mercifully stopped to thrust out a stirrup, which Hodgson grabbed with both hands. Morris leaned down from the saddle and took the wounded officer by the collar with one hand and plunged up a narrow trail leading up the cut bank on the east side of the river. The plunging of Morris's mount caused Hodgson to loosen his grip on the stirrup, but the young trooper's own strong grip held the lieutenant firmly. Hodgson's full weight pulled against Morris's saddle, slipping it backward toward the rump of the horse. Morris continued to pull Hodgson up the cut bank and the officer's weight tugged against Morris's arm and shoulder, which caused excruciating pain to the rescuer. A few yards ahead, near the top of the cut bank, Morris saw M Company Privates Henry Turley and William W. Rye. Suddenly, Turley and his mount were hit by Indian gunfire. Turley and his horse tumbled down the bank to the edge of the water while Rye galloped on unhit. Morris then cleared the top of the bank—just as a slug penetrated the temple of the hapless Hodgson, killing him instantly. Morris released his grip and the dead officer fell at the top of the cut back about twenty feet above the water.[49] After Reno's troops had deserted the valley, a warrior found Private Turley still alive. The warrior took the trooper's hunting knife and drove it to the hilt into Turley's right eye.[50]

The Struggle up the Bluffs

German-born Corporal Otto Hagemann of Company G rode up the lower bluffs just above the retreat crossing. Hagemann was shot off his horse and killed either by warriors shooting from the west bank or by others on the slopes just above him.

***

Sergeant Ferdinand Culbertson kicked his well-lathered horse up the steep slopes and came across Corporal George Loyd of G Company, an Irish immigrant. He called to Loyd that the command needed cover fire at the retreat crossing. Minutes later, Loyd caught up with French, higher on the bluffs, and asked him to order a cover fire for the wounded trying to cross the river. "I'll try! I'll try!" an excited French replied.[51] But the officer did nothing and rode on. (Loyd died from wounds received fighting the Sioux on December 29, 1890, at Wounded Knee, South Dakota.)

In the ride up the steep slopes, the troopers clung to the necks of their horses to keep from sliding out of their saddles. Others dismounted and led their exhausted horses up the steep grade as Indian bullets pinged around them.

***

An exhausted Morris and two fellow M Company privates, William D. "Tinker Bill" Meyer and English-born Henry Gordon, were half way up the bluffs when they dismounted and foolishly stopped to rest. Suddenly, Indian marksmen on their side of the bluffs fired at the three troopers and their mounts. Gordon pitched dead with a bullet in the neck. Meyer was killed instantly with a round in the eye fired by an Indian on a horse who had trailed Reno's stragglers across the ford.[52] Morris was struck by a bullet in the left breast. The bullet passed out of Morris' body. Unable to remount, Morris grabbed a stirrup and gave his wounded horse its head. He was dragged to safety at the top of the bluffs.[53] Morris survived his serious wound. On the

127

top of the bluffs, French ordered some men to take Morris to the surgeon. The troops on the hilltops gave the bodies of Meyer and Gordon protective cover fire to keep the Indians from scalping them.[54]

Two other M Company privates, the wounded Daniel Newell, whose horse had been hit twice by gunfire at the ford, and Hobart Ryder were a short distance up the slopes when they were forced to abandoned their played-out animals. Newell and Ryder took haven in some tall sagebrush growing on the side of the slope. Later, when the Indians' gunfire had slackened, both troopers crawled to safety at the top of the bluffs.[55]

***

Hare rode hard up the bluffs—he had caught A Company on his swift mount—and tried to rally Moylan's men. "If we've got to die, let's die like men!" Hare yelled to A troop above the din. Galloping close to Moylan, Hare shouted disrespectfully to him, "Don't run off like a pack of whipped curs!" Hare galloped up the bluffs, shouted a rebel yell, and called, "I'm a fightin' sonofabitch from Texas!"[56]

Up the bluffs, Hare yelled at Moylan and some troopers, "Don't run off like a pack of whipped curs!" Reno overheard Hare and called to a badly frightened Moylan to halt some men and give cover fire to those below, but Moylan did not heed the order and Reno repeated it.

A hatless Varnum and his orderly, Private Elijah T. Strode of Company A, who was bleeding from a wound in the lower right leg, rode up a blind ravine when someone shouted to them that they were riding in the wrong direction. A few minutes later, Varnum and his orderly were galloping up a steep coulee when Strode's horse faltered. Varnum dismounted and assisted the wounded Strode. Just then Sergeant Culbertson rode up and Varnum requested assistance. Varnum managed to grab the reins of a riderless M Company horse and he and Culbertson assisted Strode into the saddle and up the bluffs.[57]

***

Dr. DeWolf, and Hare's orderly, Private Elihu Clear, in their desperate attempt to flee death, galloped up a ravine some distance northwest of the rest of Reno's retreating troops. Just as DeWolf and Clear reached the crest of a hogbacked knoll, about 300 yards northwest of what soon became the Reno-Benteen Defense Perimeter, or Reno Hill, Indian sharpshooters on the slopes began firing at them. Nick Wallace reined in his well-lathered horse on a distant slope, drew his sporting rifle, and from atop his mount fired at the warriors who were shooting at DeWolf and Clear. Wallace's shots failed to find a single mark. DeWolf and Clear were several yards below the summit of the bluffs when Indian gunfire ended their lives within a few yards of each other, near where Tinker Bill Meyer and Henry Gordon had been killed. Wallace grimaced at the surgeon's death and returned his rifle to its scabbard before continuing his ride to the top of the bluffs. Firepower from the soldiers who had gained the top of Reno Hill was galling to the warriors below, since it blocked their chance to scalp Dr. DeWolf, Clear, Gordon, or Meyer.

***

Billy Cross and William Baker, and the four full-blooded Sioux scouts (White Cloud, Buffalo Ancestor, Bear-Running-in-the-Timber, and Bear Waiting) seemed to have fled the valley without incident. The same can be said for the Ree, Black Fox. But at the retreat crossing, six of the Indian scouts were having a difficult time of it. Half-Yellow-Face and White Swan were the first of the scouts to retreat across to the east side of the Little Bighorn. White Swan rode across to the east side and fell from his mount near the river with a wound in the right hand.

Young Hawk, his grandfather Forked Horn, Red Foolish Bear, and Goose, on exhausted mounts which had left them far behind Reno's retreating battalion, took haven in a thick grove of cottonwoods, felled logs, and piled driftwood along the east bank of the river. The four Rees were joined by Half-Yellow-Face and these scouts prepared themselves for a fight to the death against Sioux and Cheyenne warriors. Goose took a shot in the right hand and called to Young Hawk that he was wounded. Young Hawk assisted Goose from the latter's horse and propped him against a cottonwood. Goose's horse was shot down just after the Ree dismounted. Young Hawk, stripped of his coat and Army blouse, and with Goose's cartridge belt, vowed to die fighting the Rees' mortal enemy, the Sioux. Leaving his own mount in the care of Goose, Young Hawk started back into the fray when Half-Yellow-

Face crawled over to his position and said, "My friend [White Swan] is being killed, he is just on the edge of the thicket." Young Hawk and Half-Yellow-Face then crawled out under heavy gunfire to drag White Swan, who lay exposed to enemy marksmen, to the cover of the grove. While White Swan was on the riverbank, a bullet whistled in and struck him in the foot.

The Indians tried to burn the scouts out of their sheltered area, but the grass was too green to burn. Young Hawk, particularly, did some heroic fighting. The teenager stood in front of the brush and fired his carbine at the warriors on the opposite bank. A Sioux warrior, mounted on a gray horse, charged close to Young Hawk's position. The young Ree fired twice at the warrior and unhorsed him with the second shot. His grandfather, Forked Horn, did little fighting. From a prone position behind a rotted log and some driftwood, Forked Horn reprimanded his grandson for being so foolish as to expose himself to the Sioux and Cheyenne gunfire.

The six Indian scouts bravely held the Sioux and Cheyenne at bay for most of the afternoon while some Indian women exhorted the warriors to finish off the scouts. Late in the afternoon—after the arrival of the pack train on the bluffs—the six scouts ascended the slopes. On the way up, Young Hawk's horse was killed by a Sioux or Cheyenne sniper. The unfortunate Goose was mistaken for a hostile warrior on the hilltop by a panic-stricken trooper, who mangled the Ree's wounded hand with a carbine butt. But the scouts reached the top of the bluffs without further casualties.

Red Bear (Good or Handsome Elk), too, rode up from the valley. On the top of the slopes, he happened across White Cloud, who also had fled from the valley during Reno's retreat. The two scouts then came across White-Man-Runs-Him, Goes Ahead, and Hairy Moccasin, who had lingered on the bluffs after Boyer had dismissed them. The three Crows inquired of the whereabouts of their fellow Crows Half-Yellow-Face and White Swan before moving on. About this time, Half-Yellow-Face, who had veered farther southward in his flight up the slopes, reached a point near the mouth of Reno Creek where he met and joined Benteen's battalion. Boy Chief, Strikes Two, Little Sioux, and Bull-Stands-in-Water were joined on the slopes by the seven scouts who had failed to cross the river with Reno. One Feather, Red

Star, Red Bear, Pretty Face—he had deserted the pack train—and the four friendly Sioux scouts also joined the aforementioned of scouts. The 45-year-old Stabbed, who seems to have taken command away from Soldier, and who was Bobtailed Bull's second-in-command, spoke, "What are we doing now, we scouts? We ought to do what Custer told us to do if we were defeated. He told us to fall back to the Powder River, where the rest of the scouts are and the wagons and provisions."[58] On the movement up the slopes, Boy Chief's horse was wounded by soldiers firing from the top of the bluffs as they mistook the Indian scouts as hostile warriors. Stabbed removed his hat and waved it at the soldiers to cease firing.

Stabbed then ordered a rear guard action against the Sioux while others took the captured ponies on. The Rees Stabbed, Soldier, Little Sioux, Strikes-the-Lodge, Strikes Two, and Boy Chief and the Sioux, White Cloud, Bear-Running-in-the-Timber and Bear Waiting made up the rear guard. When no Sioux came up from the valley, the Ree horse herders (Bull, Bull-Stands-in-Water, Charging Bull, Red Bear, Red Star, Red Wolf, One Feather, Pretty Face, and White Eagle, together with the Sioux, Buffalo Ancestor) moved their coveted horse herd out at a gallop toward the Rosebud. Little Sioux stopped briefly on a slope and gazed northward where, some two miles or so in the distance, he saw many mounted Sioux blanketing the sides of a sloping hill. Gunfire echoed in the distance. On the twenty-sixth, the latter band of scouts were joined by scout Billy Cross. Black Fox caught up the group on June 27.

Atop the Bluffs

Reno's exhausted mount had nearly collapsed on the wild ride up the steep slopes from the east cut bank some 700 yards from the river. The major later reached the summit of these high bluffs hatless and without revolver or carbine. The handkerchief still was tied around Reno's forehead. Reno borrowed a revolver, rode to the edge of the bluffs, and began firing at some Indians 900 yards in the distance.

Dr. Porter, disgusted by the rout from the river valley, asked Reno, "Major, the men were pretty demoralized by the rout, weren't they?" Reno flushed with anger at the surgeon's remark. "No! That was a cavalry charge, sir!" Reno bellowed. (Except that Reno "charged"

131

away from most of the Indians.) Nevertheless, Dr. Porter testified at the Reno Court of Inquiry that "the command was demoralized . . . [and] seemed to think they had been whipped. . . ." Reno always maintained that his actions in the river valley were correct. He later defended his *retreat* from the valley by saying, "I saw I could not stay there unless I stayed forever." French merely called the retreat a *sauve qui peut* ("every man for himself") movement. But to Gerard and Herendeen, "the Rees could have stood the Indians off if Reno had stuck to the timber."[59] Reno's command had spent only forty-five minutes on the valley floor, from the time the battalion dismounted (3:15 P.M.) to the time it reached the river's ford on the retreat from the timber (4:00 P.M.).

***

Off to one side of the bluffs, a hatless Varnum, his forehead wrapped in a white handkerchief, raised his voice in loud curses as tears oozed down his cheeks. He began telling the officers of Benteen's newly arrived battalion what had happened in the valley and called for a gun, which his friend Wallace gave him. He repeatedly fired Wallace's sporting rifle at some Indians 900 yards away. But Varnum became distraught with grief at the death of his close friend Benny Hodgson. He broke down and sobbed uncontrollably.

***

Having followed Reno's shod-horse trail since somewhere near where the middle and north forks of Reno Creek intersect, Benteen's battalion now approached Reno's beleaguered command on the bluffs. Benteen and his orderly, and Weir with Company D, rode in advance of the battalion. They had seen Billy Cross riding in a southward direction when Benteen's advance reached a point opposite the bluffs where Reno's embattled command now sought haven.[60] Near a point where Reno had first crossed the river on his ride to the attack, Benteen and his orderly had viewed for the first time the remnants of Reno's command in panic and flight, desperately galloping up the slopes. When Benteen's battalion reached Reno, Edgerly saw a disheveled Reno begrimed with dust and sweat, sitting on his horse and

132

firing his revolver at some Indians several hundred yards in the distance.[61]

In a letter (July 4) to his wife, Benteen described Reno's rout from the valley: ". . . I saw an immense number of Indians on the plain, mounted and charging, some dismounted men of Reno's [battalion]; the balance of his command was mounted and flying for the bluffs. . . ."

Reno saw Benteen and hurried forward to meet him. Upon reaching Benteen, Reno blurted, "For God's sake, Benteen, halt your command and help me! I've lost half of my men!"[62] Benteen glanced about the hilltop and saw Moylan "blubbering like a whipped urchin."[63] Although Custer haters by nature, Reno and Benteen cared little for each other. Still, this was an emergency.

"Where's Custer?" Benteen asked a bewildered Reno as the senior captain looked around at the terror-filled faces of Reno's men.

"I don't know," Reno said curtly.

Benteen then handed Reno Custer's last message. Reno read the note and returned it to Benteen. The subject of Custer was dropped for the moment.

A dour-faced Hare grabbed Godfrey's right hand firmly and said excitedly, "We've had a big fight in the valley; got whipped like hell and I am damned glad to see you." Hare blamed Custer for the whole debacle at the Little Bighorn. Writing a fellow officer in 1893, Hare wrote that Custer's battle tactics were "defenseless" and that anyone trying to defend them displayed his own "incompetency."[64] Both Benteen and Weir privately admitted to Hare that, in their opinions, Reno had made a mistake by not remaining in the valley.[65]

Private Charles Windolph, of Benteen's Company H, went to the edge of the bluffs and gazed at the valley below. He could see hundreds of Indians still shooting at stragglers at the retreat crossing while other stragglers were climbing the slopes. Windolph glanced about the hilltop and saw "disorganized and terror stricken" men.

Wallace, the itinerary officer, had failed to note the official time of Benteen's arrival on the hilltop. It was about 4:15 P.M.

***

Some time after Benteen arrived on the hilltops, Reno and Dr.

TABLE 7

RENO BATTALION: TOTAL CASUALTIES ON REACHING THE BLUFFS

	Killed	Wounded	Missing In Action
Officers	2	0	1 (DeRudio)
Enlisted Men	29	12[*]	18[**]
Civilians and Scouts	6	2	3
Total:	37	14	22

[*] Private Frank Braun, Company M, who died on October 4, 1878 at Fort Lincoln is included in this total.

[**] Fifteen of these troopers later rejoined Reno's command on the blufftops. The remaining three troopers were never seen alive again. This meant that with the twenty-nine enlisted men killed outright in the valley, together with Private George E. Smith, whose horse had carried him into Indian ranks, and who was never seen again, and two troopers left behind in the timber—Private John E. Armstrong of Company A and Private John J. McGinnis of Company G—and never seen alive again, plus the aforementioned Braun, actually brought Reno's total killed in the valley to thirty-three.

TABLE 8

RENO BATTALION: ENLISTED MEN'S CASUALTIES BY COMPANY

Killed		Wounded		Left In Timber (MIA)	
Co. A	7	Co. A	5	Co. A	1
Co. B	1	Co. G	2	Co. G	10
Co. G	10	Co. M	5[*]	Co. I	1
Co. K	1	Co. M	6		
Co. M	10				
Total:	29		12		18

[*] Includes Braun.

Porter led a detail of troopers down to where the body of Hodgson lay. (The Indians had moved away from Reno's position to fight Custer.) Reno secured Hodgson's West Point class ring and a few other items from the lieutenant's body. Dr. Porter picked up Hodgson's pocketbook, which had fallen from the officer's pocket. Reno's party took advantage of the fact that few, if any Indians now remained at or near the crossing and refilled their canteens in the river. Hodgson's body was left where it had fallen and Reno's group returned to the summit of the bluffs after an absence of twenty-five to thirty minutes.

13

Stragglers in the Timber
Late Afternoon

After abandoning his horse, DeRudio climbed into a hollowed-out hole in the riverbank and hid. While he was in hiding, three stray bullets came dangerously close to hitting him. The Indians set fire to the woods in an effort to burn out any straggling bluecoats, but the fire died out before setting the timber ablaze.

DeRudio saw a warrior approach his hiding place. The Italian drew his revolver, but held his fire as the Indian suddenly moved away. Later, DeRudio left his hole and lurked through the woods. He saw several Indian women mutilating a dead or dying sergeant (Considine) with stone-head hammers a short distance away on the prairie. The sergeant was naked below the waist. One squaw jerked his penis full length and severed the organ with a large hunting knife. The scrotum went next—a valuable tobacco pouch when the testicles were removed and the skin was stretched and tanned. Two of the women gleefully danced around the body as the mutilation was in progress. DeRudio quickly put a hand to his mouth to silence his gagging. Any noise could mean death.

In another part of the woods, Private Tom O'Neill watched more fiendish squaws doing their grisly work on the genitals of Reno's dead. O'Neill became violently ill at the sight and nearly fainted. Custer's promise (via Cooke) to Reno, "I will be there to support you," kept running through O'Neill's mind. This thought kept his hopes up.

Later in the day, DeRudio found O'Neill and these two men, sometime after that, happened across Gerard and Billy Jackson in the woods. Gerard and Jackson tied their horses, but one was a mare and the other was a stallion and they began acting up. So the men tied the heads of the two horses together in an effort to cut down on their noise. Gerard said he was going to ride his horse bareback and try to cut

135

through the Sioux and rejoin the command. DeRudio protested that such actions would be a sure way of revealing the others' hiding place, so Gerard changed his mind. During the late afternoon, the four men hid beneath a burning sun in a sandy depression among some bushes near the riverbank. They watched in fear as several Indians passed them. The horses of Gerard and young Jackson were tied some way back in the woods with their mouths tied shut to keep them from whinnying. Certain death waited at the slightest sound. Warriors lurked in the area scalping, mutilating the dead, and seeking Reno's stragglers. Gerard later admitted that he toyed with the idea of disregarding his saddle and making a ride for it because his horse was very strong and swift, but DeRudio strongly opposed such a maneuver when the squawman voiced the idea. DeRudio feared Gerard's action would give away the others' hiding place.

In the meantime, Herendeen had fifteen other men gathered around him in the timber. The soldiers had met one another here and there in the woods and eventually had all come together. The scout reassured the more panic-stricken of the troopers that he, personally, had been in similar situations before, had kept his wits about him, and had survived. Herendeen said if they followed his orders, he promised every one of them would come through alive. Sergeant Charles White, bleeding from his elbow wound, promised to kill any man who didn't obey Herendeen's orders. But one of the troopers with Herendeen was a headstrong fellow, the Norwegian-born Private John "Big Fritz" Sivertsen of Company M—actually he was only five feet ten inches tall. Sivertsen cut out from the group. Sivertsen crossed the river alone and scaled the bluffs to rejoin Reno's command at 4:30 P.M.

William Slaper and fellow M Company private, German-born Ferdinand Widmayer, who got his information secondhand as he was not present at the Little Bighorn, told historian Walter Camp that Company M Sergeant Patrick Carey, reported to have been left behind in the timber, was, in fact, not left behind.[2] First Sergeant Ryan, however, stated that both Sergeant Carey and Sergeant White had been left in the timber.[3] Ryan was in a position to know who was missing from his company immediately upon reaching the bluffs on the east side of the river. First sergeants carried and kept their company muster rolls.

TABLE 9
MEN WITH HERENDEEN IN THE TIMBER[1]

1	Sgt. Charles White, Company M
2	Sgt. Patrick "Patsy" Carey, Company M
3	Pvt. John E. Armstrong, Company A
4	Pvt. John J. McGinnis, Company G*
5	Pvt. Henry Petring, Company G
6	Pvt. Benjamin Johnson, Company G
7	Pvt. Samuel McCormick, Company G
8	Pvt. John Lattmann, Company G
9	Pvt. Andrew J. Moore, Company G
10	Pvt. Hugh McGonigle, Company G
11	Pvt. Eldorado J. Robb, Company G
12	Pvt. John "Big Fritz" Sivertsen, Company M
13	Pvt. Markus Weiss, Company G
14	Blacksmith Walter 0. Taylor, Company M
15	Trumpeter Henry C. "Cully" Weaver, Company M

* The decapitated heads of the Privates Armstrong and McGinnis were found in the village after the battle. McGinnis's head was on a pole. Were they the two troopers with Herendeen in the timber who had refused to abandon their hiding place when Herendeen's group left the woods?

A quick muster check of the dead and missing would have been taken then. [I opted for Ryan's memory on this point.—author]

Herendeen's little group hid in the woods. Sergeant White, because of his wounds, began to make loud cries, but the Indians did not locate the little band. The Indians did fire the woods to burn out any stragglers, but the wind changed directions and Herendeen's group was in no danger from the flames.

Two troopers with Herendeen's group never left the timber. Both of these men—Armstrong and McGinnis—refused to desert the woods when Herendeen's group finally vacated the timber in their breakout to reach the bluffs in the late afternoon. One was perhaps captured by the Indians lurking in the woods, as the head of a G Company corporal was found beneath a cooking kettle in the abandoned village on June 27.[4] The unidentified second trooper was discovered and killed by Indians on the early morning of June 26. This unfortunate trooper undoubtedly was the one recalled by Black Elk, a 13-year-old Oglala. Black Elk said that this man was flushed from some bushes when the Sioux set the surrounding grass afire. This happened along the west

137

bank of the river. Black Elk said he and some other Indian boys shot arrows at the trooper, who was killed.[5]

Late in the afternoon, Herendeen's little band finally deserted the sanctuary of the woods. The men could see two company guidons fluttering on the summit of a distant hilltop. They started for this summit, but were fired on from a distance by three or four warriors. Herendeen fired one shot at these Indians but told the others not to fire. Herendeen's group was not molested on its ascent of the bluffs.

14
Custer's Last Stand
3:30–5:30 P.M.

After Custer halted briefly in Cedar Tail Coulee and dispatched his last *known* courier (Trumpeter John Martin of Company H), his battalion (minus four Company C stragglers plus McIlhargey and Mitchell, Reno's couriers to Custer) was made up of the following:

TABLE 10
CUSTER'S BATTALION

I. Headquarters Staff:
  George A. Custer, Lt. Col., commanding regiment
  Thomas W. Custer, aide to Lt. Col. Custer
  William W. Cooke, 1st Lt., regimental adjutant
  George E. Lord, 1st Lt., asst. surgeon
  William H. Sharrow, Sgt. Maj.
  Robert H. Hughes, Color Sgt., Company K (U.S. colors)
  John Vickory, Flag Sgt., Company F (Custer's regimental flag)
  John J. Callahan, Cpl., Company K, acting hospital steward
  Henry Voss, Chief Trumpeter
  Henry C. Dose, Trumpeter, Company G, General Custer's orderly
  Thomas S. "Boss" Tweed, Pvt., Company L, orderly to Cooke
  Francis F. Hughes, Pvt., Company L, Dr. Lord's orderly
  Headquarters Total: 12 (Officers - 4 Enlisted men - 8)
II. Battalion (non-headquarters):
  Company Officers - 9
  Non-staff Enlisted Men - 188 (Cos. C, E, F, I, & L)
  Attached Civilian Personnel - 3
  Mitch Boyer, scout
  M. H. Kellogg, correspondent
  Harry A. "Autie" Reed[**]
  Battalion Total: 200
  Total in Custer's immediate command: 212[*] (counting everybody)

---

[*] Total included McIlhargey and Mitchell, couriers from Reno, but not the stragglers Fitzgerald, Brennan, Thompson, and Watson.
[**] Reed, the 18-year-old nephew of General, Captain, and Boston Custer, had no official capacity with the campaign. He merely had accompanied his uncles on a summer's outing.

The battalion would soon have one additional man with the arrival of Boston Custer from the pack train.

The 196 enlisted men of Custer's battalion (including eight staff) had at least 24,304 rounds of combined carbine and revolver ammunition depending on how much was spent en route on hunting and individual whimsical target shooting. This fact meant that the battalion had the sustained fire power of six hours of continuous battle. Lack of cartridges, just like tired horses, was not a factor in Custer's defeat. Nor was cartridge failure a factor. The cartridge for the 1873 Springfield "Trapdoor" carbine had a less than 2 percent failure rate for nearly 96,500 rounds fired.1 The number of spent Springfield carbine cartridge casings uncovered by archaeological surveys on the battlefield in 1984 and 1985 attests to the successful firing of Custer's carbines.

***

What, if any, battle plan did Custer have at this point? The surviving officers of the regiment all said that he had none, or at least, he never revealed any. Other than stating that Custer wanted to cross the Little Bighorn at some point at the upper (northern) end of the village while Reno "kept the Indians busy" at the south (lower) end, most historians have agreed that it is difficult to know Custer's precise plans. Speculation abounds in this area. Custer, however, *did have* an original battle plan, and it can be stated, if one takes into account his troop deployment up to the point of his battalion entering Medicine Tail Coulee and the fact that Custer was a *cavalry* commander in both mentality and experience.

The standard military text of Custer's day, *The Art of War* (translated from the French by U.S. Army officers Captain George H. Mendell and First Lieutenant William P. Craighill) was well known by 1876. The chapter "Tactics and Technique of Cavalry," gave the usual mode of attack under the heading, "Tactical Employment of Cavalry." This mode was the Pivot-Maneuvering Force-Reserve maneuver. The *Pivot* (Reno) holds the enemy (the Sioux) in place by gunfire and movement and keeps the enemy occupied. The *Maneuvering Force* (Custer) moves to a suitable line of departure from which it launches a determined attack against the enemy's flank and rear. The *Reserve* (Benteen and the ammunition packs) is held until it can be employed

140

as the situation demands (Benteen—"Come on . . . be quick"). Custer had learned well. It was Reno and Benteen who were to be the fatal links in the battle chain.

Medicine Tail Coulee

Minutes after dispatching Martin to Benteen, Custer had continued his movement down Medicine Tail Coulee, a wide natural turf route leading to a floodplain ford across the Little Bighorn.

In the ride down the coulee, the frenzied mount of Irish-born Private Frank "Yankee" Hunter, of Company F bolted ahead of the entire battalion. Several of Custer's troopers laughed at the desperate effort of Hunter, in his attempt to regain control of his horse. The frantic animal carried its rider down the ravine to where the Medicine Tail's mouth opened onto the river's east bank. The "spooked" horse carried Hunter, across the stream and over a marshy pony trail leading from the west bank of the river—a few warriors lurking in the brush opposite the ford surprisingly let Hunter, pass unmolested—and bolted southward carrying its rider through the circle of Hunkpapa tepees. Hunter, was inexplicably unscathed. He finally regained control of his wild mount and galloped up the valley across Reno's battlefield in the bottoms, recrossed the river to its east bank, galloped up the slopes, and joined Reno's command after 4:00 P.M.2 Hunter, was an authentic survivor of "Custer's Last Stand."

Custer continued his movement toward the mouth of the Medicine Tail where the ford was located. He could now see five mounted Sioux scurrying ahead of the battalion down the coulee. Company E—the famed "Gray Horse Troop"[3] with its white and gray horses—led the battalion's advance down the sagebrush-shrouded ravine. The five Sioux in the battalion's front crossed the river and disappeared into some cottonwoods along the opposite riverbank. On the west side of the stream, these five Sioux joined a handful of warriors: Northern Cheyenne Bobtail Horse of the Elkhorn Scraper Warrior Society; Roan Bear, of the Fox Warrior Society; Calf, of the Crazy Dog Warrior Society; and White Shield, a warrior of extreme physical courage who had played a prominent role in Crook's Rosebud fight; with the Oglala, White Cow Bull (Buffalo). White Shield was armed only with a bow and a quiver of arrows while the other warriors named here carried rifles and/or carbines.

In a supreme act of courage, Bobtail Horse and his four companions stood their ground on a low ridge near the river as the troops of the "Long Hair" (Custer) trotted to the river. Forevermore, these five warriors were called the "Suicide Boys" by the Northern Cheyenne.

Foolish Elk, an Oglala warrior, told Walter Camp (on September 22, 1908) that he could not understand how such a small force of soldiers (as Custer had) stood a chance against such a large village.

Riding at the head of the Gray Horse was the buckskin-shirted First Lieutenant Algernon E. "Fresh" Smith, the handsome, 33-year-old acting commanding officer of Company E, who had been detached from A Company for that command. Smith's left arm was so crippled from an 1865 Civil War wound that he could not raise the limb above the shoulder and needed assistance to put on and remove his blouse and coat. Failing to earn a living in civilian life for two years after the war, while recovering from his severe wound, the hard-lucked Smith had reentered the Army for a livelihood. Tragically, none of his children had survived infancy.

Bobtail Horse's group and the other warriors lurking behind the low ridge some distance opposite the ford—now known as Medicine Tail Coulee ford (and historically [but inaccurately] as Miniconjou Ford) because it was erroneously thought that the Miniconjou tepees sat just opposite the ford—now opened fire on the Gray Horse Troop as it reached the flat of the ford. (Actually, the Sans Arc tepees sat approximately two-fifths of a mile opposite the mouth of the ford.) Lieutenant Smith shouted his men forward and quickly pulled a rifle and fired across the stream at the warriors there. A few of Smith's troopers returned the gunfire of the Suicide Boys and their allies. Some of the Gray Horsemen's bullets whistled over some of the Hunkpapa tepees.[4]

White Cow Bull squeezed off a round at the advancing Smith. The bullet tore into Smith and he pitched into the river. Twenty-seven-year-old Frederick Hohmeyer, the goateed, German-born first sergeant of Company E, barked a command and two Gray Horse troopers quickly dismounted, and into the water, and pulled Smith to the riverbank while under hostile gunfire. From his viewing distance, Curley, the Crow scout, saw this incident and erroneously believed that the two troopers who dropped into the water had been shot.[5] Smith was lifted onto a horse. Smith, hunched over in the saddle and bleeding, was taken back up the coulee to where Dr. Lord waited. How long Smith survived with his wound isn't known.

Years later, Bobtail Horse—he later crossed the river and captured two gray-hued cavalry horses—and White Cow Bull claimed that the buckskin-shirted soldier chief shot at the river crossing was General Custer.[6] Since no warrior knew Custer on sight—even the General's usually long hair had been sheared five weeks before—this claim was based on the facts that the officer who was shot wore a buckskin blouse (buckskins were Custer's normal campaign dress) and rode a sorrel horse with a white-blazed face and four white stockings. Custer's sorrel, Vic, which he rode into battle, had a white-blazed face, but only three white stockings. Several officers with Custer, including Smith, wore buckskin blouses and/or jackets, although in the warmth of the afternoon the jackets had been removed for comfort. Custer is known to have ridden into battle wearing a blue, double-breasted military blouse and buckskin trousers. This day, his buckskin jacket had been removed and was tied behind his saddle.[7] His trousers were fringed buckskin. If Custer had been killed at the ford, command of the battalion would have passed to the senior captain present, Myles Keogh. Adjutant Cooke and the headquarters staff, therefore, would have been found dead near Keogh rather than near Custer's body, where they were found. This was a point of military procedure.

Further, Lieutenant Smith's body was not found among the bodies of his troop. Smith's body, partially stripped, was found behind a dead horse on what is presently Monument Hill on June 27. It would have been a point of honor for Smith to have died with his command when it was destroyed, unless he had been severely wounded earlier. There simply could not have been any other reason why Custer would have held a combat-experienced troop commander out of action when the latter's company was fighting for its existence. In this case, Smith was the buckskin-clad officer shot and unhorsed at the ford.

Custer halted his advance at the river. From back in the battalion, the frenzied mount of a sergeant or corporal plunged ahead down the coulee, passed the head of the Gray Horse, and splashed across the stream and on to the opposite flats—where both rider and horse were killed. On June 27, Kanipe saw a dead sergeant's body and the carcass of his horse across the river in the then abandoned village.[8]

The scout Curley witnessed the Gray Horse's action at the river before he left the area:

"The White Horses were the first company. They came down [the] ravine to its mouth, and one man on a gray horse with stripes on his arm rode down into [the] river, went across and rode into the village very fast, right into the Indians. . . ."[9]

Foolish Elk, the Oglala, told Camp (September 22, 1908) that he had heard the story that one trooper had been carried across the ford by his horse and into the village, where he was killed.

Custer Turns Away from the Ford

Against all the rules of his psychological nature and his overwhelming penchant for invariably "riding to the sound of the guns," Custer "went back on" a lifelong belief and halted his advance in the face of less than a dozen warriors. Custer was one of the finest cavalry commanders in U.S. military history, jumping in rank from captain to general of volunteers during the Civil War. He had been a brigade and later a division commander during the Civil War, where he had learned that cavalry is an *offensive weapon* which becomes *immediately deficient on the defensive*. These were the words of the "Beau Saber's" (Custer's) former West Point professor, Dennis Hart Mahan, who taught at the U.S. Military Academy from 1832 to 1871, and was the foremost American military strategist, and who had written: "A body of cavalry which awaits a charge of [another body of] cavalry [mounted warriors were light cavalry] or is exposed to the fire of infantry [dismounted warriors] . . . must retire or be destroyed." True, Custer had graduated thirty-fourth out of a class of thirty-five at West Point; but not for any lack of innate intelligence, as his brilliant Civil War record will attest. His studies simply were of little interest to him.

The flamboyant, dashing Custer of Civil War fame had halted his battalion with only a few warriors in his immediate front. Some students of the battle have suggested that the more mature Custer, fooled by the real number of Indians at the ford and thereby thinking there were hordes when there were few, abandoned his "always-charge-the-

144

enemy" philosophy, decided to fall back, and awaited the arrival of Benteen and the ammunition packs on higher ground. Perhaps, for Custer once had stated that "I am not impetuous or impulsive . . . When [past] engaged in . . . a great emergency . . . my mind worked instantly . . . to bear on the situation."[10] Whatever Custer's reason for halting his attack at the ford, it died with him. It is interesting to note that the military manuals of the day offered nothing on troop deployments in Indian battles per se.

Two Moons stated that Custer and his men got "nearly to the river on their horses" and were fired on by warriors "along the west bank. Here Custer stopped momentarily . . ."[11]

Oglala War Chief Low Dog (1848–1932) also recalled Custer's action at the ford:

"[Custer's command] started to ford the river and enter the camp. . . . A soldier's horse became unmanageable and carried him across the river into the village, just beyond the ford, where he was killed. Custer then appeared to have changed his mind . . . and moved off as though making [to] the lower end of camp, to attack there. . . ."[12]

Despite the oral testimony of the "Suicide Boys," Crow scout Curley, the Northern Cheyenne Chief Two Moons, the Oglalas War Chief Low Dog and Chief He Dog, and other warriors such as Foolish Elk, Tall Bull, a Cheyenne, the Hunkpapa warrior, Horned Horse, and Two Eagles, a Brulé, many still doubt that Custer's battalion had seen *any* action at the Medicine Tail Ford. The Hunkpapa warrior Horned Horse told Walter Camp how Custer's battalion was stopped at the ford by a "tremendous [gun]fire." He Dog stated that there was some fighting near the ford—Custer got within 200 yards of the ford—but in his opinion it didn't amount to much. "No general fighting [there; only] fifteen or twenty Sioux on the east [west] side of the river and some of the soldiers replied, but not much shooting there." Two Eagles told Walter Camp's interviewer (December, 1908) that "[near the ford] Custer was attacked by a large force" and driven to the north after a "short fight only." Foolish Elk told Camp (September 22, 1908) that the soldiers [Company E] sat on their horses [at the ford] and fired their carbines into the village. The Southern Cheyenne Tall Bull told Camp (July 10, 1910) that Custer's men were at the ford

145

"within easy shot of [the] village."[13] The physical evidence of a fight at the ford, albeit it in small quantities, is conclusive. At least fifteen .45 55-caliber cartridge casings (ejected from Springfield carbines) and many .45-caliber revolver bullets (fired from Army Colts) have been found in the vicinity of the ford.[14]

One theory is that the action in Medicine Tail Coulee was a diversionary tactic by E Company intended to draw the village's warriors attention away from Custer's real objective while he and the remainder of the battalion tried to ride downriver to the so-called Crazy Horse Ford, about two and a half miles north of the Medicine Tail Ford, and cross his battalion there. One belief is that Custer hoped to ride farther northward, strike at and capture the noncombatants moving into Squaw Creek, which was nearly opposite Crazy Horse Ford, so as to insure his safety from further attack from the warriors in the village, for warriors would never endanger their women and children by then attacking Custer, if the latter held the noncombatants. Custer, it is said, knew of this second ford's presence via Boyer's intelligence. Since Curley and other Indian sources all say that Custer's casualties were next to nil at the Medicine Tail Coulee ford, it is extremely doubtful if Custer, who invariably thought offensive tactics, would have turned his battalion away in the face of such weak opposition without another offensive battle plan in mind—such as the Squaw Creek possibility. But turn away Custer did, for whatever reason.

Some, however, claim that no part of Custer's battalion didn't reach the river. Lone Bear, an Oglala, however, told Camp (January, 1909) that the soldiers "did not get down to the river." The Miniconjou Lights told Camp that Custer's battalion got to only within a quarter of a mile of the river. Standing Bear, the teenaged Miniconjou, made contradictory statements. In 1907, Standing Bear stated that Custer made no effort to cross the river, but in 1910 he stated that Custer's soldiers advanced nearly to the river where Indians forced them back.[15] DeRudio told Camp (in 1910) that on June 27 he saw the shod tracks of only two horses at the ford indicating that their riders had turned them abruptly.

Custer's change from an offensive mode to a defensive one—or so it seemed to the Indians—doomed Custer from grasping victory. By turning away from the village (regardless of whether he wished to strike at a point farther north), Custer made the Indians less afraid of him—Indians feared a charging cavalry unit at their village—and demonstrated that their "medicine was good" for a fight.

From his position on the opposite (west) bank of the river, White Cow Bull, who had never before fought the white man, was surprised to see the bluecoats halt their charge, then fall back. White Cow Bull's earlier anxiety now passed.[16]

Soon the whole village was aware that more soldiers (Custer's) had come near enough to threaten their village. But by then, Reno's flight from the valley floor had freed a large number of warriors, who turned back down the valley to meet this new bluecoated threat.

***

With the fall of Smith, command of the Gray Horse Troop now fell to its "green as grass" acting executive officer, Second Lieutenant James G. "Jack" Sturgis, a curly-headed, 22-year-old officer only a year out of West Point and the son of General Sturgis, the Seventh Cavalry's colonel and commanding officer. Jack Sturgis, who also was the regiment's acting assistant engineer, earlier had been detached from Company M to serve in his dual capacities. Less than a year before, young Sturgis had walked young ladies of St. Louis beneath sprawling oaks at Jefferson Barracks. Now he was having his first combat command, even before he had the time to think about it.

Custer led Companies F and C (in that order) in a sharp right exit from Medicine Tail Coulee's mouth, which intersected with the mouth of North Medicine Tail Coulee (also called today Deep Coulee) a short distance to the north of Medicine Tail's mouth. Company E allowed the other two companies to pass into the mouth of North Medicine Tail Coulee and then brought up the rear of the retreat. As for Custer's other two companies, I and L, they simply did not have time to exit the coulee with F, C, and E because of the warriors who soon came up Medicine Tail Coulee. Custer, as seen by Curley (told to Walter Camp in 1909), exited Deep Coulee about 900 feet from its mouth. The west bank of the river at this time (according to Curley) was thick with dismounted warriors and back in the village Curley saw that hundreds of mounted warriors were coming on. When Custer exited Deep Coulee he did not strike for higher ground right away. Curley told Camp

147

in 1908 that when Custer "withdrew from the ford, he proceeded downriver for some distance [across open country] and then struck out [to the right] for higher ground in columns of fours [Companies F and C]." Curley estimated (for Camp in 1909) that Custer proceeded downriver for 1,000 feet, but undoubtedly the distance was much farther (based on Cheyenne accounts). It is believed by the author that Custer might now have realized that his only chance for survival until the anticipated arrival of Benteen and the packs was to strike farther northward parallel to the river to a point opposite Squaw Creek, make a crossing there, and capture the noncombatants, who, even then, were fleeing up that dry creek, thereby, neutralizing any further attack on his command. At the Washita in 1868, Custer had done much the same thing when he captured noncombatants while some 8,100 Indians occupied that valley and allowed Custer and his regiment to march away with a brilliant victory without attacking him. But warrior pressure on his three companies—Company E already was functioning in rear guard action and (as we will see momentarily) Keogh's two companies were in stark isolation (they could not have held out while Custer carried out any downriver Squaw Creek action)—thwarted any such plan. Custer did an oblique movement to higher ground to the north. When Custer did his oblique movement, Curley told Camp (1908), "the Indians were in [his] front and in the ravines on both sides, and a strong force of Indians were coming up the rear."

Two Moons agreed. He told interviewer Richard Throssel (published 1911) that Custer moved downriver but that warriors pressured his rear before he turned toward a high ridge. Such warrior pressure on his command doomed any Squaw Creek activity.

Whatever plan Custer might have had in mind quickly evaporated. The Indians poured across the ford and moved up Medicine Tail Coulee, dismounted, and sniped at the trio of Custer's companies moving northward. Missus Spotted Horn Bull, a Hunkpapa cousin of Sitting Bull, watched this action from her pony's back on some benchland behind her camp on the west side of the river. Soon hundreds of warriors also filed on foot up Deep Coulee. From this coulee, the warriors also fired on Custer's retreating companies. Kate Bighead, who enjoyed watching a battle, later crossed the river on horseback and trailed the warriors up Deep Coulee. En route, she sang strong-heart songs for her young nephew, who earlier had ridden into battle.

Prior to his oblique movement toward the north, Custer suffered two casualties. While only about 100 yards or so from the river, correspondent Kellogg was killed and Trumpeter Henry Dose, Custer's orderly, was killed on a flat near the ford. Kellogg's fully-clothed body was found on June 29 on the side of a grassy slope more than 1,300 yards west of Custer Hill. Kellogg's scalp and one of his ears were missing from his body when it was found; otherwise his remains had not been mutilated. Dose's naked body was found in a kneeling position. Numerous arrows were sticking in his back and sides.[17]

Sturgis and the Gray Horse covered the retreat of Custer by firing a volley of shots at the warriors emerging from Deep Coulee.[18] Low Dog and his Oglalas pressed the rear of the Gray Horse. Low Dog recalled:

"The bluecoats held their horses' reins on one arm while they were shooting, but their horses were so frightened that they pulled the men all around and a great many of their shots went up in the air and did us no harm."[19]

Lights (also called Runs-After-the-Clouds), the Miniconjou, also witnessed the action at this part of the battlefield. He recalled in 1909:

"One company had gray horses [E Company] in the re-treat. . . . They were in the [south] fighting front; at that point they were mixed up with the other horses. At this point the company's [platoons] would alternate in covering the retreat of the others."[20]

Curley also described the scene to Camp in 1909: "[the] Sioux were thick upon both . . . [of Custer's] flanks . . . [the] firing . . . [was] heavy . . . going up from [the] river, Sioux [were] on all sides except [the] front." (By "front," Curley meant to the north, for the fighting was to the rear or south of Custer's retreating companies.)

Keogh's Command (Companies I and L)

Meanwhile, Companies I and L had been several yards back up Medicine Tail Coulee when Custer's other companies began their exit from the ravine at a point closer to the ford. I and L had not had the time to exit the gulch with F, C, and E because the hostiles had surged in great numbers up the ravine. Pressed backward, Troops I and L, under the command of

149

Captain Keogh, moved back up the gully. Keogh's two companies started into a blind draw to the north of the main branch of the coulee, but quickly realizing his mistake, Keogh turned his squadron back out of the draw and moved out of the coulee via a gouged-out cut bank to the north. His squadron (two companies) then moved directly northward across what is now Luce Ridge. This ridge is about a mile and a half east of the river and is named for Captain Edward S. Luce, Superintendent at the Custer Battlefield from 1941 to 1956.

Before turning away, scout Curley witnessed the initial action of Keogh's two companies:

"The men in the lead [were] motioning with their hands to go northeast, when the companies [I and L] broke from the main column . . . The Indians crossed [the river] . . . and . . . rode right up to the command, firing . . . The soldiers kept firing all the time while they were moving from the mouth of the coulee."[21]

Moving along Luce Ridge, Keogh briefly halted his squadron of two companies and fired a volley of shots at those warriors exiting Medicine Tail Coulee. (In 1943, Superintendent Luce discovered forty-eight cartridge shells on this ridge at three-foot intervals, which indicated a dismounted skirmish order.) Keogh hurriedly remounted his command and swung eastward and then sharply northward in a curve off Luce Ridge onto what is now known as Nye-Cartwright Ridge. Keogh's squadron at this time must have lost four troopers and a trio of cavalry horses. Many year later, the skeletal remains of these four troopers and the trio of horses were found.[22] Nye-Cartwright Ridge lies between Deep (North Medicine Tail) Coulee and Medicine Tail Coulee and begins about one and a half miles east of the river. The ridge is named for Colonel Elwood L. Nye, D.V.M., and Robert G. Cartwright, two students of the battle, who discovered cartridge casing artifacts on the ridge. Some students of the battle call this ridge Blummer Ridge after Joseph A. Blummer, who first discovered seventeen cartridge casings there in 1928. Blummer and Cartwright discovered twenty-eight more cartridge casings on the ridge in 1929.

Since Companies I and L never succeeded in getting any closer to Custer's remaining three companies than a quarter of a mile, it is extremely doubtful if Custer exercised any *real* command over these two companies during the battle. He might have tried, however. The bodies of four troopers were found at an angle between Luce Ridge and Nye-Cartwright Ridge. Perhaps Custer had sent a messenger and a three-trooper escort in an effort to communicate with Keogh. It is also possible that Keogh communicated with Custer. The bodies of two I Company men, Irish-born Private Edward C. Driscoll and Welsh-born Private James Parker, were found among the dead on Custer Hill; perhaps these men might have been assigned as orderlies to two officers who died on Monument Hill, or perhaps they succeeded in fleeing from Keogh to Custer. Keogh, by seniority second-in-command of the Custer battalion, exercised an independent command from necessity in his belabored effort to rejoin Custer and the other three companies.

Keogh, despite periodic bouts of drunkenness—Mrs. Elizabeth C. B. Custer, the General's wife, once referred to him as "hopelessly boozy"—and the fact that his troop was known as "Wild I" throughout the regiment—he once purchased ten gallons of Scotch whiskey for his company—was one of the best fighting officers in the Seventh Cavalry. A brevet lieutenant colonel and a fourteen-year veteran of the U.S. Army, Keogh had left his native Ireland and St. Patrick's College—despite the college name, it was only a boarding school—at Carlow, Ireland, in 1860, eventually traveling to Italy (via Austria), where he joined an Italian infantry regiment in the Army of Pope Pius IX on November 9, 1860. For the previous three months, Keogh had served as a second lieutenant in an Irish battalion fighting for the Pope. Keogh then served in the Italian unit (later designated as the Pontifical Zouaves) as a second lieutenant fighting for the Papal States, until his resignation on February 20, 1862.[23] Two months later, Keogh was a major in the Union Army. While serving in the Pontifical Zouaves, Keogh was awarded the military (not religious) medal Pro Petri Sede, "For the Chair of Peter," for gallantry in battle.[24] It always has been believed that this medal was found on Keogh's body, suspended on a chain around his neck, after the battle. But this was not true, since the medal was a breast-sized medal and is now in the possession of the Keogh family. Since Keogh was of the Roman Catholic faith, he must have had some medal chained around his neck—eyewitnesses have testified to that—when his body was found on June 27.

It is commonly believed that Keogh had served in the Swiss Papal Guard and had been decorated with the "medal" Agnus Dei personally by Pius IX. Vatican officials deny that Keogh was ever in the Papal Guard or that he was decorated by the Pontiff.[25] The *Agnus Dei* (Lamb of God) ordinarily is not a medal, but rather a waxed figure of a lamb emblematic of Jesus Christ and consecrated by His Holiness, the Pope.[26] Keogh, of course, was not Swiss-born and could not have served in the Papal Guard. Keogh *was awarded* the Cross of the Order of St. Gregory for his distinguished military service to the Pontiff. Keogh simply patterned himself after the hero in his favorite piece of fiction, *Charles O'Malley, the Irish Dragoon.*

Keogh moved his squadron of two companies westward along Nye-Cartwright Ridge (also called Blummer Ridge after its discoverer) in an effort to rejoin the rest of Custer's battalion. From this ridge, Keogh saw many warriors coming out of upper Medicine Tail Coulee and a smaller number of warriors exiting the head of Deep Coulee, which buttressed the western rim of Nye-Cartwright Ridge. These warriors began to occupy a line of hills 300 yards from Keogh's position. Keogh was in immediate danger of having his command cut off by warriors from both coulees. Keogh quickly deployed his men in skirmish order and fired three successive volleys of shots at the warriors. (This trio of volleys startled those on Reno Hill.) Keogh also had another more immediate problem. A band of forty to fifty Cheyenne under the Northern Cheyenne Chief Wolf Tooth had been roaming five miles from the battlefield when they had received word (via their scouts) that soldiers were preparing to attack the village. Wolf Tooth and his warriors now occupied a ridge of hills between Deep Coulee and Medicine Tail Coulee, and from a distance of about 300 yards, sniped at Keogh's left flank as he moved his squadron northward. In 1970, local resident and battle historian, Henry Weibert, discovered forty-two spent cartridge shells on what is now Weibert Ridge.

In 1938, Robert Cartwright, a keen student of the Custer Fight, and Colonel Elwood Nye, U.S. Army, discovered 102 empty cartridge casings in piles of three at dismounted skirmish intervals on Nye-Cartwright Ridge.[27] In 1946, more than 250 cartridge casings were found on the ridge. In 1968, 1969, and 1971, a total of 158 cartridge shells were found in groups of three on this ridge. More than 500 cartridge casings have been found on this ridge by various people since Blummer's original discovery in 1928.

152

Deep Gully (now Deep Ravine formerly Gray Horse Ravine) • G: Custer Ridge • H: Co. E's position (Gray Horse) • K: Keogh's position • C–D: Calhoun Ridge

Dry Coulee (now North Medicine Tail Coulee) • Ford B: At the mouth of Medicine Tail Coulee where the Gray Horse was repulsed by the "Suicide Boys." • C–D: Calhoun Ridge

Edgerly Peaks (now Weir Point) • South Coulee (now Cedar Coulee) • R: Reno's first
skirmish line in the valley

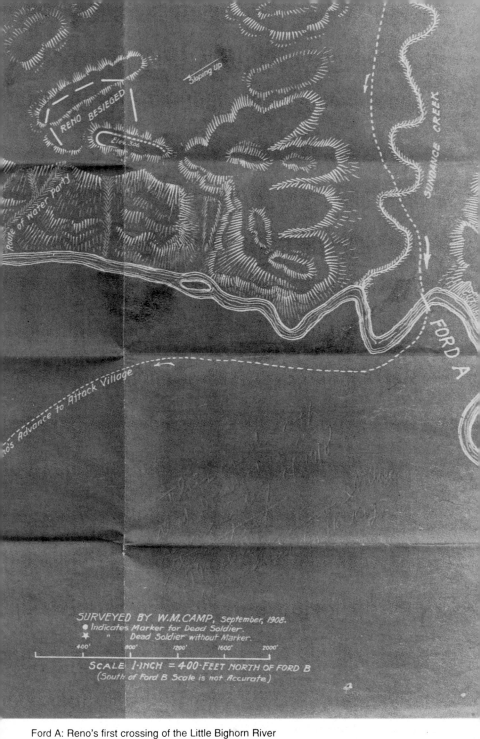

Ford A: Reno's first crossing of the Little Bighorn River

Custer Battlefield National Monument, Crow Agency, Montana

Brevet Major General George A. Custer commander of the regiment, in the center with the buckskins, on an 1875 picnic with his officers, their ladies and friends.

U.S. Signal Corps photo no. 111-SC-83837 in the National Archives

Brigadier General Alfred H. Terry,
Field Commander of three
columns—Terry, Gibbon, and Crook.

Brevet Major General John
Gibbon.

Major Marcus A. Reno, junior major and second in command to Custer.

First Lieutenant Charles C.
DeRudio of Company A,
commanding officer of
Company E.

Second Lieutenant Charles A.
Varnum of Company A,
supervisor of scouts.

First Lieutenant Donald McIntosh of Company G, acting commanding officer.

Captain Thomas H. "Tucker" French of Company M, commanding officer.

First Lieutenant Edward G. Mathey of Company M to Company B's pack train.

Two doctors with Reno's command: left, James M. DeWolf and right, Henry R. Porter.

Custer Battlefield National Monument

162

Captain Thomas W. Custer of Company C, brother of and aide to Custer.

Custer Battlefield National Monument

First Lieutenant
William W. Cooke,
regimental adjutant.

National Park Service
Department of Interior

First Lieutenant James "Jimmi" Calhoun of Company L, executive officer, to Company L as acting commanding officer.

First Lieutenant George E. Lord of Company F, assistant surgeon.
Custer Battlefield National Monument

Captain Thomas M. McDougall of Company B (Pack Train), commanding officer.

Captain Myles W. Keogh of Company of I.

Second Lieutenant Benjamin H. "Benny" Hodgson of Company B, to Reno's headquarters.

Trumpeter Private John Martin (née Giovanni Martini) of Company H pictured here as a sargeant.

Captain Thomas B. Weir of Company D, commanding officer.

Captain Frederick William Benteen of Company H, commanding officer.

First Lieutenant Edward S.
Godfrey of Company K, acting
commanding officer.
Custer Battlefield National Monument

Second Lieutenant Luther R. Hare
of Company K.
Custer Battlefield National Monument

George B. Herendeen, scout with Reno's battalion.

Charles A. "Lonesome Charlie" or "Lucky Man" Reynolds, scout with Reno's battalion.

Frederic F. Gerard, interpreter.

Michel "Mitch" Boyer (half Sioux), scout with Reno's battalion.

Goes Ahead, a Crow scout.
Custer Battlefield National Monument

Hairy Moccasin, a Crow scout.
Custer Battlefield National Monument

171

Curley, a Crow scout.

Goose, a Ree (Arikara) scout.
Custer Battlefield National Monument

Bloody Knife, a Ree, one of Custer's scouts.
Custer Battlefield National Monument

SITTING BULL.

Sitting Bull, the famous Cheyenne chief.

D. F. Barry, 1885

Two Moons, a Northern
Cheyenne chief.

Low Dog, Oglala
(Sioux) war chief.

Hump (High Back Bone), a Miniconjou war chief.

Red Horse, a Miniconjou chief.
Custer Battlefield National Monument

Crow King, a Hunkpapa (Sioux) chief.

Gall, a Hunkpapa chief.

Some warriors who fought Custer.
Custer Battlefield National Monument

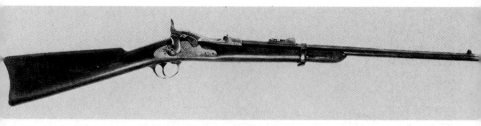

SPRINGFIELD CARBINE MODEL 1873

Caliber	45
Bore	Rifle
Method of Loading	Breech
Firing Mechanism	Firing Pin in Block
Length	Inches – 41.3
Weight – w/o Bayonet	Pounds – 6.87
Bullet, Lead, Elongated	Grains – 405
Powder, Musket	Grains – 55
Velocity	Foot Seconds – 1,100

The *Far West*.

Valley of the Little Bighorn.

Medicine Tail Coulee (center background) where Custer entered on his ride to the river.

Near the spot where Custer tried to cross the river and was repulsed by the "Suicide Boys."

Looking toward Monument Hill from the Grey Horse Company E position.

Looking at the battlefield from the Last Stand Area near where Brevet Major General George A. Custer fell.

It is doubtful if Keogh's trio of volleys took many Indian lives, but they did cause the warriors lurking in both coulees to scramble for cover deeper in the gulches.

The firepower from Keogh's command on Nye-Cartwright momentarily took the pressure off Companies F, C, and E in their movement to what is now Custer Ridge. Keogh and his squadron, however, were still very much in danger.

While the warriors were sheltering, lower in Deep Coulee, Companies I and L cut across the head of this ravine in their continued effort to rejoin Custer and the other companies now reaching Custer Ridge. The line of spent cartridge casings found over the years clearly shows a discernible route for Companies I and L: from Nye-Cartwright, across upper Deep Coulee, on a line to present Calhoun Ridge, where disaster first struck the squadron.

When Companies C and F finally reached the high ridge to the northeast (Custer Ridge) they were seen by the Cheyenne Two Moons, who heard a bugle call, and then saw the companies dismount and take their horses back over the ridge out of sight. Red Feather, an Oglala, also viewed the dismounting on Custer Ridge. Company E at this time was still on the lower slopes, where Sturgis had dismounted the troop and formed a skirmish line.

The South Skirmish Line

After reaching the slope of a narrow hogbacked ridge, Custer Ridge, his final "command post," a now worried Custer surveyed the situation through DeRudio's field glasses. The ridge, much steeper in 1876 than today, gave Custer a good look at the scene. Sturgis and the Gray Horse were down the slopes, dismounted and engaged in rear guard action with the Indians. C Company was hurriedly dispatched down the slopes, according to Cheyenne testimony (*Deep Ravine Trail*, CBNM) to support Sturgis's company. Acting Commander of C Company was Second Lieutenant Henry M. Harrington, a 27-year-old, swarthy-complected graduate of West Point (1872), who was Custer's favorite "shavetail." The official commanding officer of Company C was Captain Tom Custer, but according to Sergeant Richard P. Hanley, Private Peter Thompson, both of C Company, and Harrington's daughter, Grace Aileen Harrington, Harrington commanded C Company at the Little Bighorn campaign. Tom

185

Custer preferred serving as a staff (aide) officer to his brother and was so attached. An irregular skirmish line of troopers now occupied a position south by west about 2,000 feet between what is now Monument Hill and the headcut of a deep, flat-bottomed ravine now known as Deep Ravine but historically called the Gray Horse Ravine. (That this skirmish line existed—it is doubted by some students of the battle—is based on clearly discernible, combat-related artifacts discovered by an archaeological survey team in 1984.)

Deep Ravine—one of the deepest ravines on the Custer Battlefield—is a drainage area of approximately 7.95 million square feet (about 183 acres) running south by west of the present Last Stand Monument. The headcut of the ravine is 400 yards from the monument. From its headcut to its mouth, which emptied at the river, Deep Ravine was 1,000 yards as the crow flies. This ravine—not to be confused with Deep Coulee (formerly North Medicine Tail Coulee)—is not as deep today as it was in 1876. Company C occupied the northernmost sector of what has been called South Skirmish Line. Sturgis and the Gray Horse Troop were fighting on the south by west extremity of the line. This troop seems to have been engaged continuously since its retreat from the ford. This thin blue line was manned by only 71 troopers—each trooper held his own horse—35 of whom were of the Gray Horse.[28] The remaining troopers on the line belonged to C Company. Several yards stretched between each trooper on the line. The South Skirmish Line was not formed to check any warriors surging up Deep Ravine itself, for two reasons: (1) no Indian threat came from this ravine, and (2) if it had, the skirmishers would have been foolishly aligned perpendicularly to the enemy's attack.

This movement to a South Skirmish Line eventually cost Custer a good portion of his command.

***

A slight puff of hot breeze gently stirred the heavy clumps of sagebrush. Off to the west was a mounted Lame (Walking) White Man (1839–1876), a war chief of the Elkhorn Society and one of a few Southern Cheyenne living among his northern brethren, who was wearing only moccasins and a blanket wrapped around his waist. A brother-in-law of Tall Bull, Lame White Man called in a loud voice,

186

"Come on! We can kill all of the bluecoats!"[29] Hump (also High Back Bone—1848–1908), a Miniconjou war chief in Lame White Man's group, yelled above the din to his warriors, "Hi-yi-yi!" Several other warriors picked up Hump's yell with a crescendo. Hundreds of warriors, many on foot, moved forward in a massive wave. Those warriors who were mounted whipped one another's horses forward. Wooden Leg (he seemed to be everywhere) described the rush on the South Skirmish Line (to Dr. Thomas B. Marquis, p. 231) as not a traditional surge, but rather as one where "all around, the Indians began jumping up, running forward, dodging down, jumping up again, down again, all the time going toward the soldiers."

Jack Sturgis and the chin-whiskered, First Sergeant Hohmeyer, who was serving his third enlistment, steadied their men against the sea of bronzed humanity moving toward them. More than one profane trooper in the lot must have exclaimed, "Jesus Christ!" at the sight of the surging warriors.

The warriors, mostly armed with bows and arrows, war clubs, battle axes, tomahawks, and lances, eventually fell en masse at a point between Companies C and E. It should be noted that in 1984 and 1985, archaeological surveys revealed that more Indians than previously thought were armed with firearms in the battle. Modern archaeology identified 209 non-Army guns fired in the battle, of which 119 were repeating rifles and carbines. Of the repeating long guns fired in the Custer portion of the battle, 66 were Henrys and Winchesters and two were Spencers.[30] (One of these Winchesters was known to have been fired by Tom Custer, since he carried one into battle.) Archaeologists project the number of Indian firearms in the Custer Fight at between 354 to 414, of which a projected 198 to 232 were repeating carbines and rifles. Still, Kate Bighead stated that the majority of the Indians in the Custer Fight (two-thirds) were armed mostly with traditional Indian weapons and not with firearms.[31] When the Sioux and Northern Cheyenne surrendered in 1877–1878, they turned in 410 guns, of which 39 were Henrys, Winchesters, and Spencers, and 160 were muzzle-loaders.[32]

The warriors of Lame White Man and Hump, by their sheer force of numbers, penetrated the South Skirmish Line and drove a wedge between Companies C and E. This enfilade maneuver rolled back C

Troop. Few C troopers made it north to Custer Ridge. Many fled willy-nilly. Two-thirds of the troop, about twenty men, fled southwestward to what is now Greasy Grass Ridge, where they were killed.

Harrington and at least seven enlisted men of C Company also are known to have been driven into the sectors of Calhoun and Keogh. Harrington (according to He Dog, Red Feather, and others) broke from the South Skirmish Line on a sorrel-hued horse with stockinged legs (Company C rode sorrel horses). Harrington was clad in white canvas riding trousers with buckskin fringe on the outer seams. Several warriors pursued Harrington. Both He Dog and Red Feather claim that the officer's horse was too swift for their ponies and that he easily outdistanced his pursuers. This soldier, they said, rode hard toward the north yelling and whipping his horse with a revolver. Now and then he turned in the saddle and fired at his pursuers. Once, the revolver discharged accidentally. As the warriors were about to give up the chase, Harrington placed the muzzle of his revolver to his head and shot himself to death.[33] Harrington's body officially was never found, or at least identified, after the battle even though a diligent search was made for it.

More than one Indian told a story of how a particular trooper was outdistancing his pursuers when suddenly the trooper being chased stopped and shot himself to death. But with Harrington's suicide, it seems a whole-cloth invention in the "if he had only kept riding and not shot himself" mold to hide what really happened. Guilt (one major cause of suicide) is psychological and takes a defined period of time—and not a matter of minutes—to develop. The fear which might have caused Harrington to desert the field of combat also would have kept him from "on-the-spot" suicide. While the Indians always denied that any of Custer's command was taken prisoner, this was not true. Reno, for one, had a strong opinion as to the fate of Harrington:

"I am strongly of the opinion that . . . he was burned at the stake, for while the great battle was going on I and some other officers looking through field glasses saw the Indians miles away, engaged in a war dance about three captives. They were tied to a stake, and my impression was that Lieutenant Harrington was one of them."[34]

Ironically, Mrs. Grace B. Harrington had a premonition that her husband would be captured alive and horribly tortured to death. Someone must have told Mrs. Harrington of her husband's suspected fate as shortly afterward her mind snapped and she disappeared for two years, only to be found in Texas suffering from amnesia.

It was more likely Corporal John Foley, another Company C trooper desperately trying to outride Lame White Man's destruction, who killed himself in this manner to escape imminent capture. Several warriors galloped after Foley, who rode parallel to the river, 300 yards from the stream. The 26-year-old Foley rode to the top of the first rise along Medicine Tail Coulee. At this spot, he suddenly pulled his revolver and blew his brains out.

Foley's body was found in a position known as three-quarters in advance of the dead of C Troop.[35] Seventh Calvary First Lieutenant (later Colonel) Herbert J. Slocum visited the battlefield in 1886 and was told by Gall that a noncom had shot himself and fallen off his horse. From this information, historian Walter Camp surmised that this noncom was Corporal Foley.[36] Considering the factors of where Foley's body was found and the area in which Gall said the noncom was riding when he shot himself, this soldier must have been Foley.

Company C's veteran sergeants were among the seven enlisted men who failed to regain Custer Ridge when the mass of warriors rolled up on their company. First Sergeants Edwin Bobo and August Finckle and Sergeant Jeremiah "Darby" Finley (he was a veteran of the Washita fight of 1868), shooting their revolvers, frantically rode toward what is now Calhoun Ridge in their desperate attempt to escape the carnage of C Troop. Bobo and the goateed Finley both had served with Custer and the Seventh Cavalry even before the Washita fight. Southeast of Calhoun Ridge proper, the 35-year-old, Irish-born Finley and his horse were killed by the Indians on the western rim of the ridge. One hundred yards or so north of Finley's body, the 31-year-old, German-born Finckle and his mount were killed. The bodies of Finley and Finckle were horribly mutilated. Finley's headless body contained a dozen arrows when found. Near his body were twenty spent cartridge casings indicating that he had sold his life dearly. The 31-year-old, goateed, Bobo obviously had managed to reach Keogh's troop as he was identified among the dead of Company I and his dead horse was found in a gully between Keogh's and Calhoun's final positions.[37] Bobo was later killed in Keogh's attempted exodus to reach Custer.

Private John Brightfield of C Company, a young recruit, broke from Lame White Man's enfilade and veered southwestward to Greasy Grass Ridge, the spot where the 20 troopers of Company C was destroyed. Brightfield met his death there. He was shot twice in the chest and once in the left forearm. Frenzied warriors rushed the prostrate Brightfield and finished him with several blows to the skull and legs. (Perhaps it was this trooper's almost complete skeleton which was found in that area by an archaeological team in 1985.)

Private Nathan Short, another young C Company recruit, rode eastward in panic and desperation with several Indians in pursuit. Although seriously wounded, Short feverishly whipped his possibly wounded horse and rode clear of the battlefield. He eventually galloped back toward the Rosebud. Several weeks later, Short's skeleton, clad in the remnants of a tattered cavalry uniform, was found along with the skeleton of his horse and his Springfield carbine near the junction of the Rosebud and Yellowstone rivers. Short's campaign hat, with the number '50' marked on the inside band—his habit of marking his clothing—also was found near the remains.[38] Was Short one of two starving troopers existing on raw frogs reportedly found and killed by the Indians on the Rosebud?[39]

Custer's youngest recruit, 17-year-old Private Willis B. Wright of C Company—he had lied about his age as a 16-year-old enlistee—also made a successful breakout from Lame White Man's enfilade and rode to Keogh's sector, with whose command his body was later found. Some bones of what was a very young trooper—possibly those of Wright—were found by archaeologists in Company's I sector in 1984.[40]

Gray Horse Troop

The Gray Horse and C Company troopers fired and reloaded their single-shot carbines as fast as possible at the massive number of warriors. Eight Gray Horse troopers were killed where they knelt and stood in skirmish order.[41]

In the charge forward, Hump's horse went down with a bullet while another slug tore into the war chief's leg above the knee and exited his hip as he fell.[42] Hump's Miniconjous forked around their fallen leader and surged forward. As Hump lay withering in pain, his day's fighting at an end, he shouted his charging warriors on, "Hi-yi-yi!"

The Hunkpapa warrior Little Bear, wearing only a breechcloth, whipped his horse up a lower slope toward the surviving Gray Horse troopers who galloped in a frenzied panic southward toward Deep Ravine. Suddenly, a Gray Horse bullet tore into a leg of Little Bear, exited the limb, and passed into his horse. Rider and mount went down instantly. Little Bear rolled free of his dying horse and staggered to his feet. The soldiers' bullets zinged around him as he tried to hobble away. Elk Nation, a fellow warrior, rode through the din to reach Little Bear. Elk Nation gave Little Bear a hand up on his mount and the two warriors then galloped away over the rolling slopes on the back of Elk Nation's pony.[43] Many brave men fought on both sides that bloody Sunday afternoon.

The warriors of Lame White Man, Hump, and Red Horse—he had returned from gathering turnips—pressed the fleeing Gray Horse down the narrow ten-foot deep cuthead of Deep Ravine, which eventually drops to twenty feet at its deepest point today; it was at least six feet deeper in 1876. The ravine floor was relatively flat and ranged in width from fifteen to twenty feet. Today the width of the ravine's headcut is much larger because its north wall has slumped since 1937. Twenty-seven horsebacked and dismounted troopers—some troopers had lost their frenzied mounts—frantically plunged down the grassy, steep-walled embankments, which formed a cul-de-sac.[44] Brush and scrub trees filled the ravine. Cheyenne crossing the mouth of Deep Ravine blocked any hope of escape. Stumbling Bear, the Miniconjou, vividly recalled thirty-one years later that the men and horses in Deep Ravine were mixed up together on top of one another.[45] From the top of the cut banks, the Indians poured a murderous fire at the troopers in the ravine. Several of these troopers used their revolvers as they no longer had the time to load and reload their carbines. The fleeing Company E men were killed in the cul-de-sac ravine. They hadn't much chance to escape. Red Horse later stated: "We finished up this party right there in the ravine."

Moylan, who later viewed the bodies at this part of the battlefield, described the carnage in Deep Ravine:

"I could see where they [the soldiers] had passed down the edge [of the ravine] and attempted to scramble up [the other side], but the marks extended only half way up the bank." [46]

McDougall also viewed the bodies in Deep Ravine and said that "the men were lying on their faces and appeared to have been shot mostly in the side. . . . only a few of the men could be recognized." [47] A Company Trumpeter, Private William G. Hardy recalled for Walter Camp that the bodies of the Gray Horse were piled on top of each other in the ravine. Hardy viewed handprints halfway up the ravine walls. These troopers were buried in a mass grave in the ravine. Archaeologists attempted in 1984 and again in 1985 to locate the remains of the troopers in Deep Ravine, but failed in their efforts to uncover any remains or any equipment the men carried with them into the ravine. Since these men, for the most part, were interred in the ravine, four possibilities exist: (1) the bodies were washed out by erosion a century or more ago; (2) they are now buried deeper beneath the ravine floor by alluvial deposits than previously thought; (3) they are buried elsewhere in the ravine where archaeologists have not searched, or (4) [a recent and remote theory] these men actually were killed and buried in a neighboring coulee—now called Cemetery Ravine—about 800 feet northwest of Deep Ravine.

At least one trooper initially escaped the carnage in upper Deep Ravine by riding down to the mouth of the gulch. Sergeant John S. Ogden of Company E must have escaped to the mouth of the ravine, for his body was found near the river.

Company E's horses were stampeded down the mouth of the coulee across the river, where they were captured by squaws and other noncombatants.

Lame White Man's enfilade against the South Skirmish Line was made at the cost of many Indian lives. Some Indian survivors of the battle recalled it as the fiercest fighting of the battle and said that the greatest number of warriors killed had occurred at this part of the battlefield. One of those killed was Lame White Man. Lame White Man pursued C Company's remnants toward Calhoun's sector. From there, Lame White Man moved his pony into Keogh's sector, where he was killed on the western slope opposite Keogh's position when he was struck in the chest by a bullet. Lame White Man later was mistaken for a Crow or Ree scout and scalped by Little Crow, a Hunkpapa warrior.

Civilian packer John Frett unwittingly confirmed that the fighting on the South Skirmish Line had cost the Indians many casualties. Frett, who viewed the carnage there after the battle, counted sixteen dead Indians in what is Deep Ravine and a short distance away Frett viewed a tepee containing the bodies of nine more Indians, while still a little farther away lay another eight to ten dead Indians.

One Cheyenne who gave his life in the bloody ravine fight against Custer's Gray Horse was Noisy Walking, the 18-year-old nephew of Kate Bighead, son of Cheyenne chief and shaman White Bull (Ice) (1834–1921), and friend of the young Cheyenne, Wooden Leg. Noisy Walking fell mortally wounded into the ravine—he had been shot three times—where a frenzied trooper, before being killed, repeatedly stabbed the young warrior. After the battle, Noisy Walking was carried by travois to his camp, where he died during the night.

***

What became of Sturgis and Sergeant Hohmeyer in Deep Ravine? Hohmeyer's bloated, naked body was found among the stench and gore of the ravine. He was identified only by a single sock lettered with his name. Sturgis's remains were never officially found, or, at least, never identified. On June 27, Sturgis's shirt, undershirt with a single bullet hole, blood-soaked underdrawers, and spurs were discovered in the village. Private George W. Glease (born George W. Glenn) of Company H told Walter Camp that he had recognized the charred head of Sturgis in the village.[48] In 1926, Varnum also is said to have admitted that Sturgis's head was found in the village. Several unidentified, charred heads of white men were found in the deserted village after the battle.[49] It is possible that Sturgis's body was overlooked amid the sickening gore in Deep Ravine, but other evidence points to his being a torture-prize of the hostiles.

Sergeant Ryan stated (Hardin *Tribune,* June 22, 1923) that "we found [in the village] what appeared to be human bones, and parts of blue uniforms, where the men had been tied to stakes and trees."

Sturgis's blue flannel shirt with his initials was found in the village with the collar still buttoned (*Winners of the West,* October 30, 1926). There was only one way to remove a shirt with the collar still buttoned! Nearby Sturgis' shirt were the charred remnants of a fire and a few charred heads. While the Indian participants of the battle always denied taking any captives or torturing any of Custer's men to death, such denials simply are not to be believed. The amount of blood soaking the drawers of Sturgis indicated that he was wearing them when butchered and it is very unlikely that some Indian would carry away bloody underwear to his or her village as a trophy.

***

While this carnage was taking place, several of C Company's horses and all but a few of those of Company E's, which had not been killed, were stampeded into the ranks of the Indians' with their saddlebags of reserve cartridges. The loss of this ammunition was a severe blow to Custer's command.

Crazy Horse Breaks the Keogh-Calhoun Line

Just about the time that the Gray Horse Troop fled into Deep Ravine, the great Crazy Horse, fresh from routing Reno, led his Oglalas down the valley around the extreme northern end of the huge village and moved across a ford now bearing his name. At first, he had feared a Custer attack at the north end of the camp. Crazy Horse led his warriors around what is now Last Stand, or Monument Hill, and entered a ravine running on the back side of Custer Ridge; that ravine is now called Crazy Horse Ravine. Crazy Horse had rallied his warriors earlier by saying, "Today is a good day to fight. Today is a good day to die. Cowards to the rear! Brave hearts follow me!" (Indians fought as individuals in battle and were free to move about as the mood struck them.)

About this time, the warriors under a yelling Crazy Horse charged on an east-to-west line and drove a wedge between Companies I and L, cutting off what little hope Lieutenant Calhoun and Company L had of rejoining Keogh, whose company continued its desperate fallback in the direction of Monument Hill. White Bull, Sitting Bull's 26-year-old Miniconjou nephew, was among the warriors who drove the wedge. Crazy Horse and his men drew some gunfire from both I and

194

L, and Crazy Horse was fired on several times as he rode through some dismounted troopers, but he was not hit. Crazy Horse's contempt for the marksmanship of the Seventh Cavalry was so daring that he was admired by Arapaho warrior Waterman as "the bravest man [he] ever saw."[50] White Bull at this time pulled a trooper off his horse as the trooper attempted to shoot White Bull with his carbine. Crazy Horse counted coup on the soldier.

Extermination of Companies L and I

Extermination of Company L came only with an intense, heavy fight. Lieutenant Jimmi Calhoun, a former infantry officer, had been detached as the executive officer of Company C to command L Company prior to the campaign. The puffy-faced, 30-year-old Calhoun had married the younger sister of the Custer brothers and also was the brother-in-law of Captain Moylan. Hunkpapa War Chiefs Gall and Crow King (?–1884) yelled "Hi-yi-yi!" above the din and led their warriors against the forty-two troopers of Calhoun. Moving Robe Woman, the Hunkpapa woman, told writer Stanley Vestal that she saw a soldier holding the reins of eight to ten horses.[51] Calhoun must have desperately needed more men on the firing line as a single horse holder normally held only four mounts. Calhoun made his final stand three-quarters of a mile southeast of Custer Hill, on a ridge that henceforth bears his name.

Calhoun's immediate concern was the numerous warriors of the Hunkpapa leaders Gall and Crow King, who had poured up Deep Coulee and spilled out of the ravine to the east and south of his command. This part of the engagement was the most intense of all the battle. From a ridge—now called Henryville after the Henry rifles used by Indian marksmen on the ridge where their many cartridge casings were found by archaeologists in 1984—300 feet east of Calhoun Ridge, the Sioux poured an intense fire at Calhoun's men. Along lower Greasy Grass Ridge, some 700 yards to the southwest of Calhoun Ridge, other warriors poured heavy gunfire at the Company L men on the lower western slope of Calhoun ridge, which was some 300 yards closer to the marksmen on Greasy Grass Ridge, which actually was the western terminus of Calhoun Ridge. Calhoun's five or six horse holders must have turned loose the company mounts, for Flying By, the 26-year-old son of Miniconjou Chief Lame Deer, saw some of the soldiers set free their horses. Many of the company's mounts were stampeded into the Indian ranks by warriors yelling and waving blankets and buffalo robes. Squaws caught many of the runaway cavalry horses.

Probably about the time L's horse holders were killed, the company's first sergeant, James Butler, who had kept his horse, started out on a wild ride toward the river. The Oglala Respect (Fear) Nothing saw this man riding away from Calhoun Ridge and being killed a long distance away.[52] The 34-year-old Butler, a New Yorkborn "top kick" with flowing muttonchops, had been a member of the Army since 1871.[53] Finding his way to the river blocked by swarms of screaming warriors, Butler kicked his mount—thought by some to have been a blooded animal[54]—southward. Actually, Butler was riding the horse of Company I Sergeant Milton J. Delacy (an 1877 [sic] deserter from the regiment) who had been detailed with the pack train. Butler plunged into Deep Coulee and galloped up the other side. He met two warriors returning from the fight with Reno. Low Dog, a Sioux who is not to be confused with the Oglala chief of the same name, and Little Sun, a Cheyenne. The two warriors tried to head off the galloping Butler, but he managed to avoid them and rode on. While Butler was still some distance from Medicine Tail Coulee, Low Dog, a skilled marksman, dismounted and took deliberate aim at Butler with his rifle. Low Dog squeezed off a shot which dropped Butler and his horse as he rode up a small knoll.[55] Butler rolled down the knoll and hurriedly scrambled to his feet. The point where Butler was unhorsed and killed was about one and a half miles from what is now Weir Point. Butler did not surrender his life without a fight. Found near Butler's bullet-riddled body were nineteen spent cartridge shells, which indicated that he had sold his life at some cost. The battlefield marker were Butler's body was found is approximately 600 yards west of Medicine Tail Coulee ford.

***

Flying Hawk, an Oglala warrior who joined the Custer fight on Calhoun Ridge—he was the younger brother of Kicking Bear and another nephew of Sitting Bull—stated that he was with Crazy Horse. He said they came "up a gulch [Crazy Horse Ravine] in the rear of [behind] the soldiers on [Calhoun] hill," whereupon the soldiers, when fired upon, "broke and ran as fast as their horses could go to some soldiers that were further along the ridge toward [Custer's position]."[56]

But all hope was lost for Calhoun's men when Crazy Horse split Companies I and L.

Amid swirling alkaline dust and thick, acrid-smelling gunpowder smoke, which rolled skyward in huge billows, L Company was finished off along what is now Calhoun Ridge—named after Calhoun—while in a desperate exodus, fighting its way, mostly on foot, through to the Keogh sector. At least one warrior, Red Feather, the Oglala, stopped his pursuit of these retreating troopers to gather saddlebags he found filled with cartridges and coffee. Based on the later findings of skeletal remains and cartridge casings, eight L troopers were killed on the western rim of Calhoun Ridge, where Calhoun evidently had dispatched them.[57] The men of L gave a good account of themselves. Some, who still had their horses, tried to break through to Custer, according to Flying Hawk. Others stood their ground. Numerous piles of spent cartridge shells were found at intervals between the bodies. Some of the casing piles contained as many as thirty to forty cartridge shells. This amount of cartridge casings indicated that most of the L Company troopers had removed their reserve ammunition from the company mounts before the company horse holders were killed and their mounts stampeded. Moylan counted twenty-eight spent shells around the body of one Company L trooper. Moylan saw other cartridge casing piles containing as many as forty shells.

This spoke well of the men of L Company and its commanding officer, Jimmi Calhoun, an officer commissioned from the ranks in 1867, a rarity in the Indian-fighting Army of the post-Civil War era. He had been plagued by periodic bouts of alcoholism—so common in the frontier Army—and chronic gambling, and after a near forced retirement from the Army, Calhoun's miliary star was on the decline. But Custer, a man always willing to help a "down-and-out" officer, effected Calhoun's transfer to the Seventh Cavalry in 1871. Under the watchful eyes of the Custer family, the jaunty Calhoun had become a capable and dependable officer. He was a polite and well-mannered ladies' man who never spoke for effect. Calhoun invariably wore both his kepi and campaign hat, jauntily on the right side of his head with the brim slanted forward over the eye.

The full-bearded, one glass-eyed Second Lieutenant John J. Crittenden of the Twentieth U.S. Infantry was on detached service [since Fort Lincoln] as the acting executive officer of Company L, from his regiment at Fort Lincoln, because the Seventh Cavalry was short of officers. The full-bearded, 22-year-old Crittenden came from a very distinguished family. He was the son of Brevet Brigadier General Thomas L. Crittenden, colonel of the Seventeenth U.S. Infantry; grandson of former U.S. Senator John J. Crittenden of Kentucky; nephew of former Confederate Major General George B. Crittenden; and a second cousin of Thomas T. Crittenden, late brigadier general of volunteers. He had lost the sight of one eye in a cartridge explosion the previous autumn as a newly commissioned officer from civilian life.

Calhoun and Crittenden were killed in the rear of their men. One must wonder if, as he neared death, Calhoun recalled a letter he had written to Custer five years earlier, which said, in part, "If the time comes, you shall not find me wanting." Custer never did. One-eyed Johnny Crittenden fell dead a few yards from Calhoun while emptying his revolver at the advancing warriors. Crittenden's body was riddled with numerous arrows. One penetrated the socket that held his glass eye. Calhoun's body was so horribly mutilated that he could only be identified by a filling in a tooth.

At least one L Company private seems to have escaped the immediate carnage on Calhoun Ridge. This trooper made it to Deep Coulee (North Medicine Tail), where he made his final stand. In 1904, a boot still encasing some human foot bones was discovered there by Joseph Blummer. The initials "J. D." were still legible inside the boot. In 1928, the skeleton of this trooper was discovered in the coulee near where the boot and foot bones had been found. A metal arrow head was still embedded in one of the cervical vertebrae. Numerous spent cartridge casings were found with the remains, indicating the trooper fought for several minutes before he was killed. This trooper is believed to have been John Duggan of Company L.[58] At least one L trooper, Irish-born Private Charles Graham, broke out of Calhoun's death trap and reached Company I, with whom he perished.

The warriors of Gall and Crow King stood over the dead of Calhoun. The ax-wielding Gall, fresh from driving Reno's command from the valley floor, was fighting with great sadness. His two squaws and three children had been killed in Reno's aborted attack on the village. Gall spared no wounded cavalryman he came across, dealing each a fatal head-cleaving blow in his private agony.

***

I Company's destruction came swift and sudden as it, too, made a desperate exodus toward Custer Hill.

Keogh's company originally numbered thirty-six. This number was before the missing Troopers Driscoll and Parker, and possibly Sergeant James Bustard, departed the troop. Keogh also had the fugitives from C Company, Sergeant Bobo and the teenager Wright, and at least Graham from Company L. A hot breeze swirled the heavy dust on Calhoun Ridge where Gall and Crow King rolled their warriors over the dead of Calhoun's command northward against Keogh. A little, tawny-hued bulldog named Joe Bush, the troop mascot, loyally remained with I's troopers. Crazy Horse and Two Moons closed from the north and east while Gall and Crow King pressed from the south.

Company I's formation quickly deteriorated into disarray. Foolish Elk gave an overall view of the Keogh sector: "The men on horses did not stop to fight . . . [and] the men on foot . . . were shooting as they passed along [the ridge] . . . The Indians were so numerous that the soldiers . . . knew that they had to die."[59] White Bull, Sitting Bull's nephew, recalled that some of the soldiers mounted their horses after a bugle sounded. Some of Keogh's men, White Bull recalled, "ran like rabbits." Four of Keogh's men rode southward—they were killed—in a hopeless attempt at a breakout, through the warrior cordon. One goateed Company I trooper, perhaps Blacksmith Henry A. Bailey fled northward on a short-lived escape attempt into Crazy Horse Ravine. He was cut off two ravines east of the present Company I markers and killed. In 1984, archaeologists found, at this trooper's death site, three spent carbine casings, one Colt revolver casing, one Colt revolver bullet embedded in the ground, and a deformed bullet from an Indian gun.[60] Evidently this trooper either was out of carbine rounds or had no: had the time to reload, and pulled his revolver just as he was killed, convulsively shooting his revolver into the ground.

Archaeologists have found a paucity of Springfield carbine casings and a dearth of Colt revolver casings in the Keogh sector,[61] which suggests that Keogh's men were in retreat, not having the time to reload their single-shot Springfields, or use up many revolver rounds before they were overrun. The Indians, for their part, seem to have fought Company I close in, employing their traditional weapons, for relatively few Indian casings have been found in the Keogh sector.[62] Keogh's men scattered into irregular clusters and were killed.

Keogh and several enlisted men were clustered in a slight depression at the end. The gallant Keogh awaited the finality atop a 14-year-old gelding, the bay-hued Comanche, a company mount. A brace of English-manufactured gold-mounted, ivory-handled revolvers filled his hands. Clustered around Keogh were First Sergeant Frank E. Varden (a "top kick" despite a one-time desertion from the regiment), Sergeant Bobo,[63] Corporal John T. Wild, Trumpeter John W. Patton (or Patten), Private Wright, and perhaps Irish-born Sergeant James Bustard, if he was not killed near the village on the west side of the river.[64]

The warriors surged forward. Heavy clouds of dust, raised by stampeding horses and hordes of howling warriors, swirled toward Keogh and his men. Rushing horses rolled into Keogh's little band, quickly followed by numerous warriors. Screaming warriors rushed forward and fired into the ranks of Keogh's huddled troopers, killing them in a bunch. Keogh's left knee and leg were shattered by a bullet and he was shot a total of three times and killed before he could rise. Keogh's body was stripped (save for socks), but otherwise not touched by the Indians. Comanche was badly wounded, but survived and was found after the battle on June 27. He survived to live out his life to 1891 as an honored regimental hero, erroneously billed as "the sole survivor of Custer's Last Stand." Today Comanche is preserved through taxidermy in the L. L. Dyche Museum at the University of Kansas, Lawrence. The little bulldog and numerous cavalry horses also survived the slaughter.[65] The bulldog Joe Bush was found alive among the bloated dead of Company I two days later, a lone sentinel.

Somehow the executive officer of Company I, First Lieutenant

James E. Porter, a goateed West Point graduate (1869), who was no relation to Dr. Porter, managed to break out of I's death trap when the company's deterioration occurred. His remains were never found, or at least officially identified, after the battle, although there is one unconfirmed report that his headless body was found in the village, a possible torture victim. His buckskin blouse, with two bullet holes, was found among the debris in the village two days later. The Indians told of one soldier, whom they believed to have been an officer, who fled on horseback through the ring of warriors to the east. A handful of warriors pursued this man for two or three miles. Finally, one of the warriors, a Cheyenne named Old Bear, fired a shot at this man, dropping him.[66] Judging from the two bullet holes in Porter's buckskin blouse, they were made from a single bullet which entered behind the right shoulder, passed through his body, and exited his chest near the heart. Porter, who readily admitted that his nature was better suited for staff rather than regimental duty, had, for months prior to the campaign, sought without success an assignment to the General Staff of the Army. The Army had a name for this kind of officer—"coffee-cooler."

***

Through field glasses from Monument Hill, a quarter of a mile to northwest, Custer watched the destruction of Keogh's command with awe and foreboding. Everyone on Custer Hill must have wondered, "Where in the hell is Benteen? (When Boston Custer joined his brother's battalion from the pack train, he must have told him that Benteen was only minutes back on the main trail.) Is Reno's command dead?" Custer must have wondered. Custer now had about sixty-five men left on the hill for his "last stand." Hope faded.

Custer's remnants were surrounded save for the western side of the ridge, but there would be no mad rush by the Indians to overtake the remaining bluecoats. Instead, the warriors moved closer to Custer Hill with long-range sniping, preferring to drop a trooper here and there. Many of the Indians now were armed with carbines from the dead of both Custer and Reno. The bluecoat hope of victory had long since faded. Custer must have scanned the dusty southern horizon with

201

field glasses for the tardy Benteen. Where was the senior captain since Boston Custer had last seen him?

***

William R. Logan, the teenaged son of the Seventh Infantry's Irish-born Captain William Logan who was with Gibbon, wrote Walter Camp years later that he was at the Little bighorn with his father and Gibbon. He said he had discovered Mitch Boyer's mutilated corpse on June 27 on the eastern slope of a ridge near a coulee about half way between Monument Hill and Reno Hill,[67] which gave rise to the belief that Boyer might have been a messenger from Custer. In 1983, archaeologist Richard A. Fox, Jr., discovered skull fragments of a Caucasian-Mongoloid admixture near the middle of the South Skirmish Line on the trail to Deep Ravine. Kanipe told Camp (in 1908) that he had seen Boyer's body in Deep Ravine, which is in good proximity of where Dr. Fox found the skull fragments. The remaining teeth attached to the fragments suggest that he was a pipe smoker. The bones also suggest the man was between thirty-five and forty-five years old. The site of the skull fragments was excavated in 1984 and among the items found was a shank type, mother-of-pearl shirt button, which was common to Euro-American clothing. A video overlay of the facial bones with a bust photograph of Boyer matched exactly, indicating the bones are those of the half-Sioux Boyer.[68] Logan's description of where he said he found Boyer's body fits the general location of Dr. Fox's find of the skull fragments, except that the South Skirmish Line, where the fragments were found, was nowhere near half the distance between Custer Ridge and Reno Hill of Logan's description. Perhaps Logan's memory thirty-three years after the fact failed him as to where he remembered the location of Deep Ravine. The recent discovery of the Boyer skull fragments substantiates what Curley originally told Walter Camp in 1908, that is that Boyer had lost his horse in Custer's movement to the high slopes to the northeast. Unhorsed, Boyer was forced to cast his lot with Company E and eventually died with it.

The End of Custer

Custer now attempted a desperate breakout to the far west side of the ridge, which appeared deceptively clear of warriors. With his lone com-

202

pany still intact, F Troop with thirty-five men, he was committed to this maneuver. F Company—called the Bandbox Troop by others in the regiment because of its spit-and-polish appearance, required by its martinet commanding officer—was commanded by 33-year-old Captain George W. M. Yates, whose friendship with Custer dated from the time he served as an aide on the staff of young General Custer in the Civil War. The twice-married Yates was beset with personal tragedy when his youngest child, a son, was born mentally retarded. On the lighter side, Yates was best remembered as the best dancer among the regiment's officers and in the words of one contemporary was "a high-toned gentleman."

Yates's acting executive officer, who had been detached from Company E for that purpose, was Second Lieutenant William Van W. Reily, the 22-year-old son of a late U.S. naval officer. Reily had attended the U.S. Naval Academy from 1870 to 1872, but never had graduated. He had resigned from the Academy on October 17, 1872, in lieu of being dismissed for being deficient in academics.[69] Reily, a former civil engineer in Central America, had been commissioned from civilian life the previous autumn. He had been transferred from the Tenth U.S. Cavalry (black troopers known as the "Buffalo Soldiers") to the Seventh Cavalry in January, 1876.

The attempted breakout of F Troop soon became a disaster. Some Cheyenne accounts state that the soldiers penetrated down into the present Custer Battlefield National Cemetery—so renamed in 1992 by federal law—and to near where the stone house that formerly was the battlefield superintendent's house is today. F Company moved down to the cemetery site, out of sight of most of the warriors on the battlefield. But forty to fifty warriors suddenly appeared above the Bandbox Troop and fired on it. The galling gunfire of the Cheyenne caused Yates to quickly turn his company left and move onto the flats west of the National Cemetery and stone house site. Yates then moved his company in a retreat to a lower slope of Custer Hill. Some historians believe that Yates' action into the National Cemetery area was the initial action of the Custer battalion, based on some Cheyenne accounts. However, by the time most of the Cheyenne became engaged in the battle, Custer already had turned Companies F, C, and E northward away from Medicine Tail Coulee and most of the Cheyenne, therefore, only learned of Custer's actions as he moved northward toward their village at the far end of the camp.

Archaeological data supporting the battle action in the National Cemetery/stone house area is now nonexistent. To dig for it would entail excavating the graves, dismantling the present museum and the stone house, and upheaving the present parking areas for visitors and the National Park Service personnel.

It has been surmised that in his attempted breakout down through the National Cemetery/stone house area, Yates had every intention of moving down to the river to a northern ford. This northern ford was discovered by Dr. Fox and battlefield seasonal interpreters Michael Moore and Michael Donahue during the summer of 1990. There are two contemporary maps—Map Number 1008, Reference File, CBNM, and the map of First Lieutenant William Philo Clark, Record Group 393, National Archives—drawn from information given by Indian participants of the Custer Battle which depict the troop movement to a northern ford. Some of the Cheyennes—they were camped at the northern end of the village—not having witnessed the initial action at the mouth of Medicine Tail Coulee, historically viewed the attempted breakout to reach the northern ford as "where Custer first met the Indians." A platoon of F troopers was killed in the retreat back to Custer Hill, as revealed by the fact that only about a single platoon of this company was found with Custer. Most of the Company horses also were lost in the maneuver. Flying By told Camp (May 21, 1907) that some of Custer's men purposely let their horses free. Yates and Reily might have been wounded in the mad scramble back to Monument Hill with a platoon of F Troop.

Custer now prepared for the end. All but a few of the remaining mounts were killed for makeshift breastworks. Custer's easily recognizable horse Vic was claimed by some to have been one of the thirty-nine dead cavalry horses found on the battle ridge, although Godfrey said he wasn't. (Two dead Indian ponies also were found on the hill after.) It is doubtful that Lieutenant Cooke's thoroughbred mare, Malita, was killed at this time because its swiftness might have been needed to carry a desperate, final message. On the other hand, scores of abandoned Indian ponies and cavalry horses, lame and bleeding, were found in the Indian village and the surrounding area after the battle.

The extreme summit of the hill was a narrow, nearly level knoll in 1876, where Custer positioned seven of his best surviving marksmen behind the carcasses of six sorrel-hued horses belonging to C Company. In fact, Monument Hill was some six to seven feet higher and narrower in 1876 than it is now. The present appearance is due to the later leveling of several hillocks in the erection of the monument, the digging of the mass burial trenches for troopers, the installation of the fence, and the construction of the service road. Except for the seven marksmen at the summit, Custer's troopers occupied the slope of the ridge. Yet, the hundreds of warriors still made no sudden rush on the hill. Countless warriors popped up and down out of the tall grass and sagebrush, shooting firearms and arrows at the troops clustered on the hillside. The seven marksmen at the summit must have taken their toll on any warrior who exposed himself too much.

Through the dust and thick gunpowder, the warriors, from a distance of about forty yards, viewed an officer on the battle ridge atop a sorrel horse with three white stockings and a blaze-white face (a perfect description of Custer's Vic). This officer and some of the soldiers charged the warriors close to the north rim of the ridge and drove them down to the lower part of the ridge. This officer was described by Two Moons as wearing a buckskin blouse and having long mustaches, and who fought with a "long knife." Adjutant Cooke's long, flowing Dundreary whiskers, parted at the chin, would have been mistaken at a distance by Two Moons to have been "long mustaches." Where Cooke or any officer in Custer's battalion would have gotten a "long knife," or saber, is anyone's guess, but Cooke wore a buckskin blouse. Cooke is said to have been the regiment's best rifle marksman and fastest runner. Two Moons said he saw the long mustachioed officer repeatedly charge those warriors near the northern rim of Custer Ridge.[70]

Hundreds of warriors crept closer to the hill from all sides and shot at those soldiers. Two Moons recalled the bluecoats on Monument Hill:

"The shooting was quick . . . Some of the soldiers were down on their knees, some [were] standing . . . We circled all around them . . . We shoot . . . We shoot again . . . soldiers drop . . ."[71]

Gall told photographer David F. Barry in 1886 of these same soldiers:

"Once in a while we could see the soldiers through the dust, and finally near the end we charged through them with our ponies. When we had done this . . . the fight was over."

A murderous volley of shots killed Custer and several of his men in one bunch, among whom were Flag Sergeant John Vickory, Danish-born Corporal William Teeman of Company F, Chief Trumpeter Henry Voss, Private Francis Hughes, who was Dr. Lord's orderly, and the previously mentioned Privates Driscoll and Parker. Dr. Lord must have been killed in the same volley, as his body was found only twenty feet from that of Custer.[72] Since his headquarters staff was killed around him, it proves that Custer was not killed at the ford or earlier in the battle, otherwise the headquarters staff would have been found among the dead around the then acting battalion commander. Custer, his right hand still clutching one of his twin ivory-handled, double-action, Webley "Bulldog" revolvers, fell dead near Sergeant Vickory. The General's Remington Rolling-block .50 caliber (Model 1872) lay nearby—long silenced from lack of cartridges. Custer had several wounds. One bullet tore through his head after entering near the left ear; another slug, or a fragment of the first, struck Custer's collarbone; another struck him in the left breast, beneath the heart, after apparently having first struck and passed through his raised right forearm[73] as he was in the act of shooting. Death was instantaneous. Command of the survivors passed to Yates, if he was still alive, or to the ranking officer still living—Tom Custer.

At least one warrior could not wait for all the soldiers on the hill to go down. Bearded Man, a Cheyenne, foolishly vaulted a dead cavalry horse on the lower hillside and was instantly riddled with several bullets.[74] A Sioux warrior later mistook the dead Cheyenne for an Indian scout and scalped him. Bearded Man's body was found among the dead on Monument Hill on June 27.

***

Through a break in the thick, swirling dust and gunpowder sweep-

206

ing Custer Hill, Left Hand, one of five Arapaho warriors in the battle against the Seventh, saw a lone officer dressed entirely in buckskin with a yellow and red handkerchief tied around his neck. The officer must have been Tom Custer, the only officer among those on Monument Hill known to have been dressed thus; although brother Boston was similarly clad, his body was not found among the dead on Monument Hill. Tom Custer was standing with both hands filled with revolvers shooting at the nearest Indians on the battle ridge.[75] Tom's fifteen-shot Winchester rifle lay silent for lack of cartridges. Suddenly, Tom Custer went down with a bullet in his left side and another in one of his arms. All other officers, including Yates, Cooke, and Reily, were down. It is evident from a study of the scene that the survivors at that point now broke from Monument Hill in an "every-man-for-himself" escape attempt.

A score of soldiers fled Custer Hill, including the seven sharpshooters at the summit.[76] Several of them ran toward the river, tossing away their empty carbines and firing their revolvers.[77] White Bull, the nephew of Sitting Bull, on his movement on the lower slopes, met a blond-haired trooper, who tossed his empty carbine at White Bull before he fought White Bull in a desperate fist-punching, hair-pulling fight. As White Bull and the blond soldier rolled on the ground, White Bull's companions, a Miniconjou named Bear Lice, and Crow Boy, another Sioux, whipped at the soldier with their riding quirts. Most of their blows struck White Bull, however. Finally, White Bull broke free of the soldier, clubbed him with a rifle or carbine, and then shot him in the head and chest. In 1932, White Bull mistakenly told author-historian Stanley Vestal (real name Walter S. Campbell) that he had killed the "Long Hair" Custer, in his fight with the blond soldier sans moustache.[78] Interestingly, White Bull (1850–1947) in that same interview had told Vestal that he "did not know who [the] white general was." Since Custer had a large, drooping mustache, Vestel should have known that White Bull did not kill Custer.

As the soldiers fled the hill, they were headed in the direction of White Bull and a Cheyenne warrior, who were in a depression or coulee between them and the river. When the bluecoats neared that position, White Bull and the Cheyenne shot and killed the first two soldiers. One of the other soldiers fired back. His bullet struck White

207

Bull in the ankle and he fell into a ditch out of the path of the other soldiers.[79]

All of the other soldiers were quickly killed. Two Moons watched as one soldier with "braids on his arms" ran down from Custer Hill; he was killed before he reached the river. This man was Color Sergeant Robert Hughes, who was found in Deep Ravine where McDougall later identified his body.[80] Another fleeing trooper who made it into Deep Ravine before he was killed was English-born Private Timothy Donnelly of Company F.[81] Donnelly, however, might have been an F trooper who had bolted away when Yates' troop was fired on by the Cheyenne in F's attempted breakout.

Two Company F men might have fled Custer Hill during the final minutes, or perhaps their frenzied mounts had bolted from their company when the Cheyenne shootists fired on Yates in the National Cemetery/stone house area. The mounted Private William Brown probably fled down into and through Deep Ravine, out its mouth, and across the river. His body and the carcass of his horse were found 250 yards west of the river opposite the mouth of Deep Ravine.[82] The body of the other F Company man, Corporal John Broidy, was found on the rise above Deep Ravine, according to his fellow F Company trooper Private James M. Rooney (to Walter Camp, July 19, 1909—BYU). Broidy's right leg had been cut off and placed under his head.

Private T. S. "Boss" Tweed, Adjutant Cooke's orderly, galloped frantically from Custer Hill in his desperate attempt to escape death. Fifty yards below the battle ridge, Tweed's horse was shot. Before Tweed could rise, warriors rushed forward and finished him with axes and tomahawks. He was shot in each eye with an arrow and his crotch was split open. His badly wounded horse was found still alive on June 27.[83]

Sergeant Major William Sharrow, who had been born at sea, and another trooper, broke from Custer Hill. They started on foot, heading north on the open plains. The trooper with Sharrow was overtaken a short distance from Monument Hill. The 31-year-old Sharrow fired and reloaded on the run. He was finally killed by Crazy Horse's warriors. Sharrow's body was found the farthest north of all the soldiers on the battlefield.[84] The Oglala Flying Hawk described for Judge Eli S. Ricker, an Indian Wars historian, in 1907, what might have been the death of Sergeant Major Sharrow when he said: "This man [Sharrow?] fired two shots back [at the warriors] and was seen to fall. He got about a half mile away." (Ricker Tablets, Nebraska State Historical Society, Lincoln.)

Turtle Rib, the Miniconjou, told how he and two other warriors chased a mounted soldier across a hollow near the end of the battle, but that the soldier shot himself to death before they could catch him.[85]

Gall described a lone soldier on a hill to the southeast (one of those Company L troopers on the western rim of Calhoun Ridge) who was still alive at the end of the battle. This trooper killed several braves before he was finally killed by warriors who crawled up the sides of the hill.[86]

Boston Custer and young Autie Reed might have been among the last to flee the battle ridge (or were they killed in Yates's breakout attempt?) as their bodies were found on the lower west side of the ridge about 100 yards from General Custer's body. Both bodies were riddled with several bullets. Boston Custer was identified by a pocket diary found on his body, which was not removed when he was interred.

The Aftermath

Thousands of warriors, squaws, and children swarmed like hungry dogs over the Custer battlefield, stripping the dead soldiers of weapons, cartridges, clothing, footwear, and personal items. Yellow Nose, a Ute warrior living among the Northern Cheyenne, captured the U.S. Colors. Yellow Nose had noticed that even in the heat of battle, the bluecoats had taken great care to see that the flag did not touch the ground.

Those soldiers found alive were killed and their bodies were horribly mutilated. The common form of mutilation to Custer's dead: Squaws cut off penises and testicles (the latter for tobacco pouches). Throats were cut; stomachs ripped open; limbs were slashed or severed; skulls crushed, heads severed; bodies shot full of arrows; and stakes driven into bodies. At least one groggy trooper was decapitated alive. Another trooper was found alive in a ravine and was quickly dispatched. One frenzied Cheyenne named Black Moccasin severed both arms of one corpse and brought them back to the village. An

Indian woman named White Necklace decapitated a dead soldier in frenzied revenge for the loss of a Cheyenne niece at the Sand Creek Massacre in 1864.[87] A grieving Moving Robe Woman shot one wounded trooper to death and hacked to death another of the Long Hair's bluecoats.[88] Two other Indian women stripped a soldier who was feigning death. When they tried to sever his penis, he jumped up and began fighting them. A third squaw stabbed the soldier to death. A Cheyenne woman axed to death a live trooper who was held down by two warriors. German-born Private Gustav Klein of Company F was found alive near General Custer and had his head crushed with a large flat rock.

One wounded officer, wearing a dust-caked blue uniform and sporting a black mustache curled at the tips with wax (a perfect description of Lieutenant Reily), raised himself on one elbow behind a barricade of dead cavalry horses and stared around in wild-eyed bewilderment at the swarms of warriors on the hill. Reily's right hand still clutched a revolver. A Sioux warrior wrested the revolver from Reily's grip and fired a shot point blank into his face.[89] Other warriors shot Reily's body with numerous arrows. A warrior saw Reily's heavy gold ring with its bloodstone seal and engraved griffin and severed the officer's finger for the souvenir.

Tom Custer, blood trickling down a corner of his mouth and more blood pouring from the wound in his side, was down on his hands and knees staring wild-eyed at the Indians circling him. A former woman-izer and now a born-again Christian, Tom Custer was about to meet his Maker. Four other troopers lie semiconscious near Tom.[90] Tom and the four troopers were hacked and beaten with clubs, axes, and toma-hawks. Tom Custer was horribly mutilated. Two days later, his naked, bloated, and sun-blackened corpse was beyond recognition save for the Goddess of Liberty/U.S. Flag/initials "T. W. C." tattooed on his upper right arm. Tom's throat was cut; his stomach was cut and slashed, causing his bowels and intestines to spill out; his ears were skinned of flesh, and his head was caved in. He was scalped so thoroughly that only a tuft of hair remained on the nape of his neck. Fifty arrows bristled from his head and body.

Wooden Leg spotted Cooke's magnificent set of Dundreary whisk-ers and scalped one side of the adjutant's face. Cooke's thighs also were slashed open in several places. The adjutant's body lay between two dead cavalry horses.

Indian women stripped Dr. Lord's body below the waist, cut off the surgeon's genitals and stuffed them into his mouth. Lord's medical bag was later found in the village. Yates was scalped and his wedding ring finger cut off. He, too, was stripped below the waist. Lieutenant Smith was stripped to the waist. Smith had been found dead or dying behind a dead cavalry horse, his body was shot full of arrows.

The body of General Custer—actually found near where the present granite monument now stands and not within the present fenced area as the National Park Service erroneously marks the spot today[91]—was stripped naked (save for socks and an instep to one of his boots) and his firearms and hunting knife were carried away as spoils of combat. Blood from his wound had run down and dried on his face. The General was mutilated despite the repeated denials of that fact by the surviving officers of the regiment. The denials were made to spare the feelings of Custer's widow, Mrs. Elizabeth "Libbie" Custer. According to Cheyenne legend, however, one of Custer's index fingers was cut off and a sewing awl was jammed into each ear.[92] Realistically, Custer's body was found with an arrow shaft rammed up his penis and his left thigh slashed open to the bone.[93] William Logan, who claimed to have viewed Custer's body, stated that the mutilation was more extensive, that Custer had been scalped and that his body had been shot with numerous arrows.[94] Good taste prevented any officer from telling the General's much-devoted widow of such an atrocity to her beloved husband's body. But Custer could not have been scalped, probably because his hair was not yet long enough—since he had had his hair closely cropped prior to leaving Fort Lincoln. Custer's body was among the forty-two bodies of his command found on Monument Hill; fourteen of the bodies were Company F troopers. When Custer's naked, bloated, sun-baked body was found on June 27, it was in a sitting position and reclined against the bodies of Sergeant Vickory and Corporal Teeman. Some of the Indians had had a field day with the corpses of Custer's dead. Two Moons told how some of the bodies were dragged into the village, dismembered, and burned in a victory dance.[95] Other bodies were scattered about the battlefield. The bones of these soldiers were still being discovered in the 1980s.

211

Custer, the "Long Hair," had been rubbed out. An American military legend had passed into history.

Day's March: 32 miles in 9:30:00[96]

15

The Pack Train

Late Afternoon

It is normally believed that the pack train averaged about three miles per hour in its route from the divide; perhaps—if the mules had been reasonably bunched and all moving in unison. But there were large gaps among the mules. The train was spread over two to three miles and moving at irregular intervals. Often the train had to be halted and the mules bunched closer. Some mules undoubtedly strayed and had to be rounded up.

A mile or so passed the smoldering Lone Tepee, McDougall saw billowing smoke climbing in the sky off to the north and west. Mathey became concerned and halted the pack train on a little knoll on the north side of the northern branch of Reno (Sundance) Creek to allow the mules to close ranks.

Fifteen minutes later, Mathey again started the pack train forward. A few miles farther on, Mathey met an Indian scout traveling in the opposite direction of the pack train, whom he later said was "a half-breed." Private Augustus DeVoto of Company B, whose company's pack mules came first in the train, recalled the scout as being a Crow who spoke very poor English.[1]

When the soldiers with the train asked this scout about the other soldiers with Custer, the scout replied, "Much soldiers down."[2] The scout then moved on. If DeVoto's memory was correct as to the scout's tribe, he undoubtedly was Curley. Curley had never learned to speak good English and he was the only lone Crow traveling away from the Custer-Reno battlefields.

Mathey again halted the pack train and sent word to McDougall in the rear that a battle had been joined. McDougall left a platoon of B Company as a guard for the train and hurried forward with the other platoon to the front. Weapons were readied and the pack train again moved forward.

213

16
Movement to Weir Point
5:00–6:30–6:45 P.M.

Soon after Benteen had joined Reno at what historically has come to be called Reno Hill, at about 4:15, Weir and Edgerly both noticed that some Indian sharpshooters occupied a rock-strewn knoll some distance to the north of what is now Reno Hill, from where these sharpshooters sniped at the command. Weir, apparently without orders from Reno, led D Company to this rocky knoll, formed a skirmish line, and, within a few minutes, had driven away the warriors occupying the knoll without a single casualty to his troop.[1] Some mistakenly have referred to Weir's little sally here as his first ride to what is now Weir Point.

***

At 4:20 P.M., something caused Godfrey to look at his watch and record merely "4:20" in his memorandum book—a heavy volley of shots was heard from downriver. The salvo startled Varnum, who, just at that moment, was handing back Wallace his sporting rifle.

"Jesus Christ! Wallace! Hear that? And that?" Varnum asked as a second volley erupted.

"Jesus Christ! What does that mean?" Wallace inquired.

Sergeant Culbertson spoke to Varnum about the heavy gunfire and Varnum replied, "Custer is heavily engaged."

A third volley now sounded from downriver. Someone near Godfrey remarked at this third salvo, "Custer is giving it to them for all he is worth."[2]

In the river timber, DeRudio, Private O'Neill, and Gerard heard Custer's immense volleys while lying in the bushes. At the eruption of the gunfire, DeRudio exclaimed, "By God, there's Custer coming! Let's go out and join him." The more cautious Gerard told DeRudio to wait. Later, more heavy gunfire was heard from downriver.[3] Herendeen, from his position in the timber, also recalled having heard several heavy volleys from Custer's downriver direction. Herendeen about this time viewed a considerable number of Indians leaving the harassment of Reno and moving down the valley. In fact, the volleys were heard (albeit not very plainly) as far away as the pack train.[4] From his position in the valley, DeRudio described the gunshots as "immense volleys." (See Gerard's interview with Camp, Camp Notes—BYU, in which Gerard stated that he had heard "two volleys fired."—author) O'Neill stated that "terrific firing [came from] both up and down the river . . ."[5] On the other hand, civilian packer R. C. Churchill was of the opinion that the gunfire from downriver was not very plain. Churchill was with the pack train, some distance from Reno Hill, when he heard the shots.

On the hilltops, Reno walked to the edge of the bluffs, where Varnum and Culbertson were standing, and stared down the valley a long time without saying a word. The heavy rattle of gunfire continued all the while that Reno looked down the valley.

Moylan turned to Godfrey and Varnum and remarked, "Gentlemen, in my opinion, General Custer has made the biggest mistake of his life by not taking his whole regiment in at once in the first attack."[6] Yet Moylan, at the Reno Court of Inquiry in 1879, while trying to save the regiment from disgrace, described the gunfire as "very faint."[7] "I heard volleys [only] after the packs came up," Moylan told the court.

Godfrey, who was partially deaf, not only heard two distinct volleys of gunshots, but also heard for several minutes the rattle of guns. Godfrey even called Hare's attention to the gunfire.[8] "The volley firing was loud enough, I think, to be heard by the command generally," Godfrey recalled.

Edgerly recalled that he "heard the [gun]fire plainly." Edgerly also recalled, "We heard firing . . . heavy firing . . . by volley. . . ." Dr. Porter described the gunfire as "heavy and sharp."[9] McDougall recalled that when he arrived on Reno Hill later, "I told Major Reno about it [the gunfire]." McDougall told Reno, who had been engaged in conversation with Benteen at the time, that it sounded like a first-class battle going on downriver. And McDougall had heard this gunfire while still some distance from Reno Hill. Reno merely stared at McDougall for a while and then replied, "Captain, you have lost your lieutenant [Hodgson]. He has been killed down there."[10] Reno, according to McDougall, "did not appear to regard the seriousness of the situation." Yet, Wallace claimed to have heard no volleys despite his brief conversation with Varnum.[11] Trumpeter Martin recalled in 1922 for Custer historian Colonel William A. Graham (*The Custer Myth*, p. 291) that he heard "a lot of firing downriver" which lasted for "a half hour or maybe more."

At Reno's Court of Inquiry, he and Benteen both denied having heard any heavy gunfire from downriver other than some scattering shots.[12] "I heard no such firing," Benteen recalled. "If I had heard the firing . . . I should have known he was engaged while I was on the hill." Reno further told the Court of Inquiry, "I believe when I came out of the timber Custer's command was all dead." Yet, in his official report of the battle, dated July 5, 1876, Reno wrote of the gunfire he and his command heard from Custer's direction: *"We heard firing in that direction and knew it could only be Custer."* [Italics—author]. Reno, in fact, blamed his fellow officers for failing to inform him of the situation.

Despite the gunfire, Reno did not move toward Custer's position. The distance between Reno's position and Monument Hill was 4.2 miles. General Nelson A. Miles once timed a walk between these two points. Miles walked his horse in thirty minutes from Reno Hill to Custer Hill. Miles estimated a gallop would have reduced the time to a ten- to fifteen-minute ride. Godfrey, for one, thought it strange that Reno did not move out in Custer's direction. "The command ought to do something or Custer will be after Reno with a big stick," Godfrey commented.

An impatient Weir kept pacing back and forth, stopping only momentarily to gaze down the valley. An impetuous and hyperactive man by nature, Weir intensely disliked both Reno and Benteen and now felt that both officers were "dragging their feet" in riding out in Custer's direction. Weir was in no mood to "cool his heels" while heavy gunfire echoed from Custer's direction. When Weir queried Edgerly, about going to Custer, Edgerly replied, "We ought to go down there." Weir asked Edgerly if he was willing to ride after Custer with just D Troop. Edgerly replied in the affirmative and Weir left to seek Reno's permission.

Sometime before, Reno had dispatched Hare, by then the acting assistant adjutant general in place of Hodgson, to the pack train to hurry along the twelve ammunition–pack-carrying mules. Hare left the bluffs on Godfrey's horse—it was fresher than Hare's played-out mount—in search of the pack train. Hare found the head of the pack train about a mile to a mile and a half from Reno Hill. When Hare had reported to the pack train, Mathey had asked how Custer was doing. "They are giving us hell," Hare replied. Twenty minutes after departing Reno Hill, Hare returned to the bluffs with two ammunition-carrying mules (4,000 rounds), escorted by civilian packers Frank C. Mann and the aforementioned Churchill, Sergeant Benjamin C. Criswell of Company B, English-born Private Henry Holden of Company D, and another trooper. Sometime during the lull in activity, Reno and Dr. Porter led a detail to the river to make certain that Hodgson truly was dead and not just wounded. Reno secured Hodgson's West Point class ring and also removed keys and a gold pin from his body. Dr. Porter recovered Hodgson's pocket book and other personal items. Hodgson's gold pocket watch and chain already had been removed by a warrior. Reno's group took advantage of the opportunity to fill their canteens from the river. Reno's detail hid Hodgson's body in some brush and then returned to the bluffs. On the bluffs Reno ordered Varnum to take a burial detail below and bury Hodgson. Varnum replied that he would have to wait for the arrival of the pack train with the spades. Reno's party must have made their trip to Hodgson's body sometime between the time that some troopers, after gaining the bluffs, had descended with canteens to the river for water, only to be repulsed by Indian snipers and the arrival of the packs for Reno's party came under no hostile gunfire and were not molested. This would fit the timetables for Reno's trip as figured by both Godfrey ("Custer's Last Battle") and Varnum (*I, Varnum*, p. 116).

***

While Weir was away looking for Reno, Irish-born First Sergeant Michael Martin of D Company told Edgerly that the regiment "ought to go to the sound of the firing." In the meantime, Reno had returned from the river and he and Weir butted heads over Weir's request to ride out after Custer. Reno was in no mood for insubordination, especially from Weir, whom Reno thought an incompetent officer. Reno dismissed Weir's request as "crazy." Weir's intense hatred of Reno reached a fever pitch. Angry words passed between the two men. The most recent trouble between them dated to early May when Reno had placed Weir under arrest and asked for him to be court-martialed for some petty offenses. General Terry had refused Reno's request. All of this had happened during Custer's absence.

A rattled Weir broke off his argument with Reno and returned to his troop. Weir could no longer restrain his impatience at Reno's indecisiveness. Weir and his orderly mounted their horses and rode off in Custer's direction. It was about 5:00 P.M. Edgerly saw Weir and his orderly ride away and assumed that Weir had secured Reno's permission to move in Custer's direction. The loyal Edgerly soon mounted D Company and followed after Weir. About fifteen minutes after Weir had left Reno Hill, McDougall and the first of the pack mules arrived. Sometime later, as an afterthought, Reno dispatched Hare to catch up with Weir and tell him to open communications with Custer. In the meantime, when McDougall arrived on Reno Hill, he saw that no skirmish line had been formed, so he placed B Company on a line around the hilltop.[13]

***

At about 5:20 or 5:25 P.M., Weir and his orderly galloped atop a triangular promontory shrouded in sagebrush about one and a quarter miles north of Reno Hill, or three miles from the Custer battlefield. Edgerly and D Company rode past the right side of the promontory—now called Weir Point—when Weir hand-signaled him to return to the correct promontory. From his position, Weir viewed, through borrowed field glasses, hundreds of Indians milling about Custer and Calhoun ridges. Weir, however, failed to distinguish any soldiers. He later told fellow officers that he had seen enough Indians over by Custer "to eat up my command a hundred times." After Edgerly arrived on Weir Point, he viewed the Custer battlefield and "saw a good many Indians galloping up and down and firing at objects on the ground."

About twenty-five minutes after Weir had "sailed off" from Reno Hill for Weir Point, Benteen—he felt that Weir had "showed off" by his insubordinate movement from Reno Hill—on his own volition, led

Companies H, K, and M toward Weir in an effort to form a junction with him. Benteen had delayed his movement from the bluffs while waiting for Company M, which waited for the remaining ammunition packs to reach Reno Hill so it could replenish its cartridge supply. Interestingly enough, only one box of cartridges (1,000 rounds) was broken open by Reno's men after the arrival of the ammunition packs. When Reno learned of Benteen's unauthorized sally, he had a bugler sound trumpet calls to abort Benteen's downriver maneuver, but the strong-headed Benteen simply ignored the calls. Reno now had lost control of both of his senior captains (Benteen and Weir).

Even with McDougall's arrival with the pack mules on the hilltop, Reno still delayed his movement downriver. Finally, at about 5:35 P.M. or shortly thereafter, Reno started the rest of the command on a movement toward Custer's position. In the meantime, Varnum and a detail of six troopers now started down the slopes to recover Hodgson's body when Wallace called them back to the blufftop as the command was then moving out. Below him, Varnum saw Herendeen and twelve troopers, several of whom were wounded, struggling to climb the bluffs. The Indians, for the most part, had left Reno's position to ride downriver to fight Custer. This gave Herendeen's group a window of time to slip through to Reno. To recall, two of the men with Herendeen's original group had refused to leave the river bottoms when Herendeen departed. They were never seen alive again. And Private "Big Fritz" Sivertsen had left Herendeen's group earlier in the afternoon. In its ascent of the bluffs, Herendeen's group came across the scout Billy Cross, who, earlier, had rejoined Reno's command, but now seems to have been cutting out from the command.

In the movement from Reno Hill, Moylan's company was left with the struggle of bringing along the wounded. McDougall's troop gave assistance in this. The pack train was the last of Reno's command to leave the hilltop, some time after the original movement began. One man, Private Thomas "Billy" Blake of Company A, was left behind as the command moved away. Blake was so paralyzed with fear that he refused to move out by feigning injury.[14]

***

In the meantime, Benteen's battalion had caught up with D Company at Weir Point. Benteen's troop (H) occupied a high bluff, where Benteen planted the company guidon for any survivor on Custer Ridge to see. Benteen later made the absurd statement that the battlefield was not even visible from Weir Point. Any visitor to Weir Point will see the absurdity of this statement. The troops on Weir Point were positioned accordingly: Company M was positioned to the rear of H and Company D stood at a right angle to H and parallel to K Company. Only scattered shots now were heard from the Custer battlefield.

Edgerly, as had Weir, saw many Indians on the Custer battlefield. He could see part of Monument Hill swarming with squaws. A few of the enlisted men on Weir Point believed they saw a dismounted trooper being killed in the distance. Godfrey, however, could not distinguish any human figures on the battle ridge. But Godfrey seems to have been a minority of one in this regard. Both Wallace and Hare saw hordes of Indians milling about the Custer battlefield. Hare expressed the opinion that Custer was then fighting. Godfrey was not convinced. He led a detail of Company K in a forward gallop a quarter mile beyond Weir Point. From this closer advantage point, Godfrey viewed through field glasses hundreds of Indian ponies on the move in the valley and a large assemblage of Indians on Custer Ridge. Godfrey later wrote in *Century* Magazine (1892):

"We heard occasional shots [while at Weir Point], most of which seemed to be a great distance off, beyond the large group on . . . [Custer] hill . . ." The conclusion was arrived at that Custer had been repulsed, and the firing was the parting shots of the rear guard. "The firing ceased, the groups dispersed, clouds of dust arose from all parts of the field, and the [Indian] horsemen converged toward our position."

Through the breaks in the swirling dust clouds, Weir caught a glimpse of a guidon fluttering in a momentary whiff of hot breeze on Custer Ridge. "That's Custer over there!" Weir shouted to no one in particular. Irish-born Sergeant James Flanagan of D Company had been viewing the scene through field glasses. Handing the glasses to Weir, Flanagan cautioned, "Here, captain, you better take a look through these glasses. I think those are Indians." Weir and Godfrey— the latter from his forward position—saw hundreds of warriors moving through the swirling dust of the Custer battlefield—and converging toward Weir Point.

Benteen told Godfrey, "This is a hell of a place to fight Indians. I am going back to see Reno and propose that we go back . . . ." Benteen then skedaddled to the rear. By the time Benteen reached Reno, the area was thick with Indians.

Reno was informed of the situation and he, Benteen, Weir, and Hare quickly conferred on a plan of action. Benteen told Reno, ". . . We cannot fight here. We had better fall back somewhere." Reno agreed and ordered an immediate fallback. Hare, on his own, galloped forward to inform Godfrey of the movement back to the bluffs. Hare was a loyal friend of Godfrey.

Falling Back

The command's withdrawal from Weir Point was anything but orderly. According to Hare's testimony at the Reno Court of Inquiry, Reno ordered Companies D and M to hold the approaching Indians temporarily at bay to give the other companies time to retreat to Reno Hill. It seems doubtful—was Hare lying at the court of inquiry to protect Reno?—that a formal order of withdrawal was given. McDougall testified that he observed the troops falling back, indicating that no formal fallback order was ever given. Reno, however, testified that he told Benteen, "You look out for that side and I will the other. I [then] took D Company with me." Not all of Reno's officers were told of the fallback. Benteen, for one, immediately led his company away from Weir Point at a gallop. French of M Company learned of the movement only when he saw Benteen's withdrawal and that he called to Edgerly to fall back. Edgerly refused to fall back as he had no such orders from Weir, his troop D commander. For some reason, Weir had failed to return to his company. Edgerly quickly changed his mind, however, when he saw the command retreating.

Edgerly started D Company out at a trot, but he, himself, was one of the last to leave Weir Point. Stepping into a stirrup, he saw a lone warrior hurriedly approaching the promontory. Drawing his rifle from its scabbard, Edgerly aimed and squeezed off a shot at the approaching warrior. Edgerly then tried mounting his horse while still holding his rifle. The skittish horse kept moving in circles while Edgerly repeatedly tried to mount him. Finally, Edgerly handed the rifle to his

221

orderly, the German-born Private Charles Sanders of D Company, and mounted the horse. Several bullets pinged around Edgerly and his orderly. Sanders sat in his saddle and began laughing at what poor shots the Indians were. One bullet whistled by and struck the canteen of Corporal George W. Wylie of D Company. Another bullet cut through the staff of the company guidon, held by Wylie. Wylie dismounted, quickly retrieved the guidon, remounted, and galloped after an already fleeing Edgerly and Sanders.

In D Company's movement away from Weir Point, Swiss-born Farrier Vincent Charley was struck in the hips by a bullet and dropped from his saddle. Charley screamed for help. Edgerly told the unfortunate trooper to get into a hole and that he would return for him. But neither Edgerly nor anyone else returned to rescue this unfortunate trooper. Charley was last seen crawling after D Company.[15] Charley did not give up his life easily, though. Nine empty cartridge shells were later found near his body. Edgerly eventually caught up with Weir and told him about Charley. Weir callously replied that nothing could be done for the "poor bastard." Edgerly protested, but Weir became adamant and the matter was dropped.[16] Weir had lost his stomach for a fight.

Edgerly had taken command of D Company on its retreat from Weir Point, and the company fell back in orderly fashion even though the hostiles pressed its rear.

Godfrey dismounted his company (K), deployed the men in skirmish order, and fired a volley of shots into the charging Indians. This gallant action on the part of Godfrey and K Company allowed Edgerly and D Company to pass unmolested. Hare, who loyally remained behind to assist Godfrey, took ten K Company troopers and occupied a high bluff, from where they poured another volley at the pressing Indians. Godfrey remounted his company (including Hare's detail) and fell back with the rest of the regiment. Godfrey periodically dismounted his troop and gave a covering fire for the other companies of the retreating column of troops. This cover fire by K kept the Indians from overriding the rear of the column. Some of Godfrey's troopers panicked in this rear guard action, but he kept them in check by threatening to shoot any man who refused an order. Godfrey was the best officer among the surviving officers at the Little Bighorn and he showed it that day.

In the fallback to Reno Hill, a disgusted McDougall, fearing another "Fort Phil Kearny affair," told Benteen that "Reno was doing nothing to put the command on the defensive," and that as the senior captain, Benteen "had better take charge." Benteen merely grinned.[17] On the return to Reno Hill, Weir sought out Godfrey and thanked him for covering D Company's retreat. Weir then asked Godfrey who he would obey if it came down to a conflict in judgment between Reno and Benteen. "Benteen," came Godfrey's curt reply.[18] (The "Fort Phil Kearny affair" to which McDougall referred was the December 21, 1866, wipeout of Captain William J. Fetterman's command by Sioux and Cheyenne near Fort Phil Kearny in present-day Wyoming. Fetterman's commanding officer at the fort was the incompetent and overly cautious Colonel Henry B. Carrington.)

When the Seventh Cavalry retreated in its fallback to Reno Hill, the fighting Indian scouts came up the slopes to Weir Ridge. Young Hawk carried a stick with a white handkerchief tied to it to indicate they were "friendlies." The wounded White Swan rode his own mount while the wounded Goose rode the horse of Red Foolish Bear, who was "shank's mare." Seeing the Sioux "coming on" toward them, Red Foolish Bear swung up behind Goose and all the scouts but Young Hawk galloped away to the safety of Reno Hill. Young Hawk momentarily remained behind, flaunting the Sioux with his handkerchief-tied stick. He then outrode the Sioux to Reno Hill. Galloping to the Reno-Benteen Defense Perimeter, Young Hawk frantically waved the "white flag." The soldiers gave the young Ree cover by shooting over him at the Sioux.

The Pack Train

The pack train had gone only a short distance when word came that the command was returning to Reno Hill. During the movement, a mule toting ammunition broke away from the packers. Private James "Crazy Jim" Severs of Company M—who later served time for grand larceny at the Wyoming State Penitentiary—pursued the runaway animal for a hundred yards, caught it, and returned it to the packers, all the while exposed to gunfire from some Indian sharpshooters still lurking in the Reno Hill area.

Sergeant Richard F. Hanley of Company C reherded another runaway ammunition-packing mule back to the pack train. That mule charged eastward and halfway to the Indian lines as the mounted Hanley, with the assistance of C Company Private John McGuire, who was on foot, shooed the mule back to the packers while under a twenty-minute gunfire which ripped the ground around them with bullets. Hanley received the Medal of Honor for his heroics, but McGuire's assistance went unnoticed officially.

Entrenchment Hill: The Defense Perimeter

By 6:30 to 6:45 P.M., the surviving regiment was entrenched on two parallel ridges on Reno Hill in what came to be called the Reno-Benteen Defense Perimeter. The defense perimeter was positioned as follows: facing all along the northwest side of the perimeter was Company M; to M's right on the extreme northeast of the perimeter was Company K; on the eastern side of the perimeter stood Company D; Company G (actually, this troop had less than a platoon on duty), now under Wallace's command, also occupied the east side of the perimeter; Company A was positioned on the southeast sector of the perimeter; Company H was stretched for some distance to the extreme south of the other companies, but at a somewhat higher elevation than the others, which exposed it to greater hostile gunfire. Company B stood on the western side of the defense perimeter. The next day, Companies B and M switched positions on the perimeter. Company A was positioned in a saucer-shaped, shallow depression which was barricaded with dead horses and mules, boxes, and empty packing crates near the field hospital of Dr. Porter. Mathey, who was still commanding officer of the eighty-four soldier-packers, detached earlier by Custer and Cooke near the divide, set up a barricade of packing cases around the makeshift field hospital which Dr. Porter had located in a shallow depression between the two ridges on the defense perimeter. The mules, tied and unpacked, and the horses, which remained saddled and bridled, were corralled in two semicircles and the wounded men were placed in the swale inside of the horses and mules. Dr. Porter, the only surviving surgeon on duty, tirelessly labored for two days and nights caring for the wounded and the dying. When he wasn't caring for the dying and wounded, Dr. Porter did yeoman work with a borrowed carbine.

Several of the regiment's officers did not distinguish themselves on this "Entrenchment Hill." Moylan incurred the enmity of several of the enlisted men because he rarely stirred from behind the carcass of a dead mule amid *aparejo* packs—an *aparejo* was a mule pack with a cinch—while "blubbering like a whipped urchin" (Benteen's words). Henceforth, the men of the Seventh referred to Moylan as "Aparejo Michie." Years later, Moylan had the gall to tell Godfrey that Reno's conduct in the battle was not exemplary. First Lieutenant Frank Gibson showed no spunk, either. The executive officer of H Company hugged the ground, lying low, and refused to move about. And Mathey found a sanctuary in the field hospital; from the late afternoon of the twenty-fifth until midmorning of the twenty-sixth, he "hid out." Mathey spent his time—in Benteen's words—"gossiping away like an old lady over her tea."

Benteen's blunder was of a different nature. His H company was the only one which did not scoop out shallow carbine pits on the twenty-fifth to provide protection from Indian sharpshooters. There were few spades within the regiment, but the men also used penknives, mess kits, axes, canteens, even spoons and sticks, to dig and scoop out carbine pits, traces of which still exist today. Benteen felt that his exhausted men needed rest and did not have enough energy to engage in the rigorous task of digging carbine pits. Benteen's company paid a bloody price for its commanding officer's foolish decision: three soldiers killed and nineteen others wounded on the twenty-sixth.[19] Two of the wounded troopers died a week later. Benteen's defenders have stated that most of Company H's casualties were not shot from the front and, therefore, Benteen had no need to have his men dig protective pits. Regardless of the geographical semantics here, Benteen's troop suffered the *most* casualties on the defense perimeter *due to exposure to Indian sharpshooters.*

***

From what is now Sharpshooter's Ridge, beginning some 880 yards north of the present Reno-Benteen monument, Indian marksmen, including Wooden Leg, directed some of their heaviest sniping at the troops on the defense perimeter. Some Indian marksmen also occupied a small rocky knoll just north of the perimeter—the same knoll from which Weir had driven off some Indians prior to his movement to Weir Point. Sergeant Ryan recalled in 1923 one particular warrior sharpshooter who occupied this rocky knoll:

"While we were lying in line he fired a shot and killed the fourth man on my right. Soon afterward he fired again and shot the third man. His third shot wounded the man on my right, who jumped back from the line and down among the rest of the wounded . . . I, Captain French, and some half dozen members of my company . . . wheeled to our right and put in a deadly volley, and I think we put an end to that Indian, as there were no more men killed at that particular spot."[20]

Godfrey, for one, was horrified at the lack of protection from Indian sharpshooters. Some of the men had only thin sagebrush and scattered prickly pear cactus between them and an Indian bullet. Godfrey walked around K's line, cautioning his men not to waste their cartridges and telling them to allow only the company's marksmen to fire their weapons.

In the late afternoon on the M Company line, French approached Ryan, one of the best shots in the regiment, and asked him if he could do anything about some Indian sharpshooters on a bluff which was out of range of the troopers' carbines. Ryan's personal weapon was a .45 Sharps rifle and its range was superior to the Springfield carbine. Ryan's Sharps was mounted with a rifle telescope; he fired a few rounds to get his range and then in rapid-fire succession he triggered a half dozen shots, which scattered the red marksmen on the distant bluff.

The firepower of the Indians had been increased by the capture of carbines and cartridges from Custer's dead. These single-shot Springfield carbines—called "Trapdoor" Springfields because they featured a breechblock whose mechanism allowed it to spring upward and forward to expose the chamber for loading—were not shoddy weapons, as is commonly believed. This belief was based, in part, on French exposing himself to hostile marksmen on the firing line while extracting jammed cartridge shells—a sometimes problem with Trapdoors—with his penknife from a few of his troopers' carbines. Jamming occurred when the carbine's ejector spring pulled the head of a cartridge off and left the empty shell in the barrel. French extracted shells from only six carbines. The six were the only defective carbines out of a total of 380 in Reno's command so reported.[21] Archaeological surveys in 1984 and 1985 uncovered only three Springfield carbine shell casings which indicated forceful prying. The copper casing of the cartridge was soft, and when discharged, the shell sometimes expanded and lodged in the carbine's chamber. The copper shell casing, when combined with the tanning acids in the leather loops of a trooper's cartridge belt, produced a chemical called verdigris, which sometimes caused the cartridge to expand in the chamber. Jamming of the cartridge in the chamber could result from either factor. But the 1873 Trapdoor Springfields gave a hard kick when fired and "carried" well for 500 yards.

Less than two months after the Little Bighorn battle, First Lieutenant John E. Greer, U.S. Army Ordnance, conducted field tests of the Springfield carbine .45-70 (M/1873) and the lever-action, 12-shot Winchester .44-40 rifle (M/1873). Greer's tests proved that the Springfield carbine was a superior weapon to the Winchester rifle.[22] A repeating carbine or rifle had a rapid firing advantage, however, over a single-shot weapon when confronted by a numerically superior attacking enemy.

***

Bullets "pinged" all around the hilltop and occasionally one found a mark. Heavy gunfire came from Indian sharpshooters 500 yards from the east and the same from the north. Private Slaper recalled that the men on the defense perimeter were ordered to lie flat on their stomachs and not expose themselves. Sergeant Ryan recalled that the Indians "made several charges upon us and we repulsed them every time . . . [and] the firing became general all along the line, very rapid and at close range."[23] Benteen recalled the Indian gunfire upon the troops' position as "as lively a fire as you would like to stand up under." And Godfrey recalled the Indian gunfire as "a heavy fire." McDougall described it as "very heavy."

A spent bullet ricocheted off the head of chief packer John Wagoner. When struck, Wagoner kicked convulsively for several seconds and then sat up and rubbed his head.[24] Miraculously, the chief packer had survived his near-fatal wound. Private Slaper had a slug hit a mound of loose dirt in front of his face, showering soil into his eyes. Another slug sliced off one of Slaper's boot heels. German-born

Trumpeter Julius Helmer of K Company was hit in the bowels by a sharpshooter's bullet and died in great agony while pleading with his fellow troopers to shoot him. Helmer possibly was the aforementioned trooper referred to as being killed to the right of Sergeant Ryan.

Benteen pointed out some distant Indians to his men. English-born Private Herod T. Liddiard of Company E, a good shot, while in a prone position, took aim with his carbine at these Indians, all the while talking to the troopers near his position. An instant later, a bullet smashed into Liddiard's head, killing him instantly.[25] [Liddiard's killing possibly occurred on June 26—author] Liddiard had been one of Company E's packers with the mule train, and being a good marksman, Benteen had brought him to his sector. At dusk, First Sergeant DeWitt Winney of K Company, while sitting in his rifle pit, bobbed his head above his barricade and instantly a bullet struck him in his forehead.[26] Winney screamed, "I am hit!" and looked quizzically at Godfrey. Godfrey began to reassure Winney, but he expired before Godfrey could finish speaking.

One warrior was killed by those on the Reno-Benteen Defense Perimeter before sundown. A Miniconjou named Dog Back-bone (Ass) raised his head and was drilled in the forehead by a Seventh Cavalry marksmen.[27] The Indian gunfire continued until nearly dark.

After the horses of the command had been unsaddled and the mules relieved of their packs, Mathey, on his own authority, secured ropes and lariats and improvised a makeshift picket line for the animals by tying them to the legs of dead horses and mules.

After sundown, a lone bugle sounded "Taps" in the distance. The bugle was heard by those on Reno Hill.[28] It was an eerie sound. Was it the last of Custer's dying trumpeters paying respect to his fallen comrades?

17
Night and Day
June 25–26

The Indian village

Light rain fell off and on during the night of the twenty-fifth. The night was sultry.

From the hilltops, Reno's men could see the many campfires from the Indian encampment on the valley floor and hear the incessant whooping and yelling, frantic revels, beating of the nerve-shattering tom-toms, and the discharging of firearms. The victorious Indians were holding scalp and torture dances around the fires. In 1935, Varnum recalled the village on the night of June 25 as a "scene of demoniacal celebration and frantic revel." It was a night of "demonical screams and discharging firearms," Godfrey recalled in 1892. (Some of the tribes, however, did not hold dances this night.) The frenzied dispatching, in a most hideous manner, of several captives had occurred in the village. According to Northern Cheyenne Chief Two Moons and Little Knife, a Hunkpapa warrior, a soldier with stripes on his arm (perhaps Sergeant Miles O'Hara) was tortured to death on the night of the twenty-fifth during a wild dance.[1] Several charred heads of white men were found in the village, including the three that were suspended by wire from a single lodgepole,[2] and the charred head of a redheaded noncom, found beneath a cooking kettle.[3] The heads of Second Lieutenant Sturgis, Sergeant O'Hara, Private John E. Armstrong of Company A, and Private John J. McGinnis of Company G also were identified in the village, as was, possibly, the headless body of Lieutenant Porter of I Company.

Company I Private Gustave Korn, who had been with Reno's battalion in the valley fight, climbed the slopes under the cover of darkness and reached Reno's lines safely in the night.

Reno Hill

Pandemonium temporarily broke loose on Reno Hill after dark. Some of the men imagined that they could see a column of troops on some distant hills or ridges. Some poor wretches even believed they could hear horses' hooves, the barking orders of officers, and trumpet calls in the distance. One trooper on Reno Hill quickly sounded stable call. Some of Reno's troops discharged weapons and others sounded trumpet calls to alert the phantom column of troops. One frenzied civilian packer mounted a horse and galloped about the hill shouting, "Don't be discouraged, boys, [General George] Crook is coming." But gradually the beleaguered command realized it was only phantasma of their imaginations and settled down to digging carbine pits.

Reno was out of sight after the command's return to the hilltops from Weir Point. At sundown, Reno continued his drinking from his private whiskey stock. We know that he had consumed half a bottle of whiskey—save for Hodgson's drink on the ride down the valley—by the time of the arrival of the pack train on the bluffs because Reno greeted Mathey—so Mathey recalled—with, "Look here! I have got half a bottle yet!"

Reno's nerves were badly frayed and the incessant drum beating in the Indian camp only made him more jittery and irritable. Reno overhead Big Fritz Sivertsen ask another trooper, "What are we going to do? Stay here all night or move away?" An angry Reno bellowed, "I would like to know how the hell we are going to move away."

Sometime during the night, Varnum asked Reno's permission for himself and Irish-born Sergeant George M. McDermott of Company A to go for help. Reno refused to answer Varnum—he just stared for a few minutes—before he denied the request by telling Varnum that he (Reno) could not afford to lose two of his best marksmen and that both he and McDermott were needed on the hilltop in the event of an attack. Varnum pressed the matter, to Reno's displeasure. Reno and Varnum quarreled and the matter was settled in Reno's favor. Reno curtly dismissed Varnum with the comment, "Varnum, you are a very uncomfortable companion."[4] Varnum did persuade Reno to send the scouts for help if they would agree to risk the attempt. The following September, Reno and Varnum got into a wrestling match in the Fort

Lincoln Officers' Club when Varnum tried to break up a brawl the drunken Reno was involved in; Reno called for pistols to duel Varnum, but was prevented from doing so. In truth, Varnum and Reno despised each other. (McDermott was killed in the battle on Snake Creek near Bear Paw Mountain, Montana Territory, on September 30, 1877.)

***

The prevailing belief among those on Reno Hill was that Custer had been defeated and was "holed up" somewhere. Half-Yellow-Face and an unidentified G Company trooper both volunteered to leave the hilltop and try to reach Terry and Gibbon. During the night, Reno sent both men from the bluffs. Sometime later, both returned to the defense perimeter, having failed to penetrate the Indian sentinels.

Also during the night, Reno and Benteen held a private talk. At one point, Custer's German-born striker, Private John Burkman of Company L, overheard Reno say, "I wonder where the Murat of the American Army is now?" This was an obvious reference to Custer. But Reno had more on his troubled mind than Custer's whereabouts. Indecision stalked his footsteps and whiskey now dulled his reasoning. He suggested to Benteen that the regiment should just pick up and "skedaddle." When Benteen asked how the seriously wounded could be transported, Reno callously replied that any who could not ride would have to be abandoned. Benteen, to his credit, told Reno that he would never be a part of such a monstrous act.[5] The matter was quickly dropped.

Benteen toyed, however, briefly with the idea of officially taking command from Reno—a most serious breach of military discipline—but rejected the idea because it would have "stirred up too much trouble" in such a tight situation as the regiment found itself. Benteen had first thought of the notion on the command's return from Weir Point when McDougall had approached him and asked him to "take the lead in affairs" as the command needed "a commanding officer here pretty damn quick."[6]

***

It was near midnight and Reno probably was drunk. Both Captain McDougall and Private William Slaper denied that Reno was intoxicated.[7] The evidence seems otherwise. Reno's whiskey consumption had increased over the years, although he was known to have been a heavy drinker since his cadet years at West Point. The premature death of Reno's wife hadn't helped his drinking. At about midnight, Reno went to the pack mules. He carried a bottle of whiskey. Civilian packer John Frett saluted him and said, "Good evening." Reno braced himself against a mule and inquired of Frett in a slurred voice, "Are the mules tight?" Frett thought Reno said, "tied" and replied yes. Reno again asked Frett if the mules were tight. Frett, who, at the Reno Court of Inquiry, described Reno as "very drunk," failed to understand what the major meant by "tight" and said so. Reeking of whiskey and flushed with drunken rage, Reno screamed at Frett, "Tight, goddamn you, tight!" Reno then launched and slapped Frett across the face while spilling whiskey on the shirt front of the startled packer. Reno stepped back and picked up a carbine. Reno then threatened to shoot Frett if he found him around the packs again. R. C. Churchill, a civilian packer,[8] pulled Frett away from the drunken Reno.[9] Churchill later testified that Reno was "under the influence of liquor." That Reno was intoxicated on the night of June 25, however, does not mean that he was drunk on the afternoon of the twenty-fifth and that his decision to flee the valley had anything to do with an alcohol-muddled brain.

The Valley

In the blackness on the valley floor—there was no moon this night—Gerard and young Jackson slowly picked their way through the darkness. Both men remained mounted. DeRudio and Private O'Neill trailed behind Gerard and Jackson by clutching the tails of the horses of the two men. The four men groped their way through the maze of cottonwoods and scrub brush and had crossed and recrossed two bends of the Little Bighorn. Once O'Neill attempted to test the water's depth and plunged into the swift, cold current up to his neck and almost was swept away. DeRudio knelt by the river's edge and gave O'Neill a hand up out of the water. Once, they stumbled across McIntosh's body in the darkness. Fred Gerard, who had lived among the Arikara, his wife's people, for many years, had adopted many of the latter's customs and superstitions. During one of the river crossings, Gerard had uttered the following prayer in the Sioux

232

language and then tossed his gold pocket watch into the water: "Oh Powerful One, Day Maker! And you, people of the depths, this I sacrifice to you. Help me, I pray you, to cross safely here." Jackson, who was more white than Indian, was amused by Gerard's actions. DeRudio asked Gerard, "What were you saying? What was that splash?" The squawman ignored DeRudio's questions.

About 11:00 P.M., DeRudio, O'Neill, Gerard, and Jackson were on an island in the river when they heard Sioux voices call to them in the darkness, "Where are you going? Hold on. Don't go away. We are Sioux!" Gerard and Jackson kicked their horses and galloped into the night. DeRudio and O'Neill dropped down into some bushes and waist-high grass. Six or seven Sioux were heard to jump their horses into the river after Gerard and Jackson and called out to them, "Are you afraid? We are not white troops." DeRudio knelt and clutched his cocked revolver. The only sounds which DeRudio and O'Neill now heard—aside from their own breathing—was the rippling of the river and a light rain, just beginning to fall, which patted the leaves of the cottonwood trees clustered along the banks of the river. Minutes passed as if hours.

The Crow scouts White-Man-Runs-Him, Goes Ahead, and Hairy Moccasin, strictly adhering to Custer's orders (through Boyer) to go back and stay out of the fight, rode all night in rain and reached the mouth of the Little Bighorn sometime before first light on the twenty-sixth. There they camped. On the morning of the twenty-sixth, the three Crows crossed the Big Horn River and met some of the Crow scouts from the Terry-Gibbon column.

***

The eastern sky began to show the first gray light of dawn. DeRudio and O'Neill heard several warriors jump their horses into the river. DeRudio told O'Neill he could make out six or seven Indians who lurked at a fork in the river. To hasten these Indians' flight, DeRudio triggered two revolver shots at them. O'Neill raised his carbine and also fired a shot at these warriors. While O'Neill was reloading, DeRudio fired another shot at the now fleeing warriors.

233

June 26

In the predawn, while Gerard and Jackson, were swimming their horses from bank to bank in an effort to locate a ford, Gerard's horse plummeted in deep water and carried Gerard across the river and against a cut bank. The horse was not able to touch bottom, so he swam back for the opposite bank. Gerard's horse, a stallion, attempted to mount Jackson's mare in midstream. Both horses struggled with the swift current and knocked against each other, spilling Gerard and Jackson into the stream. Gerard swam to the east bank of the river while Jackson swam to the west bank. In the process, Gerard had lost both his rifle and his revolver. Gerard called to Jackson to run down their mounts. Jackson eventually secured the horses and led them to Gerard on the opposite bank. Later, finding it impossible to get up the east cut bank, both men recrossed to the west bank of the stream and continued up the river past where Reno first crossed the river on his ride down the valley. En route, they soon heard Sioux talking and horses splashing into the river and fled via a wide circular route out into the valley. Gerard and Jackson found a thick cluster of cottonwoods and willows, tied their horses, and fell into an exhausted sleep despite the dangers lurking about them. The pair slept until 10:00 A.M., only to be wakened by gunfire from Reno's position on the bluffs. The flash of Reno's guns was plainly visible to Gerard and Jackson from their hiding place. Later in the morning, Jackson knelt on a dry twig and it broke with a loud snap. Jackson and Gerard froze. A Sioux sentinel called to a companion, "Did you hear that?" "Yes!" came the reply. Gerard and Jackson tumbled down a slope into some heavy underbrush and landed several yards apart. Sioux voices were heard only a few yards away from Jackson. A few anxious minutes passed before the Sioux moved away. Jackson and Gerard remained in concealment, barely stirring, throughout the entire day of the twenty-sixth. The heat and the thirst was nearly unbearable, but Jackson and Gerard did not dare to move from their hiding places.

***

Dawn of the twenty-sixth found DeRudio and O'Neill tired, wet, and hungry on an island in the river. In the murkiness, DeRudio saw seven or eight figures moving along the riverbank. Believing them to be Tom Custer and some troopers, DeRudio threw away all caution and ran to the bank. There, DeRudio called to a buckskin-jacketed warrior he believed to be Tom Custer, "Tom. Send your horse across here." O'Neill, realizing that DeRudio had mistaken a handful of Sioux warriors for Tom Custer and his men, broke from the brush and tried to stop DeRudio. The Indians stopped and gazed about the river, failing to see DeRudio at first.

"Here I am," DeRudio cried. "Don't you see me?" The Indians now saw DeRudio and opened fire. O'Neill triggered a round at the warriors with his carbine. DeRudio fired two rounds from his revolver. The shots startled the Indians' ponies and the animals reared and jostled against one another. DeRudio and O'Neill darted back into the thick brush and, stooping low, ran through large clumps of grass. Several volleys—O'Neill estimated fifty shots—were fired in their direction, but fortunately neither DeRudio nor O'Neill was hit.

About 150 yards farther to the east, DeRudio and O'Neill hid in a clump of rotted tree logs and stumps. There they remained throughout the day, where they heard the rattle of gunfire on Reno Hill and heard the shouts of war chiefs in the river bottom. Several bullets were fired in their direction, but they remained hidden. The sun rose and soon the intense heat became almost unbearable. DeRudio and O'Neill suffered from extreme thirst; but they dared not move, even though the river was only a few yards away. O'Neill's mouth became so dry he lost all salvia. A minute seemed an eternity to these tortured men.

18
Entrenchment Hill
June 26

The Reno-Benteen Defense Perimeter

A light rain fell in the predawn. On the southern part of the defense perimeter, a few Company H troopers had scooped out carbine pits on their own. Two groups of Indian riflemen positioned to the south and below Company H gave Benteen's men the most trouble. Benteen still had not ordered any protective pits dug. Two Company H privates, Charles Windolph and Julian D. Jones, already had taken the initiative by digging out a shallow trench wide enough for the two of them to lay side by side. Loose dirt from their digging had been piled in front of them. Jones told Windolph that he was removing his overcoat. Jones then rolled to one side to free an arm from his overcoat sleeve, and as he did, he screamed. It was his last utterance, as a bullet had torn through some nearby boxes of hardtack and drilled his heart. The Indian who shot him occupied a knoll several hundred yards to the south.[1] A few minutes after Jones was killed, another bullet ricocheted off the hard ground. It struck Windolph in the side, giving him a flesh wound. A minute or two later, the Indian sharpshooter drilled Windolph's carbine and split the stock of the weapon.[2] Windolph later recalled that "there was no full-fledged charge [upon the hilltop], but little groups of Indians would creep up as close as they could get and from bushes on little knolls open fire [at us]." Godfrey, for protection, covered himself entirely with his bedding.

Bullets from the Indian riflemen, from the east and north, whined about the bluffs. A slug whistled through French's campaign hat, barely missing his skull. French's prized gray horse was shot in the head and staggered among the other mounts picketed near the field hospital. Private Henry C. Voight, a young German-born trooper of Company M, took the wounded animal by the bridle and led it away from the other horses. In the process, a bullet from an Indian rifleman tore into Voight's head and killed him.[3]

236

Private Richard B. Dorn of Company B stooped to waken a late-sleeping McDougall when a bullet whistled across the bluffs and tore into the top of Dorn's head, ending his life.[4]

Most of Benteen's troop—its southern line lay along an elevated saucer rim—was exposed to the continued sniping of Indian riflemen who occupied a high hill south of Benteen's sector. Benteen told his troopers, "Men, this is a groundhog case. It's live or die with us. We must fight it out with them." One Indian bullet shot off Benteen's boot heel and the senior captain exclaimed, "Close call! Try again!" Later, another slug grazed his right thumb and another just missed him. When some of Benteen's men cautioned him about drawing the Indian fire, Benteen replied, "Well, they fire so often anyway." Years later, Varnum recalled how Benteen never dodged a bullet, ignoring them all. McDougall recalled that despite the gravity of the situation, Benteen was always smiling and inspiring others.[5]

Benteen feared that the Indians would resume their attack on the defense perimeter as they had done on June 25. Benteen hustled down among the packs and got about fifteen or sixteen troopers and civilian packers on duty there to reinforce his sector under Lieutenant Gibson, the executive officer of Company H. Benteen then went to where Reno was lying on a blanket and told him, "You've got to do something here pretty quick; this won't do, you must drive them back." After considerable urging by Benteen, Reno told Benteen to take one of the companies on his (Benteen's) side of the line for a charge. Benteen replied, "All right, I will take French. Benteen brought Company M to the extreme southwest sector of the line. McDougall later recalled how Benteen kept a close watch on Reno by frequently visiting him where he (Reno) was lying and made suggestions to him. Company B also moved to the extreme north side of the perimeter.

Company C Private John B. McGuire, Jr., who was wounded in the right arm on the hilltop on June 26, recalled for Walter Camp that the Indians got close enough to the troops on the defense perimeter to shoot arrows and throw stones at them.

Sometime between 9:00 and 10:00 A.M., Benteen decided to charge those hostiles lurking below and to the west of the Company H position, near the southwest sector of the defense perimeter, before they could mount an all-out assault on the hilltop. A party of warriors had crawled up a steep ravine leading from the river. These Indians had crawled to within rock-throwing distance of Benteen's position. Benteen's belief about an impending assault by the Indians was reinforced when a Sans Arc warrior named Long Robe shot a Company H trooper and penetrated the defense perimeter to count coup before he was shot and killed.[6] A coup—pronounced "coo"—was killing, scalping, or touching an enemy in combat, and to count (or touch) coup was to add to the "score."

A steep ravine, thick and heavy with undergrowth and scrub juniper trees, meandered down to the river 1,000 yards away, and was some distance southwest of the main perimeter, but west of Benteen's position. (This ravine later would be used by the command's water carriers.) Due to the steepness of the ravine and its thick undergrowth, it was not a good access for an attack by the Indians. At the time of Benteen's concern, the upper ravine was occupied by a number of warriors. These were the closest Indians to the defense perimeter. Benteen left Gibson, acting commander of Company G, in charge of fifteen or sixteen assorted troopers and civilian packers on the Company H line. Benteen now returned to Reno—the major was still lying on his blanket—and told him, "They [the Indians] are coming to our left and you ought to drive them out." A lethargic Reno answered, "Can you see the Indians from there?" "Yes," replied Benteen. "If you can see them," Reno said, "give the command to charge. "It should be pointed out that most spent cartridge casings from Indian-used firearms have been found *several hundred yards away from the Reno-Benteen Defense Perimeter* and Reno seemed to believe Benteen's anxiety about an impending attack was just that—anxiety on Benteen's part.

In the meantime, Private Andrew J. Moore of Company G, one of Gibson's orphaned troopers, who originally had been left in the timber during Reno's retreat to the bluffs, stood to aim his carbine. Private Hugh McGonigle, another of G Company's orphans, cautioned Moore not to stand and expose himself to Indian riflemen. But Moore said he could not get a good aim without standing. A second later, Moore took a slug in the kidneys. At first, he thought he had been struck by an accidental shot fired by someone in the field hospital. Moore died later, pleading with Dr. Porter to administer him some opiates.[7]

After a lull, the Indian gunfire increased with a fury. Benteen yelled to Company H, "All ready, now, men? Now, is your time [for the charge]. Give them hell! Hip! Hip! Here we go!" Benteen now led his yelling company in an unmounted charge to the south.

French belatedly led his company on foot to reinforce Benteen's rear during the charge. The warriors threw clods of dirt and arrows by hand at the charging troops. A Sans Arc warrior named Eagle Hat jumped up when he saw the charging soldiers and scampered into the "water carriers' ravine." Benteen spied the Sans Arc warrior and squeezed off a revolver shot at the fleeing Indian. The slug slammed into Eagle Hat's spine, killing him instantly.

Benteen advanced some 100 yards before Reno called him back to the line. Despite Reno's in-name-only-authority, Benteen had taken command of the defense perimeter.

Several warriors were stationed near the defense perimeter. When Benteen charged, they fired some rapid volleys at his men. Benteens's company, in truth, suffered the most casualties to Indian riflemen because he had not had his men dig any protective pits until the early morning of the twenty-sixth after his company was being "hit" regularly by Indian marksmen. Benteen's fears of an all-out assault on the defense perimeter by the Indians never were realized.

According to the Hunkpapa Gall, the Indians never had any intention of an all-out assault on the Reno-Benteen Defense Perimeter. Gall stated that the shamans (medicine men) in the village believed the "medicine" was not right for an attack. Yet, the Indians' "medicine" was good enough to defeat Reno in the valley and wipe out Custer downriver. The truth is the Indians rarely made a mass attack on a large body of entrenched troops.

During Benteen's return to the defense perimeter, Private James J. Tanner of Company M sustained a mortal wound, according to Sergeant Ryan and Private Newell.

Ryan, nearly a half century later, described for the Hardin *Tribune* [June 23, 1923] the rescue of Tanner:

> [He] was badly wounded . . . and lay on the side of the bluffs in an exposed position. There was a call for volunteers to bring him down, and I grabbed a blanket [and] with three other men, rushed to his assistance, rolled him into a blanket, and made quick tracks in getting him from the side of the bluffs to where our wounded

lay. Fortunately, none of the rescue party received anything more than a few balls through their clothing.

Poor old Tanner, they got you!" blubbered Private Newell, Tanner's close friend, to the stricken soldier back in the field hospital. "No, but they will in a few minutes," Tanner bravely gasped. He closed his eyes and died within a few minutes. Newell broke down and sobbed uncontrollably.[8]

Varnum was another casualty of Benteen's charge. One bullet tore into the calf of one of Varnum's legs. The other bullet cut along the trouser of his other leg, denting his boot and bruising his anklebone. Varnum returned from the charge and dropped into a carbine pit as other bullets pinged the loose dirt around the hole.[9]

In the afternoon, Benteen finally busied his company digging trenches for protection. Dead horses and mules were laboriously dragged to this parapet as added cover.

After Benteen's charge, the command was ordered back to the cover of their carbine pits. Edgerly and two D Company troopers, Thomas W. Stivers and Patrick M. Golden (or Goldan), an Irish immigrant, huddled together in an enlarged rifle trench. Golden's insides were jelly. All afternoon of the previous day, he had whined and cried and whimpered repeatedly that "if they [the Indians] come back, they will kill me." He refused to budge from his trench. A bullet suddenly thudded into the trench, spraying loose dirt on its three occupants; another slug embedded itself in Golden's temple. He died instantly.[10]

***

Indian bullets continued to whine about the blufftops throughout the day. Dr. Porter, the only surviving surgeon, later recalled for his parents his harrying experience: "I established a hospital in the center of the mules and horses, where the wounded were brought in faster than I could attend. Men and animals were killed and wounded all around me, and the horses fell over on my wounded men." In the distance, the troops on the defense perimeter could see Indian riflemen stand erect to fire and then drop down behind the bush.

To conserve cartridges, troopers had been ordered not to fire without the permission of their officers. Sixty-four members of Reno's command (including two civilians) were struck by the marksmanship of Indian riflemen in the two days the battle was waged on the bluff. Indian targets were 363 officers and enlisted men plus an assortment of civilians and Indian scouts. The slightest movement by any of the defenders brought a sharpshooter's bullet whizzing across the blufftops. Reno and Godfrey ventured to the pack train and, as they walked, several Indian bullets whistled at them. Reno, narrowly missed by a bullet, said to Godfrey, "I'm damned if I want to be killed by Indians. I have gone through too many battles."

Not all of the Seventh Cavalry thought Reno befuddled and cowardly. Company M Private William Slaper recalled a Reno whom Slaper admired "during the entire fighting on the hill" and who "did not seem to be at all ruffled." Reno's walking about the hilltop seemingly oblivious to the Indian sharpshooters was something, Slaper recalled, which "encouraged his fellow-officers as well as the troopers."[11]

***

Throughout the day, Indian sharpshooters continued taking a toll of the troopers bunched on Reno Hill. Corporal George Lell of Company H stood, but suddenly doubled over with a slug in the stomach. He was carried to the field hospital, where he begged for water. Knowing that his life was ebbing, Lell begged his comrades to "lift me up, boys, I want to see the boys again before I go." He was elevated to a sitting position so he could view his fellow troopers making a fight of it. A smile pressed Lell's lips as he gazed above the hilltop. He then was laid down and died before sundown.[12]

A few yards away from where Lell was hit, Company H Private Thomas E. Meador was lying on the defense perimeter when a bullet from an Indian sharpshooter struck him in the chest, passed entirely through his body, and exited his back, just above the hip.

Sometime during the day, three troopers were so seriously wounded by Indian marksmen that they died several days, or weeks, later: Private William M. George of Company H (died July 3); Private James C. Bennett of Company C (died July 5); and Irish-born Private David Cooney of Company I (died July 20). The Indians later estimated that during the two days of fighting on Reno Hill, they had fired more than 2,000 rounds at the soldiers entrenched on the blufftops.

The Water Carriers

Indian marksmen weren't the only hazard to those on Entrenchment Hill. The horses and mules of the command were crazed by thirst. Extreme heat and intense thirst plagued the troops on the treeless hilltop to the point of nearly driving many of them senseless. One poor wretch, Irish-born Private Cornelius Cowley of Company A, did go berserk from the maddening thirst and had to be forcibly tied down.

Company F Private Edwin F. Pickard recalled the torture on the hilltop: "Our throats were parched, the smoke stung our nostrils, [and] it seemed as if our tongues had swollen so we couldn't close our mouths, and the heat of the sun seemed fairly to cook the blood in our veins." [13]

Private Jacob Adams of Company H later recalled how the intense thirst had swollen his mouth so that swallowing became impossible. Men sucked pebbles, chewed grass and hardtack—blowing it out their mouths when it became too dry—to try to relieve their horrible thirst. Some troopers tried urinating into their mess cups—so crazed were they for any liquid—but could only pass a few dribbles. Godfrey recalled the thirst as "almost maddening." Some relief came from some raw potatoes and a few cans of tomatoes which the command possessed. Reno refused to allow the command's canned fruits and vegetables—the tomatoes were slipped to him—to be distributed to the most seriously wounded. Dr. Porter passed on the dire news that the wounded were in grave need of water.

The unremitting agony prompted several troopers to volunteer to descend the steep ravine west of Company H's position, which led to the river 1,000 yards away, to fill canteens and cooking kettles with water. The ravine route to the river was down steep, heavily underbrushed and scrub-treed terrain. It was a long and arduous trek. The heart of the ravine offered good protection from Indian gunfire, but the water carriers were exposed to Indian riflemen in moving to the head of the coulee. That final twenty to thirty yards from the mouth of the ravine to the river was open and unprotected. Over this stretch, the water carriers were exposed to Indian marksmen.

Benteen chose the four best marksmen from his company and positioned them to provide protective gunfire for the water carriers.

Benteen's four marksmen were Sergeant George H. Geiger, German-born Saddler Sergeant Otto Voit (a deserter from the 13th U.S. Infantry then serving in the Seventh Cavalry under the alias Frank May), Blacksmith Henry W. B. Mecklin, and the aforementioned Private Windolph. This quartet of troopers stood, atop knolls at either side of the head of the water carriers' ravine, and while exposed to Indian sharpshooters for more than twenty minutes, provided cover fire for the numerous water carriers. All four of these men earned the Medal of Honor for their gallant sharpshooting. Windolph died in 1950, the last surviving white participant of the Battle at the Little Bighorn.

One sharpshooter giving cover fire to the water carriers, who did not earn the coveted Medal of Honor was Private Pigford of Company M. Pigford spotted a warrior in a cottonwood tree across the river. Pigford triggered a round from his carbine and dropped the Indian from the tree. This dead Indian was found on June 27 with a wound in his thigh and his neck broken in the fall from the tree.

Several water carriers volunteered for more than one trip to the

TABLE 11
WATER CARRIERS WHO EARNED THE MEDAL OF HONOR
FOR SECURING WATER FOR THE WOUNDED*

Sergeant Rufus D. Hutchinson, Co. B
Sergeant Stanislaus Roy, Co. A (French-born)
Private Neil Bancroft, Co. A
Private Abraham B. Brant, Co. D
Private Thomas J. Callan, Co. B
Blacksmith Frederick Deetline, Co. D (German-born)
Private Theodore W. Goldin, Co. G
Private David W. Harris, Co. A
Private William M. Harris, Co. D
Private James Pym, Co. B (English-born)**
Private George D. Scott, Co. D
Private Thomas W. Stivers, Co. D
Private Peter Thompson, Co. C (wounded) (Scottish-born)
Private Frank Tolan, Co. D
Private Charles H. Welch, Co. D

* Except as noted here, these medals were awarded October 5, 1878: Bancroft left the Army before he was awarded his medal and never received it. Callan's medal was awarded October 24, 1878. Goldin's medal was awarded December 21, 1896.
** Pym was shot and killed in 1893 by his wife's lover fifteen years after his Army service.

TABLE 12
WATER CARRIERS WHO WERE NOT AWARDED THE MEDAL OF HONOR IN SPITE OF SECURING WATER FOR THE WOUNDED

Sergeant John Rafter, Co. K
Sergeant Louis Rott, Co. K (German-born)
Corporal George H. King, Co. A (fatally wounded; died July 2, 1876)[*]
Private Jacob Adams, Co. H
Private Ansgarius Boren, Co. B (Swiss-born)
Private Charles Campbell, Co. G
Private Thomas W. Coleman, Co. B
Private Augustus L. DeVoto, Co. B[14] (Italian-born)
Private Edmond Dwyer, Co. G
Private John Foley, Co. K
Private John M. Gilbert, Co. B
Private Edward Housen, Co. D (killed)
Private William D. Nugent, Co. A
Private Edwin F. Pickard, Co. F
Private William C. Slaper, Co. M.
Private James Weeks, Co. M
Private James Wilber (real name James W. Darcy), Co. M (wounded)
Saddler Michael P. Madden, Co. K (wounded) (Irish-born)
Paints-His-Face-Half-Yellow, scout[**]

[*] King family tradition says that Corporal King received his fatal stomach wound as a water carrier. It is interesting to note that King was promoted to sergeant posthumously to retroactively date from May 17, 1876, the date the regiment left Fort Lincoln, and his gravestone at the Custer National Cemetery so state's his sergeant's rank. Such an honor for an enlisted man of that era was rare. He did something to merit that distinction.

[**] Medal of Honor regulations prohibited civilian and scout personnel of the Army from being awarded the medal. Medals of Honor erroneously issued to a few scouts of the Indian Wars later were revoked for this reason.

river. Benteen's quartet of sharpshooters gave heavy cover fire as the water carriers made their several trips down the ravine and to the river.

Upon reaching the mouth of the ravine, the water volunteers hid in the brush. Then, one by one, at irregular intervals, they took turns dashing to the river. The first man fetched a kettle of water for the others, but the first kettles dipped also scooped up mud. Still, many of the carriers plunged their heads into the river and drank their fill in gulps. For all of these men, it was their first drink of water in thirty-six hours, mud and all. Indian riflemen, lurking in the cottonwoods on the opposite bank, fired away at the water carriers as they drank at the

TABLE 13
OTHERS WHO WERE AWARDED THE MEDAL OF HONOR
AT THE BATTLE AT THE LITTLE BIGHORN

Sergeant Benjamin C. Criswell, Company B, for recovering the body of Lieutenant Hodgson (on June 27), bringing up the ammunition under fire, and other brave deeds.

Sergeant Thomas Murphy, Irish-born, Company K, for gallantry in action.

Private Henry Holden, English-born, Company D, for bringing up the ammunition.

Private Charles Cunningham, Company B, for declining to leave the line for medical treatment after suffering a neck wound on June 25.

river's edge. Several of the drinkers seemed impervious to the bullets which rippled the water near them.

Private Augustus DeVoto, who had been with the pack mules, exposed himself to Indian marksmen by wading into the river and filling a big cooking kettle with water. DeVoto carried the kettle to the bank and also filled several canteens; all the while, Indian riflemen fired away at him.[15] Private William Nugent, Company A, stripped to his underwear, plunged down the broken ravine, sprinted across the open flat to the riverbank, and submerged his head beneath the water while simultaneously submerging the many canteens he toted. Bullets zipped into the water around him. Finally, near-suffocation forced Nugent's head above the water.

Benteen stood on a knoll viewing the gallantry of the water volunteers. He was joined by Hare. Indian sharpshooters pinged and zinged away at the two officers. When Hare asked him if it were wise for them to expose themselves to the Indians, Benteen smiled and commented, "If they are going to get you, they will get you somewhere else if not here." Benteen, a fatalist, also had told Varnum, "When the bullet is cast to kill me, it'll kill me, that's all." Little wonder why Private William Morris, Company M, later said: "Benteen was unquestionably the bravest man I ever met." Herendeen also called Benteen "one of the bravest men I ever saw." This was echoed by Gibson, Benteen's executive officer: "[Benteen] is one of the coolest and bravest men I have ever known." Indeed, a fatalistic Benteen was

245

impervious to the instant death striking the hilltop in the form of Indian sharpshooters' bullets.

The gallantry of the water carriers cannot be understated. Private Peter Thompson, Company C, made three separate runs to the river. Thompson made his second and third treks to the river despite being struck in the right hand by an Indian bullet on his first trip for water. Private James Wilber (James W. Darcy), Company M, was hit in the left leg on his trip to the river.

Saddler Mike Madden, Company K, a lovable Irishman with a thick brogue, was in the first group of water carriers to descend the ravine. A bullet struck Madden's right leg below the knee and he crumpled to the ground with a double fracture of the limb. Half-Yellow-Face, the Crow scout who had descended the ravine with some of the water carriers, helped get Madden on his back and into some brush out of sight of the hostile marksmen. It was too dangerous to carry Madden back up the ravine under the rifle fire of the Sioux and Cheyenne, so Half-Yellow-Face had to leave him in his hiding place until sundown, when Madden was carried back to the hilltop. The next day Dr. Porter amputated Madden's leg without anesthetic. The Irishman's only painkiller after surgery was a few long gulps of brandy. Smacking his lips, Madden smiled and reputedly told Dr. Porter after guzzling the brandy, "Doctor, cut off me other leg." Godfrey became so choked with emotion at Madden's bravery that he promoted him to sergeant on the spot. After the successful removal of his limb, Madden was carried a short distance away, where he lustily emptied his bowels.

Two troopers lost their lives in the sorties to the river. Private Edward Housen of Company D dipped his bucket into the river as he drank his fill of water. From across the opposite bank, a distance of twenty to thirty yards the young Cheyenne warrior Wooden Leg squeezed off a shot just as Housen raised himself from the riverbank. Wooden Leg's bullet struck Housen and he pitched into the river and began struggling. A Sioux warrior went into the stream and clubbed Housen to death with his rifle.[16] The other water carrier fatality, Corporal George H. King of Company A, who was shot in the stomach, died on July 2.

The water was a godsend to the thirsty men of Reno's command, especially for the many wounded who suffered the most for water. Many of the wounded were delirious from the lack of water. A thirsty Moylan called to Canadian-born Private James Weeks of M Company on the latter's return from the river and asked for a drink of water. "You go to hell and get your own water," Weeks shouted to Moylan. "This water is for the wounded!"[17]

The Shooting Stops

Throughout the day, from about 11:00 A.M. to 3:00 P.M., the Indian rifle fire gradually slackened, although Indian sharpshooters continued to find a mark now and then. At 3:00 P.M., the shooting stopped altogether. Shortly before the cease of hostilities, civilian packer Frank Mann stood in his carbine pit near Company A working his carbine behind a three-foot stack of boxes of hardtack. Now and then Mann raised his head above the top of the boxes for a better aim. An Indian marksman to the southeast spied the packer's bobbing head and squeezed off a shot, just as Mann was sighting his carbine. The Indian's slug struck Mann's temple and he died without a sound.[18]

Sergeant Ryan, however, had the distinction of having fired the last round of the engagement. French ordered Ryan to place a few well-directed shots in the vicinity of high knoll just north of Reno Hill. Ryan recalled the incident for the Hardin *Tribune* in 1923.

"I fired a couple of shots (with a .45 Sharps telescopic rifle) until I got range . . . of the Indians. Then I put a half dozen shots in rapid succession, and those Indians scampered away from that point of the bluff, and that ended the firing on the part of the Indians in that memorable engagement, and the boys set up quite a cheer."

In the meantime, Reno had attempted to send out messengers (some Indian scouts) to Terry and Gibbon, but nothing came of it.

Sometime before sundown, the Indians struck their village camp. Indians, especially large villages, moved every two or three days for sanitation reasons. The encampment also wanted to move for fear of other soldiers in the immediate area (Terry and Gibbon). The Sioux had torched the grass in the valley about 2:00 P.M. to cover their movement downriver. Awestruck, the men on Reno Hill, viewing the large dust clouds raised by the huge movement, at first stared dumbfoundedly at the enormous size of the village and its pony herd. The procession was still in view at nightfall.

Wallace said that "it was the largest body of Indians I ever saw. . . ." Herendeen agreed. "This was the largest camp I ever saw, by a great deal. . . ." Hare described the village's movement as a "dark moving mass" which "took a long time [to pass]," according to Wallace.

Benteen estimated the column of Indians at three miles. The huge pony herd of the camp looked to Edgerly like "a great brown carpet being dragged on the ground." Edgerly later stated the village pony herd was the densest body of animals that he had ever seen. Hare estimated the herd at between 20,000 and 25,000 ponies. Moylan crawled from behind his dead mule and suggested that the huge Indian pony herd appeared to be an enormous buffalo herd. From their hiding place in the valley, DeRudio and O'Neill viewed the passing village from only 50 yards away. DeRudio later said that the Indian column took several hours to pass downriver. From their hiding place, Gerard and Jackson saw some Sioux in a gully opposite them. Soon a great horde of Indians, women and children included, passed near where Gerard and Jackson hid. The two men saw wounded warriors being carried on travois while dead warriors were tied on the backs of their ponies. Squaws wailed death chants for lost warriors. At the sight of the Indians on the move, the realization that the Indians were moving away suddenly hit Reno's men on the hilltop and they gave three lusty cheers.

The "pull out" by the Indians at the Little Bighorn was due to their intelligence of the approaching Terry-Gibbon column of troops. Kate Bighead, Missus Spotted Horn Bull, and Wooden Leg all testified in later years that the many soldiers (Terry-Gibbon) approaching the battle area was the reason that the Indians deserted the field of combat.[19] Respect (Fear) Nothing, the Oglala, viewed the approaching Terry-Gibbon column with captured field glasses from the Custer battlefield on the late afternoon of June 26.[20] Lone Bear, an Oglala, stated the reason the Indians did not attack Reno was that "he was too firmly entrenched."[21] The Miniconjou Lights stated simply that the village fled when it heard more soldiers were coming.[22] This was also confirmed by the Hunkpapa, Horned Horse, who stated that "we heard that more soldiers were coming up the river, so we had to pack up and leave."[23]

At dusk the surviving horses and mules of the regiment were driven to the river and watered for the first time since the afternoon of the twenty-fifth and turned out to graze. All of the surviving stock was again watered on the morning of June 27.

During the evening, Reno moved his command a short distance to the north to get away from the overpowering stench of the dead horses and mules. The command dug in on either side of a big ravine. That evening, the dead on Reno Hill were interred.

A still-cautious McDougall remained concerned that the Indians might not all be gone, or at worst, return, so his Company B spent a portion of the night digging a trench for better protection.

***

About an hour before midnight, Gerard and Jackson, both a little worse for wear, scaled the bluffs to reach Reno's command. To keep from being shot by a "jumpy" sentinel, Gerard called out, "Hello! Hello, there!" as he approached the defense perimeter.

A voice replied, "Hello! Hello! Who are you?"

"Gerard!" came the reply.

"Gerard is coming in!" the sentinel cried.

Gerard was ravenous after not having eaten for nearly forty-eight hours and wolfed down hardtack and cold coffee. The squawman retched only minutes after eating and drinking.

249

19

Terry and Gibbon to the Rescue

June 27

At about 3:00 A.M., an exhausted DeRudio and O'Neill crept out of the valley and scaled the bluffs. When about 200 yards from the campfire on Reno Hill, DeRudio called out, "Picket, don't fire! It is Lieutenant DeRudio and Private O'Neill." Both men then ran the remaining distance to reach Reno's command. DeRudio, of course, wasted little time in recounting to his fellow officers his "lurid adventures" in the valley. French listened with disgust to the Italian's wild tales and seriously toyed with the idea of shooting him on the spot. French, instead, walked away, only in retrospect to regret not having shot DeRudio on the spot.[1] In a July 10, 1876, letter to his wife, Benteen wrote that DeRudio "deserves no credit for being caught in the woods and after being left there—kept there."

***

On June 27, an early morning fog hung over the Little Bighorn valley, but the morning soon turned sunny and warm. The hills, ridges, and burned-out valley at the village site, for the first day in two, was silent of gunfire. About 9:30 A.M., the dust clouds raised by the approaching Terry-Gibbon column were sighted by the "battered bastards" of Reno's command. At first, those on the hilltop thought that the Indians were returning. Carbines were quickly readied and the horses brought under protection. Godfrey, French, Varnum, and others scanned the distant horizon with field glasses. Reno dispatched three unnamed volunteers to see if the dust clouds were raised by the Indians returning or if by soldiers; if by Indians, the volunteers were instructed not to return to Reno Hill but to ride on in search of Terry and Gibbon. Reno also dispatched the Ree scout Forked Horn and his grandson, Yellow Hawk, to investigate the dust clouds. An anxious hour passed before Varnum recognized the fluttering, dust-covered

250

guidons of what mistakenly was thought (by those on Reno Hill) to be Crook's column. Hare and Wallace were quickly dispatched to meet the advancing troops. Neither officer stopped to saddle their mounts before riding out.

Tears of joy and relief filled the eyes of many on Reno Hill. A bleary-eyed Moylan no longer controlled his emotions and he wept unashamedly. Most of Reno's men gave three loud cheers in unison at the sight of the approaching troops. Some men shook hands and congratulated one another for surviving what would prove to be *the* ordeal of their lives. Many men silently gave thanks to their Creator. Private Edward Pigford later summed up the collective feelings of those on Reno Hill when he stated, "I never saw anything in all my life that looked as good to me as Terry's men."

Later in the day, the survivors of the Seventh Cavalry learned of the fate of Custer and his battalion four and a quarter miles away. The earlier joy and festive mood turned sour and ugly; happiness and thanksgiving soon became remorse and mental anguish. A dumbfounded Terry lamented, "I find it impossible to believe that so fine a regiment as the Seventh Cavalry should have met a catastrophe." Later, to *Far West* skipper Grant Marsh, Terry lamented that the whole affair was "a terrible blunder; a sad and terrible blunder." An equally horror-struck Captain Walter Clifford of Gibbon's Seventh Infantry also lamented, "Let us bury our dead and flee from this rotting atmosphere."

Benteen's feelings, however, were mixed. Viewing Custer's mutilated, bloated, and blackened corpse, Benteen commented to one of Terry's staff officers, "What a big winner the U.S. government would have been if only Custer and his gang [officer clique] could have been taken [out by the Indians]."[2] Even Custer's death had not diminished Benteen's hatred of the man.

DeRudio, on the other hand, was thankful that he had been with Reno instead of Custer. "No one would now be alive had we not been led by a coward," DeRudio later commented.[3] Gibson wrote his wife that "if it hadn't been for Benteen every one of us would have been massacred [because] Reno did not know which end he was standing on. . . ."[4] Varnum was less harsh: he simply wrote later that Reno had made "a poor showing" at the Little Bighorn. So was Herendeen. He

TABLE 14
RENO'S CASUALTIES ON THE HILLTOPS

	Killed	Wounded Who Survived
Officers	0	2[*]
Enlisted Men	17[**]	43
Scouts/Civilians	1	1
	18	46

[*] Benteen and Varnum.
[**] Includes four troopers who later died of their wounds.

merely stated that it was Benteen who had saved the fight on the hill.[5] McDougall later stated that Reno was "thoroughly incompetent to handle the situation [at the Little Bighorn]."[6] Sergeant Ryan, who had little reason to like Benteen—who once broke Ryan from a noncom and refused to endorse French's recommendation for a Medal of Honor for Ryan—recalled that "Captain Benteen . . . saved Reno from utter annihilation, and his gallantry cleared the ravines of Indians."[7]

***

Sergeant Benjamin Criswell and four other men of B Troop (Augustus DeVoto, Private Stephen L. Ryan, Farrier James E. Moore, and Saddler John E. Baily) went down to the riverbank and recovered the naked and bloated remains of Lieutenant Hodgson. They laboriously carried Hodgson's body across carbines to its burial on the hilltop.[8]

The Seventh Cavalry's total casualties at the Little Bighorn was 272 men killed, including 15 officers; 59 surviving wounded, including two Ree scouts, and a civilian packer; 344 Army horses killed and lost; and numerous government mules lost and killed in the single biggest defeat of the U.S. Army in the post Civil War West. The

TABLE 15
KNOWN WARRIOR CASUALTIES IN HILLTOP FIGHT

Dog Backbone (Ass), Miniconjou
Eagle Hat, Sans Arc
Long Robe, Sans Arc

TABLE 16
RENO'S TOTAL CASUALTIES AT THE LITTLE BIGHORN
(Valley & Hilltop Fights)

	Killed	Wounded Who Survived
Officers	2	2
Enlisted Men	50*	54
Scouts/Civilians	7	3
Total with Reno	59	59

* Includes five troopers who died later of their wounds.

Indians' victory had not been easy; Reno reported to the Army's Chief of Ordnance that the regiment had expended 38,038 rounds in the battle. Undoubtedly, some of these rounds found their marks.

There are no accurate statistics available for the number of Indian casualties in the battle because Indians removed their dead and wounded from the battlefield. Any attempt at trying to produce a casualty count for Indians at the Little Bighorn falls into the "wild guess" category. Some Indian sources place the warrior dead in the battle at the ridiculously low total of forty to seventy. This total, of course, is based only on the names recalled by other warriors in their old age. The other extreme, equally ridiculous, puts the warrior dead in excess of 700. The bodies of nearly two score (forty) Indians were found in burial dress in and around the village after the battle. Later reports by the Indians themselves said wounded warriors died for weeks after the battle. But Custer and his men undoubtedly gave a good account of themselves and sold their lives at considerable expense. Sitting Bull, himself, later admitted that many of the Sioux tepees had been emptied of warriors by the "Long Hair's" men.

***

The defeat of the "Long Hair" was the high-water mark of Indian

TABLE 17
THE CUSTER BATTALION'S TOTAL DEAD

Officers	13
Enlisted Men	196
Scouts/Civilians	4
Total with Benteen	213

253

resistance on the North American continent. But the significance of Custer's destruction on the Little Bighorn is in the fact that it brought the American public's attention to the bloody Indian problem during the country's Centennial Summer. It produced a public outcry that resulted in $200,000 in Congressional appropriations for the Army and an authorization for an additional 2,500 enlisted men which otherwise might not have been obtained. More importantly, Custer's defeat interrupted an American populace's celebration of its Centennial Summer and refocused Americans' attention on, not how far they had come as a people and a nation in the preceding 100 years, but, rather, on how far they needed to go to achieve the hopes and dreams of that Centennial Summer. Those hopes and dreams of a century-old America, of growth, stability, and economic prosperity also, unfortunately, included the subjugation of the Plains tribes; the former three never could be achieved while the latter remained a task unfilled. But, in the end, the Indian was doomed by the very thing he fought to preserve—his centuries-old way of life.

20
Taps
Victory and Defeat

The Little Bighorn was a battle badly planned and in some ways badly fought.[1] A Proceedings of the Court of Inquiry in the case of Major Marcus A. Reno concerning his conduct at the Little Bighorn River, June 25 to 26, 1876 (National Archives) was held at Chicago, January 14 to February 12, 1879. The inquiry was held at the request of Reno because of the ugly publicity tainting his character as an officer in the wake of Custer's annihilation. Reno, however, called for an official inquiry only after the statute of limitations for prosecution had expired. The court officially exonerated Reno of any misconduct during the battle, but it did so with "damn faint praise." It held:

> The conduct of the officers throughout was excellent, and while subordinates, in some instances, did more for the safety of the command by brilliant displays of courage than did Major Reno, there was nothing in his conduct which requires animadversion from this court.

The court's verdict did not vindicate Reno. He went to his grave in 1889 with the specter of Custer haunting his character.[2] He died friendless, in poverty, and disgrace.

The Reno Court of Inquiry was a military coverup or "whitewash." DeRudio, decades later, stated that the surviving officers of the regiment, except French (who did not testify in person but by deposition), Weir (who died in 1876), and Gibson (who also did not testify), deliberately protected Reno at the inquiry,[3] presumably to save the honor of the regiment. The wily Benteen also admitted that he had coyly "held back" in his testimony to protect Reno.[4] Godfrey told Gerard that he (Godfrey) had been threatened (by persons unnamed) with "pigeonholed" charges if he testified to Reno's cowardice during the battle.[5] To Godfrey's credit, he accused Reno of "nervous timidity" on the witness stand. Godfrey further testified that he was not "impressed with any of Reno's qualifications" nor did Reno's conduct "inspire the command with confidence in resisting the enemy." French, a few years after the battle, became so despondent over the Custer tragedy that he contemplated suicide.[6] French suffered from delirium tremens and probably would not have made a good witness. At the time of the Reno Court of Inquiry, he was sitting out a court-martial sentence for conduct unbecoming an officer and a gentleman.

***

The sweet victory on the Greasy Grass brought no lasting salvation to the red race. The Little Bighorn was merely a candle in the wind—the red man's apocalypse. By January, 1891, the red race had been vanquished on the North American continent. Custer's demise on the Greasy Grass only had delayed the inevitable. It is a credit to the Indian that his race even survived that conquest.

***

A federal peace commission in September, 1876, informed the nonrecalcitrant Sioux chiefs that Congress—as of August 15—had restructured the Laramie Treaty of 1868 to exclude the Black Hills from the Sioux lands.

> . . . There were no cowards on either side . . .
>
> *Sitting Bull*

> I am much grieved, for I expected if I did not defeat you, to hold out much longer, and give you more trouble before I surrendered. I tried hard. . . . I am no coward. I am an Indian.
>
> *Black Hawk, a Sioux*

> Only the mountains live forever.
>
> *from an old Indian prayer*

In Remembrance

To those gallant Americans, red and white (and one black man), who took different roads to the Little Bighorn and fought for their country as they envisioned that country should be.

256

TABLE 18
SEVENTH CAVALRY NECROLOGY
(Prominent Battle Participants Only)

1876	Weir
1882	French
1889	Reno
1890	Wallace
1898	Benteen
1901	Wm. Jackson
1903	Dr. Porter
1904	Young Hawk
1909	McDougall
	Moylan
1910	DeRudio
1913	Gerard
1914	O'Neill
1915	Mathey
1918	Herendeen
1919	Gibson
	Goes Ahead
1922	Hairy Moccasin
	J. Martin (Trumpeter)
1923	Curley
1926	Kanipe
1927	Edgerly
1929	White-Man-Runs-Him
	Hare
1932	Godfrey
1936	Varnum

Appendix
Tables of divisions, companies, Indians, etc.

TABLE 19
THE 7TH U.S. CAVALRY
Battle of the Little Bighorn

Terry: 3 regiments
Custer — Reno — Benteen

CUSTER
    Bvt. Maj. Gen. George A. Custer, commanding regiment
    Capt. Thomas W. Custer, aide to Custer, of Co. C
    1st Lt. William W. Cooke, regimental adjutant
    1st Lt. George E. Lord, asst. surg.
    Sgt. Maj. William H. Sharrow, of Co. F
    Color Sgt. Robert H. Hughes, of Co. K
    Flag Sgt. John Vickory, of Co. F
    Cpl. John J. Callahan, acting hospital steward, of Co. K
    Chief Trumpeter Henry Voss, of Co. F
    Trumpeter Henry C. Dose, Custer's orderly, of Co. G
    Pvt. Thomas S. "Boss" Tweed, Cooke's orderly, of Co. L
    Pvt. Francis F. Hughes, Lord's orderly, of Co. L

Companies C, E, F, I, and L

Company C
    Capt. Thomas W. Custer, CO to Gen. Custer's HQ staff
    1st Lt. James "Jimmi" Calhoun, XO, to Co. L as acting CO
    2nd Lt. Henry M. Harrington, acting CO
    1st Sgt. Edwin Bobo
    1st Sgt. August Finckle
    Sgt. Jeremiah "Darby" Finley
    Sgt. Richard P. Hanley
    Sgt. Daniel A. Kanipe
    Cpl. John Foley
    Pvt. James C. Bennett
    Pvt. John Brennan
    Pvt. John Brightfield
    Pvt. John Fitzgerald
    Pvt. John B. McGuire
    Pvt. Nathan Short
    Pvt. Peter Thompson
    Pvt. James Watson
    Pvt. Willis B. Wright

Farrier John Fitzgerald

Company E, The Gray Horse Troop
    Capt. Charles S. Ilsley, CO, absent on permanent detached service
    1st Lt. Charles C. DeRudio, XO, to Co. A
    1st Lt. Algernon E. "Fresh" Smith, acting CO, of Co. A
    1st Lt. Herbert J. Slocum
    2nd Lt. William Van W. Reily, to Co. F
    2nd Lt. James G. "Jack" Sturgis, acting XO, of Co. M
    1st Sgt. Frederick Hohmeyer
    Sgt. John S. Ogden
    Pvt. Herod T. Liddiard

Company F
    Bvt Maj. Gen. George Armstrong "Autie" Custer
    Sgt. Maj. William H. Sharrow
    Capt. George W. M. Yates, CO
    1st Lt. George E. Lord, asst. surg.
    2nd Lt. William Van W. Reily, acting XO, of Co. E
    Flag Sgt. John Vickory
    Color Sgt. Robert H. Hughes
    Cpl. John Briody
    Cpl. John J. Callahan, acting hosp. steward, of Co. K
    Cpl. William Teeman
    Pvt. William Brown
    Pvt. Edward Davern, Reno's orderly, to Reno's HQ
    Pvt. Timothy Donnelly
    Pvt. Francis F. Hughes, Dr. Lord's orderly, of Co. L
    Pvt. Frank "Yankee" Hunter
    Pvt. Gustav Klein
    Pvt. Dennis Lynch, absent aboard the *Far West*
    Pvt. Edwin F. Pickard
    Pvt. James M. Rooney
    Pvt. Thomas S. "Boss" Tweed, Cooke's orderly, of Co. L
    Chief Trumpeter Henry Voss
    Trumpeter Henry C. Dose, Gen. Custer's orderly, of Co. G

Company I
    Capt. Myles Walter Keogh, CO, sr. capt. and second in command to
        Custer, this battalion
    1st Lt. James E. Porter
    1st Sgt. Frank E. Varden, top kick
    Sgt. James Bustard
    Sgt. Milton J. DeLacy, to Co. B's pack train
    Cpl. John T. Wild
    Pvt. David Cooney

Pvt. Edward C. Driscoll
Pvt. Francis Johnson (nee Francis J. Kennedy)
Pvt. Gustave Korn
Pvt. Archibald McIlhargey, Reno's striker
Pvt. John Mitchell, Reno's cook
Pvt. James Parker
Pvt. Willis B. Wright
Blacksmith Henry A. Bailey
Trumpeter John W. Patton (Patten)

Company L
1st Lt. James "Jimmi" Calhoun, acting CO of Co. C
2nd Lt. John J. Crittenden, acting XO, of 20th U.S. Infantry
1st Sgt. James Butler
Pvt. John Burkman, to Pack Train, Custer's striker
Pvt. Charles Graham
Pvt. Francis F. Hughes, to Co. F. as Dr. Lord's orderly
Pvt. Thomas S. "Boss" Tweed, to Co. F as Cooke's orderly
Pvt. Byron L. Tarbox
___ John Duggan, rank unknown

RENO
Maj. Marcus A. Reno, 2nd in command to Custer
2nd Lt. Benjamin H. "Benny" Hodgson, acting asst. adjutant gen., of Co.
   B
2nd Lt. George D. "Nick" Wallace, itinerary officer, of Co. G
Pvt. Edward Davern, Reno's orderly, of Co. F

Companies A, G, and M

Company A
Capt. James Myles "Michie" Moylan, CO
1st Lt. Charles C. DeRudio, XO of E
1st Lt. Algernon E. "Fresh" Smith, to Co. E as acting CO
2nd Lt. Charles A. Varnum, supervisor of scouts
1st Sgt. William Heyn
Sgt. Samuel Alcott
Sgt. Ferdinand A. Culbertson
Sgt. Henry Fehler
Sgt. George M. McDermott
Sgt. Miles F. O'Hara
Sgt. Stanislaus Roy
Cpl. James Dalious
Cpl. George H. King
Pvt. John E. Armstrong
Pvt. Neil Bancroft

260

Pvt. Thomas "Billy" Blake
Pvt. Cornelius Cowley
Pvt. James Drinan
Pvt. William G. Hardy, trumpeter
Pvt. David W. Harris
Pvt. James McDonald
Pvt. William Moody (also Moodie)
Pvt. William D. Nugent
Pvt. Francis M. Reeves
Pvt. Benjamin F. Rogers
Pvt. Richard Rollins
Pvt. Edward Stanley
Pvt. Elijah T. Strode, Varnum's orderly
Pvt. Thomas P. Sweetser
Pvt. William O. Taylor
—— James Sullivan, rank unknown
Trumpeter David McVeigh
Civilian Packer Frank C. Mann

Company G
   1st Lt. Donald McIntosh, acting CO
   2nd Lt. George D. "Nick" Wallace
   Acting 1st Sgt. Edward Botzer
   Sgt. Martin Considine
   Cpl. Otto Hagemann
   Cpl. George Loyd
   Cpl. James Martin
   Pvt. Charles Campbell
   Pvt. Edmond Dwyer
   Pvt. Theodore W. Goldin
   Pvt. Benjamin Johnson
   Pvt. John Lattmann
   Pvt. Samuel McCormick
   Pvt. John J. McGinnis
   Pvt. Hugh McGonigle
   Pvt. Andrew J. Moore
   Pvt. Thomas F. O'Neill
   Pvt. Henry G. Petring
   Pvt. John Rapp, McIntosh's orderly
   Pvt. Eldorado J. Robb
   Pvt. Benjamin F. Rogers
   Pvt. Henry Seafferman
   Pvt. Edward Stanley
   Pvt. Markus Weiss
   Farrier Benjamin J. Wells

Trumpeter Henry C. Dose, Gen. Custer's orderly
Saddler Selby Crawford

Company M
Capt. Thomas H. "Tucker" French, CO
1st Lt. Edward G. Mathey, to Co. B's pack train
2nd Lt. James G. "Jack" Sturgis, acting asst. eng., to Co. E as acting XO
1st Sgt. John M. Ryan, acting XO
Sgt. Patrick "Patsy" Carey
Sgt. Miles F. O'Hara, guidon bearer
Sgt. Charles White
Cpl. Henry M. Cody (a.k.a. Henry M. Scollen)
Cpl. Frederick Streing
Pvt. Frank Braun
Pvt. Jean B. Gallenne
Pvt. Henry Gordon
Pvt. Henry Klotzbucher, French's striker
Pvt. George Lorentz, French's orderly
Pvt. George B. Mask, Hodgson's orderly, of Co. B
Pvt. John H. "Snopsy" Meier
Pvt. William D. "Tinker Bill" Meyer
Pvt. William E. Morris
Pvt. Frank Neely
Pvt. Daniel Newell
Pvt. Edward A. [or D.] Pigford
Pvt. Roman Rutten
Pvt. Hobart Ryder
Pvt. William W. Rye
Pvt. James "Crazy Jim" Severs
Pvt. John "Big Fritz" Sivertsen
Pvt. William C. Slaper
Pvt. George E. Smith
Pvt. John Sullivan
Pvt. David "Sandy" Summers
Pvt. James J. Tanner
Pvt. Rollins L. Thorpe
Pvt. Henry Turley
Pvt. Henry C. Voight
Pvt. James Weeks
Pvt. Ferdinand Widmayer (was not there)
Pvt. James Wilber (also James W. Darcy)
Trumpeter Charles "Bounce" Fischer
Trumpeter Henry C. "Cully" Weaver
Blacksmith Walter O. Taylor

BENTEEN

Companies B, D, H, and K

Company B (Pack Train)
Capt. Thomas M. McDougall, CO
1st Lt. Edward G. Mathey, acting CO, of Co. M
2nd Lt. Benjamin H. "Benny" Hodgson, to Reno's HQ
Sgt. Benjamin C. Criswell
Sgt. Milton J. DeLacy, of Co. I
Sgt. Rufus D. Hutchinson
Pvt. Ansgarius Boren
Pvt. Thomas J. Callan
Pvt. Thomas W. Coleman
Pvt. Charles Cunningham
Pvt. August L. DeVoto
Pvt. Richard B. Dorn
Pvt. John M. Gilbert
Pvt. George B. Mask, to Co. M as Hodgson's orderly
Pvt. James Pym
Pvt. Stephen L. Ryan
Farrier James E. Moore
Saddler John E. Baily

Chief Packer
John C. Wagoner

Civilian Packers
R. C. Churchill
John Frett
Frank C. Mann

Company D
Capt. Thomas B. Weir, CO
2nd Lt. Winfield S. Edgerly, acting XO
1st Sgt. Michael Martin
Sgt. James Flanagan
Cpl. George W. Wylie
Pvt. Abraham B. Brant
Pvt. Patrick M. Golden (also Goldan)
Pvt. William M. Harris
Pvt. Henry Holden, to Pack Train
Pvt. Edward Housen
Pvt. Charles Sanders
Pvt. George D. Scott
Pvt. Thomas W. Stivers
Pvt. Frank Tolan

263

Pvt. Charles H. Welch
Blacksmith Frederick Deetline
Farrier Vincent Charley

Company H
    Capt. Frederick William Benteen, CO
    1st Lt. Francis M. "Frank" Gibson, XO
    Sgt. George H. Geiger, water carrier sharpshooter
    Sgt. Otto Voit, saddler, water carrier sharpshooter
    Cpl. George Lell
    Pvt. Jacob Adams
    Pvt. William M. George
    Pvt. George W. Glease (née George W. Glenn)
    Pvt. Julian D. Jones
    Pvt. Thomas E. Meador
    Pvt. Charles Windolph, water carrier sharpshooter
    Blacksmith Henry W. B. Mecklin, water carrier sharpshooter
    Trumpeter John Martin (née Giovanni Martini)

Company K
    1st Lt. Edward S. Godfrey, acting CO
    2nd Lt. Luther R. Hare
    1st Sgt. DeWitt Winney
    Sgt. Robert H. Hughes, to Co. F as color sgt.
    Sgt. Thomas Murphy
    Sgt. John Rafter
    Sgt. Louis Rott
    Cpl. John J. Callahan, to Co. F as acting hosp. steward
    Pvt. Elihu F. Clear, Hare's orderly
    Pvt. John C. Creighton
    Pvt. John Foley
    — John F. Donahue, rank unknown
    Trumpeter Julius Helmer
    Saddler Michael P. Madden

TABLE 20
FRIENDLY INDIANS

CROW
  Curley, scout
  Goes Ahead, scout
  Hairy Moccasin, scout
  Half-Yellow-Face (a.k.a. Paints-His-Face-Half-Yellow), scout
  White Swan, scout
  White-Man-Runs-Him, scout

SIOUX
  Bear Waiting, scout
  Bear-Running-in-the-Timber, scout
  Buffalo Ancestor, scout, horse herder
  White Cloud, scout
  William "Billy" Cross (1/2 Sioux), scout

REE (Arikara)
  William "Billy" Baker (1/2 Arikara), scout
  Black Fox, scout
  Bloody Knife, scout
  Bobtailed Bull, scout and leader of the Rees
  Boy Chief, scout
  Bull, scout, horse herder
  Bull-Stands-in-the-Water, scout, horse herder
  Charging Bull, scout, horse herder
  Forked Horn, oldest scout
  Goose, scout
  Little Brave, scout
  Little Sioux, scout
  One Feather, scout, horse herder
  Pretty (or Good) Face, pack train, horse herder
  Red Bear (Good or Handsome Elk), scout, horse herder
  Red Foolish Bear, scout
  Red Star, scout, horse herder
  Red Wolf, scout, horse herder
  Soldier, scout
  Stabbed, scout
  Strikes Two, scout
  Strikes-the-Lodge, scout
  White Eagle, scout, horse herder
  Yellow Hawk, scout
  Young Hawk, scout & grandson of Forked Horn

TABLE 21

CHEYENNE
- Bearded Man
- Black Moccasin
- Crooked Nose
- Little Bird
- Little Sun
- Little Wolf, chief
- Noisy Walking
- Old Bear
- Sitting Bull, chief
- Tall Bull
- Whirlwind
- White Bull, chief, shaman
- White Bull
- White Necklace
- Wooden Leg
- Yellow Hair

NORTHERN CHEYENNE
- Bobtail Horse, suicide boy
- Calf, suicide boy
- Roan Bear, suicide boy
- Two Moons, chief
- White Shield, suicide boy
- Wolf Tooth, chief

SOUTHERN CHEYENNE
- Kate Bighead
- Lame (Walking) White Man, a war chief
- Twin Woman, wife of Lame White Man

OGLALA
- Black Elk
- Chief Red Cloud
- Dewey Beard (Iron Hail)
- Eagle Elk
- Flying Hawk
- Foolish Elk
- He Dog, a war chief
- Kicking Bear
- Lone Bear
- Low Dog, war chief
- Red Feather
- Running Eagle

Thunder Hawk
White Cow Bull
White Cow Bull (Buffalo), suicide boy

MINICONJOU
Bear Lice
Crow Boy
Dog Back-bone (Ass)
Dog-with-Horns
High Horse
Hump (High Back Bone), war chief
Iron Thunder
Lame Deer, chief
Lights (Runs-After-the-Clouds)
Red Horse, chief
Standing Bear
Stumbling Bear
Turtle Rib
White Bull

HUNKPAPA (Sioux)
Black Moon
Crow King, chief
Elk Nation
Gall, chief
Good Bear Boy
Horned Horse
Iron Hawk
Little Bear
Little Crow
Moving Robe Woman
Missus Spotted Horn Bull
One Bull

SANS ARC
Eagle Hat
Elk Stands Above (High)
Long Robe

BRULÉ
Two Eagles

ARAPAHO
Left Hand
Waterman

UTE
Yellow Nose

SIOUX (at the retreat)
    Crow Boy
    Low Dog (same name as the Oglala)
    Running Eagle
    Runs Fearless
    Runs-the-Enemy
    Young Skunk

TABLE 22
INCOMPLETE LIST OF SURVIVORS

SOLDIERS

Maj. Marcus A. Reno, 2nd in command to Custer
Capt. Frederick Wm. Benteen, Co. H
Capt. Thomas H. "Tucker" French, Co. M
Capt. Thomas M. McDougall, Co. B, pack train
Capt. James Myles "Michie" Moylan, Co. A
1st Lt. Charles C. DeRudio, Co. A
1st Lt. Edward S. Godfrey, Co. K
1st Lt. Edward G. Mathey, Co. M, to Co. B's pack train
2nd Lt. Winfield S. Edgerly, Co. D
2nd Lt. Luther R. Hare, Co. K
2nd Lt. Charles A. Varnum, Co. A, supervisor of the scouts
Cpl. George W. Wylie, Co. D
1st Sgt. William Heyn, Co. A
1st Sgt. John M. Ryan, Co. M
Sgt. James Flanagan, Co. D
Sgt. Daniel A. Kanipe, Co. C
Sgt. Stanislaus Roy, Co. A
Pvt. James P. Boyle, Co. unknown
Pvt. John Brennan, Co. C
Pvt. John Burkman, Co. L, Custer's striker
Pvt. John C. Creighton, Co. K
Pvt. Augustus L. DeVoto, Co. B, pack train
Pvt. John Fitzgerald, Co. C
Pvt. George W. Glease, Co. H
Pvt. Theodore W. Goldin, Co. G
Pvt. William G. Hardy, Co. A, trumpeter
Pvt. Frank "Yankee" Hunter, Co. F
Pvt. Hugh McGonigle, Co. G
Pvt. William E. Morris, Co. M
Pvt. Daniel Newell, Co. M
Pvt. I. D. O'Donnell, Co. unknown, Custer's striker
Pvt. Thomas F. O'Neill, Co. G
Pvt. Henry G. Petring, Co. G
Pvt. Edward A. Pigford, Co. M
Pvt. James M. Rooney, Co. F
Pvt. Stephen L. Ryan, Co. B
Pvt. William C. Slaper, Co. M
Pvt. William O. Taylor, Co. A
Pvt. Peter Thompson, Co. C
Pvt. James Watson, Co. C
Pvt. Ferdinand Widmayer, Co. M, absent

Pvt. Charles Windolph, Co. H
John E. Baily, Co. B, saddler
Frederic F. Gerard, interpreter

INDIANS
Black Elk, Oglala
Bobtail Horse, northern Cheyenne, chief
Charlie Corn, tribe unknown
Curley, Crow, scout
Flying Hawk, Oglala
Foolish Elk, Oglala
Good Voiced Elk, tribe unknown
Hairy Moccasin, Crow, scout
He Dog, Oglala, war chief
Hump, Miniconjou, war chief
John Stands-in-Timber, tribe unknown
Left Hand, Arapaho
Lights, Miniconjou
Lone Bear, Oglala
Low Dog, Oglala, war chief
Margot Liberty, Cheyenne
Missus Spotted Horn Bull, Hunkpapa
One Bull, Hunkpapa
Soldier, tribe unknown
Tall Bull, Cheyenne
Turtle Rib, Miniconjou
Two Moons, northern Cheyenne, chief
White Bull (Ice), Cheyenne, chief and shaman
White Cow Bull (Buffalo), Oglala, suicide boy
White Shield, northern Cheyenne, suicide boy
White-Man-Runs-Him, Crow, scout
Wooden Leg, Cheyenne

SCOUTS (Reno's)
2nd Lt. Charles A. Varnum, Supervisor
2nd Lt. Luther R. Hare, of Co. K, Varnum's asst.
George B. Herendeen, scout
Charles A. "Lonesome Charlie" or "Lucky Man" Reynolds
William "Billy" Baker (1/2 Arikara)
Michel "Mitch" Boyer (1/2 Sioux)
William "Billy" Cross (1/2 Sioux)
William "Billy" Jackson (1/4 Blackfoot)

INTERPRETERS
Frederic F. Gerard (for Rees), married a Ree
Isaiah "Teat" Dorman, black

Notes

1. The Gathering Storm

1. John S. Gray, *Centennial Campaign* (Fort Collins, CO: The Old Army Press, 1976), p. 320. A study of Sioux agency records for the period are interesting. "Agents were notoriously dishonest and/or inaccurate in reporting their agency figures. Agents at the five Teton Lakota (Sioux) agencies had inflated their census rolls by a combined 125 percent!"—Gray, p. 316.

2. Thomas Two Moons to Richard Throssel in the Billings [Montana] *Daily Gazette,* July 2, 1911. Interview.

3. Contrary to popular belief, Custer and other Civil War generals were not demoted in rank after the war. They merely reverted to their Regular Army (lineal) ranks after having been mustered out of the Union Army. Custer's brevet rank of major general, such as other brevets, except for rare circumstances, became for all practical purposes in 1869 (and thereafter) an honorary rank.

4. Colonel (later Major General) Robert P. Hughes, "The Campaign Against the Sioux in 1876," *Journal of the Military Service of the United States,* vol. 18, no. 79, January, 1896. Hughes had married a sister of Brigadier General Alfred H. Terry, and as a relative, was extremely protective of Terry (then deceased) in this article. Hughes, as a captain of the Third U.S. Infantry, was Terry's chief of staff in 1876. The officer Custer spoke to was Captain (later Brigadier General) William Ludlow, Terry's chief engineer.

5. Mari Sandoz, *The Battle of the Little Bighorn*, (Philadelphia and New York: J. B. Lippincott, 1966), pp. 31, 54-55, 77, 181-182.

2. Prelude to War

1. Colonel Charles Francis Bates, *Custer's Indian Battles* (Bronxville, NY: privately published, 1936), p. 28.

2. Boyer's surname was Boyer (and not "Bouyer" as commonly believed) according to Boyer's baptismal record, uncovered in the South Dakota Historical *Collections* by the eminent historian John S. Gray, Ph.d., M.D.—Gray, *Custer's Last Campaign, Mitch Boyer and the Little Bighorn Reconstructed* (Lincoln and London: University of Nebraska Press, 1991), pp. 7-8.

3. Captain E. S. Godfrey, "Custer's Last Battle," *Century Magazine*, vol. 43, no. 3, January, 1892.

4. New York *Herald*, July 23, 1876. The *Herald* stated this as a quote from a letter written by "a prominent officer killed in Custer's Last Charge." The "prominent officer" is believed to have been Custer himself.

5. Major James S. Brisbin, Second U.S. Cavalry, to the New York *Herald*, June 28, 1876.

6. Report of Captain Edward W. Smith, Eighteenth U.S. Infantry, July 1, 1876, Acting Assistant Adjutant General, Department of Dakota, National Archives, Washington, D.C. Smith was Terry's acting assistant adjutant general.

7. Brevet Major General John Gibbon to Brigadier General Alfred H. Terry, November 5, 1876. Letters Received, Department of Dakota, National Archives.

8. Godfrey to Bates, March 19, 1926, William J. Ghent Papers, Library of Congress, Washington, D.C. Copies of Terry's original maps are in the author's possession through the courtesy of the late W. Kent King. See W. Kent King, "Mappings of an 'Unknown' Land, Battle Road of the Dakota Column," talk given at Dakota State College, Madison, South Dakota, April 6, 1979, reprinted as *Mappings of An 'Unknown' Land, Battle Road of the Dakota Column* (Jessup, MD: privately published, 1981), pp. 1-30; idem, *Massacre: The Custer Cover-Up: The Original Maps of Custer's Battlefield* (El Segundo, CA: Upton & Sons, 1989), pp. 56-74.

9. King, *Mappings Of An 'Unknown' Land, Battle Road of the Dakota Column*, pp. 1-30; idem, *Massacre: The Custer Cover-Up*, pp. 56-74.

10. Roger Darling, *A Sad And Terrible Blunder* (Vienna, VA: Potomac-Western Press, 1990), p. 2.

11. Brisbin to Godfrey, January 1, 1892, Godfrey Papers, Library of Congress, Washington, D.C.

12. Brisbin to Godfrey, January 1, 1892, Godfrey Papers. Custer made the comment to Irish-born First Lieutenant John Carland, Sixth U.S. Infantry.

13. Dan L. Thrapp, *Encyclopedia of Frontier Biography* (Glendale, CA: The Arthur H. Clark Co., 1988), vol. 3, p. 1385.

14. A now-missing affidavit of Mary Adams, January 16, 1878, reported by Major General Nelson A. Miles,
    Personal Recollections and Observations, (New York: The Werner Co., 1896). Quoting that Mary Adams was aboard the *Far West* on June 21-22 and not at Fort Abraham Lincoln is attested to by several sources: H. A. "Autie" Reed (Custer's teenaged nephew) to his parents, Mr. and Mrs. David Reed of Monroe, Michigan, June 21, 1876, collection of the late Colonel Brice C. W. Custer (grandnephew of General Custer); Lawrence A. Frost, M.D., *General Custer's Libbie,* (Seattle, WA: Superior Publishing Company, 1976), p. 270; Sergeant John G. Tritten, former saddler sergeant, Seventh Cavalry, to Walter Mason Camp, n.d., Camp Field Notes, Robert S. Ellison Collection, Manuscript Division, Lilly Library, Indiana University, Bloomington (hereafter cited as Camp Notes—IU). Copies of these Camp Notes are in the author's possession.

    The Swiss-born Tritten told Camp that Mary Adams arrived back at the regiment's Powder River supply base on July 4 aboard the *Far West*. Richard A. Roberts, brother of Mrs. Captain George W. M. Yates of the Seventh Cavalry, had accompanied the regiment as far as the Powder River supply base, where he was forced to remain behind because he had no fresh mount. In a letter home Roberts wrote of Mary Adams's presence aboard the *Far West*.— Frost to author, June 22, 1983, at Billings, Montana. Interview. In the Elizabeth B. Custer Collection (the General's wife) at the

Custer Battlefield National Monument, (hereafter cited CBNM), Crow Agency, Montana are two check stubs signed by General Custer in May, 1876, indicating payment for wages due to two black servants, the sisters Mary and Maria Adams. Custer historian John S. Manion discovered these historic check stubs. See also: Manion, *General Terry's Last Statement to Custer* (Monroe, MI: Monroe County Library System, 1983); idem, "Did Custer Disobey?" Little Big Horn Associates *Newsletter,* vol. 18, January, 1984, pp. 5-6; Frost, "We Remember Mary," *Research Review: the Journal of the Little Big Horn Associates,* vol. 1, no. 2 (New Series), December, 1987; Letter, Tom Custer to Emma Reed (his niece), June 5, 1876, reprinted in Frost's "We Remember Mary" and his *Custer Legends,* (Bowling Green, OH: Popular Press, Bowling Green State University, 1989), pp. 200-201; Richard A. Roberts, "The Aftermath," address at Charleroi, Pennsylvania, 1913, reprinted in "We Remember Mary." It was Maria (not Mary) Adams who greeted Second Lieutenant Charles L. Gurley, Sixth U.S. Infantry, et al., at Fort Lincoln when calling on the Custer household to inform those present of the Little Big Horn tragedy. Mary Adams died in 1878 or 1879 and Maria passed away in 1939; Letter, John F. Donahue, former private, Seventh Cavalry, to the Bismarck [Dakota Territory] *Daily Tribune,* January 17, 1888. Donahue claimed to have been within earshot of Terry's final words to Custer: "You are to strike the Indians on the 26th of June in conjunction with my command, unless you think the Indians are likely to get away from you. Use your own judgment." Nothing in Terry's written orders to Custer even suggested a coordinated strike on the 26th, especially when Terry then did not know for certain where the Indians would be found on that date.

15. Charles C. DeRudio, February 2, 1910, Camp Notes—Robert S. Ellison Collection, Denver Public Library (hereafter cited DPL). Interview. First Lieutenant Charles C. DeRudio kept his saber. First Lieutenant Edward G. Mathey carried his saber wrapped in his field pack. The regiment's sabers were

left at the supply base at the conflux of the Powder and Yellowstone rivers. At this camp several soldiers, including the regimental band, were detached from the regiment and left behind. It is interesting to note that C. A. Stein, the veterinary surgeon, was so scared that Custer attached him to the supply base. Donahue goes on to claim that he later overheard Custer say: "My intentions were to give the Indians a daylight surprise on the morning of the 26th, but we have been discovered by an Indian who was fishing in the [Reno] creek, and several of us saw this Indian ride at full speed to give the alarm. Consequently we will be attacked and I would rather attack than be attacked. We will march on them at once." Donahue was a member of Company K, and as such, was with Benteen's battalion unless dutied elsewhere. I find it completely out of character for Custer and his past mode of operation to rationalize his reason[s] for his plan of attack—certainly, no surviving officer ever recalled such a statement by Custer prior to the battle. Also, it was not a lone Indian fishing in Reno Creek which triggered Custer's attack on the 25th as shall be seen later. Donahue's statement smells of enlisted men's scuttlebutt so commonplace in the American Army of that or any other era.

16. Godfrey, "Custer's Last Battle," *Century Magazine*, vol. 43, no. 3, January, 1892. Second Lieutenant George D. Wallace survived the Little Big Horn only to be killed fighting the Sioux at Wounded Knee Creek in South Dakota on December 29, 1890.

17. Ibid.

18. Dr. James M. DeWolf to his wife, June 21, 1876, CBNM.

3. Following the War Trail

1. Letter, George B. Herendeen to the New York *Herald*, January 22, 1876.

2. Herendeen to Walter Mason Camp, August 5, 1911, Walter M. Camp Field Notes, Archives and Manuscripts, Harold B. Lee Library, Brigham Young University, Provo, Utah (hereafter

cited as Camp Notes—BYU). Interview. Copies of some of these Camp Notes are in the author's possession. For Custer's comment to Herendeen as to why he [Custer] did not carry out the Tullock's Creek scout, see: letter, Camp to Mrs. Elizabeth B. Custer, August 19, 1919, Camp Papers, CBNM. Interestingly enough, Herendeen again approached Custer on the 24th and told him they were at the point for him [Herendeen] to depart on his Tullock's Creek scout. Custer surprisingly did not respond to Herendeen, but merely stared at him absentmindedly and then turned away—New York *Herald*, January 22, 1878.

3. Report of Second Lieutenant George D. Wallace, Seventh Cavalry, to the Chief of Engineers, Department of Dakota, in the *Annual Report of the Chief of Engineers to the Secretary of War, 1876,* National Archives; First Lieutenant Winfield S. Edgerly, Seventh Cavalry, in the Leavenworth [Kansas] *Weekly Times,* August 18, 1881. Interview; Captain E. S. Godfrey, "Custer's Last Battle," *Century Magazine,* vol. 43, no. 3, January, 1892.

4. Captain Michael J. Koury, *Diaries of the Little Big Horn,* (Bellevue, NE: The Old Army Press, 1968), p. 23, quoting from John C. Hixon, "Custer's Mysterious Mr. Kellogg" and "The Diary of Mark Kellogg," *North Dakota History,* vol. 17, no. 3, 1950. It was against the advice of General in Chief William T. Sherman about not taking newspaper correspondents with the expedition that Kellogg—hardly without the knowledge and consent of Brigadier General Alfred H. Terry—accompanied the Custer command. The New York *Herald* claimed Kellogg as its correspondent after his death at the Little Bighorn. Kellogg filed copy with the *Herald* for Bismarck [Dakota Territory] *Daily Tribune* editor and publisher Clement A. Lounsberry, who was the official correspondent of the *Herald.*

5. Sandy Barnard, to a group of Custer/Little Bighorn buffs, St. Louis, Missouri, March 12, 1989. Talk. Barnard is a leading authority on Mark Kellogg.

4. Journey Into Battle

1. Walter Mason Camp to Elizabeth C. B. Custer, August 19, 1919, Camp Papers, CBNM.

2. Charles A. Varnum to Albert W. Johnson, November 13, 1929, Fred Dustin Collection, CBNM.

3. Nicholas Ruleau to Judge Eli S. Ricker, 1906, Ricker Collection, Nebraska State Historical Society, Lincoln. Interview.

4. Letter, Varnum to father and mother, July 4, 1876, reprinted in Lower Massachusetts *Weekly Journal,* August, 1876.

5. Captain E. S. Godfrey, "Custer's Last Battle," *Century Magazine,* vol. 43, no. 3, January, 1892.

6. White-Man-Runs-Him, 1919, in Colonel W. A. Graham, *The Custer Myth, A Source Book of Custeriana* (Harrisburg, PA: The Stackpole Co., 1953), p. 23. Graham reports a 1919 interview with White-Man-Runs-Him.

7. Varnum to Camp, April 14, 1909, Camp Papers, BYU.

8. O. G. Libby, ed., "The Arikara Narrative of the Campaign Against the Hostile Dakota, North Dakota Historical *Collections,* vol. 6, 1920. Since neither Varnum nor Gerard, the only surviving white men at the Crow's Nest, ever mentioned this second look by Custer from a second peak, this minor sidebar was nearly lost to history. Red Star stated that Reynolds and Custer went ahead, leaving others behind (at the Crow's Nest). This second peak was within hollering distance of the Crow's Nest, for when Custer doubted the scouts had seen the village, Gerard called to the Rees, "Custer thinks it is no village."

9. Varnum to Camp, April 14, 1909, Camp Papers; Colonel T. M. Coughlan, *Varnum—the Last of Custer's Lieutenants,* ed. John M. Carroll, (Bryan, TX: privately published, 1980), p. 11.

10. Libby, ed., "The Arikara Narrative." Red Star, 1912. Interview. Red Star passed away in 1934.

11. John S. Gray, *Centennial Campaign* (Fort Collins, CO: The Old Army Press, 1976), p. 168.

12. Myles Moylan to Godfrey, January 17, 1892, Godfrey Papers, Library of Congress, Washington, D.C.

13. Appointment, Commission, and Personal File of Charles C. DeRudio, National Archives, Washington, D.C. Charles C. DeRudio was born Carlo C. di Rudio to the Count and Countess aquila di Rudio at Belluno, Italy, where his maternal grandfather had been governor.

14. Oberstaatsarchivar Osterreichishes Staatsarchiv, Kriegsarchiv, Vienna, Austria. Letter to author, April 30, 1969. DeRudio never attended, much less graduated from, the Royal Austrian Military Academy.

15. Letter, DeRudio to Secretary of War Edwin M. Stanton, August 3, 1866, A, C, and P File, DeRudio, National Archives; A, C, and P File, DeRudio, National Archives. Newspaper clipping, March 20, 1881; Washington [D.C.] *Post,* September 15, 1901; Hollywood *Citizen,* August 31, 1929; DeRudio to Officers' Club at Fort Sam, Houston, Texas, 1895. Talk; Colonel Cornelius C. Smith to *Frontier Times,* vol. 10, no. 9, June, 1933, pp. 390-391. Mrs. Elizabeth B. DeRudio, the English-born wife of DeRudio, had sought help from British nobility, many of whom signed a clemency petition for her husband, to spare him from execution. Mrs. DeRudio had secured audiences with French Empress Eugénie—she had escaped assassination in the attempt that had failed to take the life of her emperor-husband—and the Archbishop of Paris, one of Louis Napoleon's confidants, to plead for her husband's life. DeRudio's life was spared on March 15, 1858, and his sentence was commuted to life imprisonment in the penal colony at Cayenne, French Guiana. The infamous Devil's Island penal colony was nearby. DeRudio eventually escaped from Cayenne in an open boat and sailed to Dutch Guiana and eventual freedom. DeRudio also claimed service with the French Army in Algeria, North Africa. He eventually made his way to New Amsterdam and on to England.

16. Fred Dustin, *The Custer Tragedy* (Ann Arbor, MI: privately published, 1939), p. 109.

17. Lieutenant Colonel Melbourne C. Chandler, *Of GarryOwen In Glory, The History Of The Seventh United States Cavalry* (Annandale, VA: The Turnpike Press, Inc., 1960), p. 386.

18. John Burkman, former private, Seventh Cavalry and striker for General Custer, to I. D. O'Donnell, O'Donnell Collection, CBNM.

19. Hunt, Frazier and Robert, *I Fought With Custer* (Lincoln: University of Nebraska Press, Bison Books' edition, 1974), p. 76. This conversation was overheard by German-born Private Charles Windolph, a member of Benteen's company. The Hunts interviewed Windolph in 1946.

20. Edward G. Mathey, October 19, 1910, Camp Notes—BYU. Interview.

5. Benteen's Scout

1. Captain Frederick W. Benteen to his wife, July 2 and July 4, 1876, Frederick W. Benteen Collection, University of Georgia Library, Athens; Benteen to Private Theodore W. Goldin, February 24, 1892, Benteen-Goldin Letters, Thomas Gilcrease Institute of American History and Art, Tulsa, Oklahoma. Goldin served as an almost 18-year-old recruit of the Seventh Cavalry at the Little Bighorn. In his official report of his scout, dated July 4, 1876, Benteen wrote in part, ". . . there being no valley of any kind that I could see on any side."—*Annual Report,* War Department, 1876, 44th Congress, 2nd Session, House of Representatives, Executive Document no. 1, part 2.

2. Lieutenant Francis M. Gibson to his wife, July 4, 1876, Gibson-Fougera Collection, CBNM. Mrs. Fougera was the daughter of Gibson, the executive officer of Company H.

3. Ibid; Gibson to Edward S. Godfrey, August 9, 1908, Godfrey Papers, Library of Congress, Washington, D.C.; 1876 Field Diary of Lieutenant Edward S. Godfrey, Godfrey Papers; First Lieutenant Winfield S. Edgerly in Leavenworth [Kansas] *Weekly Times,* August 18, 1881. Interview; Brigadier General Edgerly, n.d., Camp Notes—BYU. Interview.

4. William O. Taylor to Godfrey, February 20, 1910, Godfrey Papers, Library of Congress, Washington, D.C. Taylor served as a private in Company A of the Seventh Cavalry and was at the Little Bighorn.

5. Gibson to his wife, July 4, 1876, Gibson-Fougera Collection, CBNM.

6. Hunt, Frazier and Robert, *I Fought With Custer* (Lincoln: University of Nebraska Press, Bison Books' edition, 1974), p. 80. The Hunts wrote the story of Private Charles (later Sergeant) Windolph, Company H.

7. Benteen to Catharine L. Benteen, July 9 and 10, 1876, Special Collections, University of Georgia, Athens.

8. Gibson to Walter Mason Camp, December 7, 1910, Camp Notes—BYU. Interview. Gibson was confused in later years as to whether or not he actually saw the valley of the Little Bighorn; Gibson to Godfrey, August 8, 1908, Godfrey Papers. Employing the fold-out map in Roger Darling's *Benteen's Scout-to-the-Left—the Route from the Divide to the Morass (June 25, 1876),* (El Segundo, CA: Upton and Sons, 1987), it is obvious that Gibson saw the valley of the Little Bighorn from his advanced position.

9. Benteen to Goldin, March 19, 1892, Benteen-Goldin Letters, Thomas Gilcrease Institute of American History and Art.

6. Reno Gallops to the Advance

1. Author. Research. Cooke's words are synthesized here, based on what the various witnesses said they heard the adjutant say to Reno. Frederic Gerard, George B. Herendeen, Dr. Henry R. Porter, Trooper Edward Davern, and, of course, Reno, all claimed to have heard Cooke's words.

2. Bismarck [Dakota Territory] *Daily Tribune,* January 17, 1888.

3. Major Marcus A. Reno, Seventh Cavalry, to Captain Edward W. Smith, Acting Assistant Adjutant General, July 5, 1876, Letters Received, Department of Dakota, National Archives, Washington, D.C.

4. Charles A. Varnum, *I, Varnum, An Autobiography,* ed. John M. Carroll (Glendale, CA: The Arthur H. Clark Co., 1982), p. 64.

5. Ibid., pp. 64-65; Colonel T. M. Coughlan, *Varnum—the Last of Custer's Lieutenants,* ed. John M. Carroll, (Bryan, TX: privately published, 1980), p. 12.

6. John McGuire, former private, Seventh Cavalry, n.d., Camp Notes—BYU. Interview; "Narrative of Private Peter Thompson, Seventh Cavalry," in the Belle Fourche [South Dakota] *Bee,* 1914. Reprinted by the North Dakota Historical Society in a volume of its *Collections.* A copy entitled "The Experience of a Private Soldier [Thompson] in the Custer Massacre" is in the Vickers Collection at the CBNM. See also: Thompson, *Narrative of the Little Big Horn,* ed. Daniel O. Magnussen (Glendale, CA: The Arthur H. Clark Co., 1974). A copy of the Thompson *Narrative* is in the author's possession; Richard P. Hanley, former sergeant, Seventh Cavalry, October 4, 1910, Camp Notes—BYU. Interview.

7. New York *Times,* July 13, 1876. Article. This piece was based on Cross' debriefing of June 18, 1876. Billy Cross later claimed to have participated in Reno's fight in the valley, but many of his statements are erroneous and admittedly he had received much of his information concerning the valley fight secondhand.

8. "Proceedings of the Court of Inquiry of Major Marcus A. Reno, Seventh U.S. Cavalry, Concerning His Conduct at Battle of the Little Big Horn River, Montana Territory, June 25-26, 1876," January-February, 1879, National Archives, (hereafter cited as Reno Court), 1894.

9. Frederic F. Gerard, January 22 and April 3, 1909, Camp Notes—BYU. Interviews.

10. William O. Taylor, former private, Seventh Cavalry, to Walter Mason Camp, December 12, 1909, Camp Notes—BYU.

11. Captain Frederick W. Benteen to Private Theodore W. Goldin, March 3, 1896, Benteen-Goldin Letters, Hodgson's clandestine lover was Mrs. Emily M. Bell, the wife of First

Lieutenant (later Brigadier General) James M. Bell, who was not present at the Little Bighorn. Reno was court-martialed in 1877 for, among other things, attempting to kiss Mrs. Bell while her husband was absent from the post and for slandering Mrs. Bell's name. Reno was sentenced to be cashiered from the Army for his offenses, but on the recommendation of the Judge Advocate General, President Rutherford B. Hayes, commuted Reno's sentence to suspension from rank and pay for two years. Reno finally was cashiered from the Army on April 1, 1880, for being drunk and disorderly in public and for peeping through a window at the daughter of his commanding officer, Brevet Major General Samuel D. Sturgis, colonel, commanding the Seventh Cavalry. However, on May 31, 1967 [yes, 1967] the Department of the Army, on a recommendation from the Army Board for Correction of Military Records, corrected Reno's military record to posthumously read he was honorably discharged on April 1, 1880.

12. Memorandum Notebook of Lieutenant Donald McIntosh, Seventh Cavalry, CBNM. A copy is in the author's possession.

7. The Indian Village

1. Standard Certificate of Death, State of Montana, for Thomas Two Moons, April 20, 1917, Montana State Department of Health and Environmental Services, Helena; a copy is in author's possession. This Indian has been called Two Moon and Two Moons interchangeably by historians. His real name was Two Moons.

2. Reno Court, p. 236; Edgar I. Stewart, *Custer's Luck* (Norman: University of Oklahoma Press, 1955), p. 350.

3. Ibid., p. 183.

4. Ibid., pp. 267-268.

5. Moylan never used James—very few military references to it.

6. Chicago *Times* Account of the Reno Court of Inquiry, p. 516.

7. Stewart, *Custer's Luck* p. 355.

8. Reno Court, p. 356.

9. Ibid., pp. 52-53, 272, 320-321.

10. New York *Herald*, January 22, 1878.

11. Stewart, *Custer's Luck*, p. 354.

12. Major Marcus A. Reno, Seventh Cavalry, to Captain Edward W. Smith, Acting Assistant Adjutant General, July 5, 1876, Letters Received, Department of Dakota, National Archives, Washington, D.C.

13. Military History File of Marcus A. Reno, Headquarters of Army, Adjutant General's Office, May 22, 1880, National Archives.

14. Brigadier General Edward J. McClernand, "With Indians and Buffalo in Montana," *Cavalry Journal,* vol. 46, no. 36, January–April, 1927, p. 36.

8. The Indian Scouts

1. "Narrative of Private Peter Thompson, Seventh Cavalry," in the Belle Fourche [South Dakota] *Bee,* 1914. In later years, Thompson told a lurid story of Custer's last fight as allegedly witnessed by him from a distance. Under all known circumstances, much of Thompson's narrative is not plausible, to say the least.

2. John McGuire, former private, Seventh Cavalry, to Walter Mason Camp, n.d., Camp Notes—BYU. Interview. Fitzgerald and Brennan often joked about their desertion from Custer's battalion.

3. Frederic F. Gerard to Camp, January 22 and April 3, 1909, Camp Notes—BYU. Interview.

4. White Bull to Walter S. Campbell, 1932. Interview. (Stanley Vestal), Walter S. Campbell Collection, Division of Manuscripts, University of Oklahoma Library, Norman.

9. Custer Rides to the Attack!

1. Will Aiken, Montana Historical Society *Collections,* vol. 4, pp. 277-286.

2. Douglas C. McChristian, historian, CBNM, talk, Hardin,

Montana, June 23, 1989, "Hurrah, Boys! We've Got Them: An Analysis of Custer's Observation Point," referring to the testimony of Luther R. Hare at the Reno Court of Inquiry.

3. Greensboro [North Carolina] *Daily Record,* April 27, 1924.

4. Daniel A. Kanipe, former sergeant, Seventh Cavalry, June 16-17, 1908, Camp Notes—IU. Interviews. Kanipe informed Camp that the correct spelling of his surname was "Kanipe." See also: Kanipe in the Greensboro *Daily Record,* April 27, 1924.

5. Kanipe to Camp, June 16–17, 1908, Camp Notes—IU. Interviews. Greensboro *Daily Record,* April 27, 1924.

6. Letter, Kanipe to Camp, July 20, 1908, Camp Notes—IU.

7. Chicago *Times* Account of the Reno Court of Inquiry, p. 618; Captain E. S. Godfrey, "Custer's Last Battle," *Century Magazine,* vol. 43, no. 3, January, 1892.

8. Augustus L. DeVoto, "Description of Reno's Fight, 1916," Camp Papers, CBNM. Kanipe was the only known courier from Custer to the pack train.

9. Letter, Kanipe to Camp, October 9, 1910. Camp Notes—IU. Kanipe gives his account of his meeting the two Ree scouts, Benteen, and the pack train.

10. John Martin, former private and trumpeter, Seventh Cavalry, October 24, 1908, and May 13, 1910, Camp Notes—IU. Interviews.

11. Lieutenant Colonel W. A. Graham, "Custer's Battle Plan, The Story of His Last Message, as Told by the Man Who Carried It. [John Martin]," *The Cavalry Journal,* July, 1923.

12. White-Man-Runs-Him to Major General Hugh L. Scott and Tim McCoy, 1919, interview, in Colonel W. A. Graham's, *The Custer Mystery, A Source Book of Custeriana* (Harrisburg, PA: The Stackpole Co., 1953), p. 23.

13. Standing Bear to Camp, July 12, 1910, Camp Notes—BYU. Interview.

14. Letter, Camp to Brigadier General Charles A. Woodruff, Feb-

ruary 28, 1910, Camp Papers, BYU. Curley claimed—or at least his interpreters claimed [this is not Camp writing this, but only a possibility according to me] as Curley had never learned much English—to have been in Medicine Tail Coulee with Custer's battalion. But Curley's fellow Crows vehemently disputed him on this point. Goes Ahead emphatically stated that not one of the Crow scouts entered Medicine Tail Coulee; Hairy Moccasin to Camp, February 23, 1911, Camp Notes—BYU. Interview. Hairy Moccasin told Camp that Curley had left the other Crow scouts at Weir Point; Colonel W. A. Graham, *The Custer Myth, A Source Book of Custeriana* (Harrisburg, PA: The Stackpole Co., 1953), p. 24. Quoting White-Man-Runs-Him to Tim McCoy, 1919. Interview. White-Man-Runs-Him stated that Curley had left the other Crows about the time that Reno's battalion became engaged in the valley fight [Curley was then at Weir Point]. Curley did linger in the area and did witness through field glasses the initial fighting of Custer's battalion. After departing Custer, White-Man-Runs-Him, Goes Ahead, and Hairy Moccasin moved southward in search of their fellow tribesmen, Half-Yellow-Face and White Swan. Since Curley had not departed from Custer's battalion prior to White-Man-Runs-Him, Goes Ahead, and Hairy Moccasin, the trio of scouts failed to understand that Curley had seen any of Custer's battlefield action, and, therefore, judged him a liar. Curley remained in the vicinity of the battlefield while his fellow tribesmen, after departing Custer, immediately rode away from the area. It is extremely doubtful that Curley was or even claimed that he was in Medicine Tail Coulee with Custer's battalion. See Chapter 14 for Curley's eyewitness accounts. [Yes, Curley told repeated accounts over the decades following the Custer fight; at least three of them to Camp, alone.]

15. Graham, "Custer's Battle Plan, the Story of His Last Message as Told by the Man Who Carried It," *The Cavalry Journal,* July, 1923; Graham, *The Custer Myth,* p. 290.

16. John Martin, former private and trumpeter, Seventh Cavalry,

to Camp, May 4, 1910, Camp Notes—IU. Interview. Some students of the battle believe that Martin was dispatched to Benteen prior to the Custer battalion entering Cedar Coulee, but Martin told Camp that he was in the coulee with Custer although after a lapse of thirty-four years Martin's memory had confused Cedar Coulee with Medicine Tail Coulee or Camp misinterpreted his statement as to which coulee he meant. Camp, however, wrote then-Brigadier General Edward S. Godfrey that "after I had spent much time with him [Martin] going over maps and sketches of the details of the topography his recollection was revived and he was able to tell the thing straight-forward."—Camp to Godfrey, December 21, 1922, E. S. Godfrey Folder, Francis R. Hagner Collection, Manuscript Division, New York Public Library. Martin later told the Reno Inquiry (1879) that Custer had intended for Benteen to attack the Indians in the center. That might have been, but Custer's primary reason for wanting Benteen "to come quick" was either to obtain the ammunition packs or keep the whole pack train under Benteen's protection. Martin told the court of inquiry that as he rode back looking for Benteen, he had seen Reno deploying his men on the skirmish line in the valley. But years later, Martin told Camp that he had seen neither Indians nor Reno.

17. Martin to Camp, October 24, 1908, Camp Notes—IU. Interview.

18. Ibid., May 10, 1910, Camp Notes—IU. Interview.

10. Shoot-out in the Valley

1. "Story of the Big Horn Campaign of 1876: as told by Private Daniel Newell, of Company M, 7th U.S. Cavalry," to John P. Everett, *The Sunshine Magazine*, September 30, 1930; E. A. Brininstool, *Troopers with Custer*, (Harrisburg, PA: The Stackpole Co., expanded ed., 1952), p. 48, quoting William C. Slaper, former private, Seventh Cavalry. Interview.

2. Edgar I. Stewart, *Custer's Luck* (Norman: University of Okla-

homa Press, 1955), p. 466; Hardin [Montana] *Tribune,* June 22, 1923.

3. Roman Rutten, former private, Seventh Cavalry, to Walter Mason Camp, n.d., Camp Notes—IU. Interview.

4. James Wilber, former private, Seventh Cavalry, n.d., Camp Notes—BYU. Interview.

5. "Story of the Big Horn Campaign of 1876: As told by Private Daniel Newell. . .," *The Sunshine Magazine.*

6. Ibid.

7. Wilber to Camp, Camp Notes—BYU. Interview.

8. St. Paul [Minnesota] *Pioneer Press,* July 18, 1886, quoting Hunkpapa Chief Gall; Colonel W. A. Graham, *The Custer Myth, A Source Book of Custeriana* (Harrisburg, PA: The Stackpole Co., 1953), p. 90.

9. Hardin [Montana] *Tribune,* June 22, 1923.

10. Fred Dustin, *The Custer Tragedy* (Ann Arbor, MI: privately published, 1939), viii-ix; Dustin, *Echoes from the Little Big Horn Fight: Reno's Position in the Valley* (Ann Arbor, MI: privately published, 1939), pp. 1-17. The latter booklet, the last of Dustin's published writing on the battle, was a revised supplement to his earlier analysis of Reno's skirmish lines in the valley, found in *The Custer Tragedy.*

11. The GarryOwen Loop did not exist in 1876. It was not drawn on the original map of the battlefield prepared that year under the supervision of First Lieutenant Edward Maguire, Brigadier General Alfred H. Terry's engineering officer. Maguire's original map remained hidden from public view for more than a century—until discovered by the late W. Kent King in the National Archives, Washington, D.C. In 1980, the author purchased a copy of this Maguire map from Mr. King. An altered version of Maguire's map was used at the Reno Court of Inquiry (1879).

12. J. W. Vaughn, *Indian Fights, New Facts on Seven Encounters* (Norman: University of Oklahoma Press, 1966), pp. 148-149.

The late Jesse Vaughn, an attorney who pioneered the use of the metal detector in the study of artifacts on Indian war battlefields, discovered cartridge casings on several famous battlefields of the Indian Wars.

13. Pinedale [Wyoming] *Roundup,* updated clipping, Agnes Wright Spring Collection, American Heritage Center, University of Wyoming, Laramie. Interview.

14. John M. Ryan in the Hardin [Montana] *Tribune,* June 22, 1923.

15. Robert J. Ege, "Isaiah Dorman, Negro Casualty with Reno," *Montana, the Magazine of Western History,* vol. 16, no. 1, January, 1966, p. 37.

16. Judge William E. Morris, former private, Seventh Cavalry, to Cyrus Townsend Brady, September 21, 1904, quoted in Brady's *Indian Fights and Fighters* (Lincoln: University of Nebraska Press, Bison Books' edition, 1971), p. 403.

17. Frederic F. Gerard to Camp, January 22 and April 3, 1909, Camp Notes—BYU. Interviews; Among the Camp Notes at Indiana University, there is a statement by Charles C. DeRudio that he saw Reno drinking at the ford and that Gerard claimed to have seen Reno finishing a bottle of whiskey on the skirmish line twenty minutes later, and that Reno was then intoxicated. Gerard was notoriously anti-Reno.

18. Vaughn, *Indian Fights,* pp. 155-157.

19. Red Feather to Major General Hugh L. Scott, 1919, National Anthropological Archives, Smithsonian Institution, Washington, D.C. Interview.

20. Edward Pigford, former private, Seventh Cavalry, n.d., Camp Notes—BYU. Interview. Ryan, former first sergeant, Seventh Cavalry, to Camp, April 7, 1920, Camp Papers, CBNM; Ryan to Camp, April 10, 1920, excerpted in *Newsletter, Little Bighorn Associates,* vol. 29, February, 1990, p. 5. A wounded O'Hara might have been one of the Sioux captives in the battle.

21. Charles A. Varnum, *I, Varnum, An Autobiography,* ed. John M.

Carroll (Glendale, CA: The Arthur H. Clark Co., 1982), p. 113; Robert M. Utley, ed., *The Reno Court of Inquiry: The Chicago Times Account* (Fort Collins, CO: The Old Army Press, 1972), pp. 52, 70, 219.

22. David Humphreys Miller, *Custer's Fall* (New York: Bantam Books, Inc. 1963), pp. 74-75; Miller, "Echoes of the Little Bighorn," *American Heritage,* vol. 22, no. 4, June, 1971, p. 31. Miller interviewed One Bull on several occasions between 1935 and 1947. One Bull passed away in 1949.

11. Benteen: "Come On...Be Quick"

1. United States Military Academy Museum at West Point, New York. Note the missing k in "pacs." The author owns a photograph of this message.

2. John Martin, former private and trumpeter, Seventh Cavalry, to Walter Mason Camp, October 24, 1908, Camp Notes—IU. Interview. Martin denied to Camp that he had told Benteen that the Indians had "skedaddled." Martin was a recent immigrant who had a poor command of the English language. It is doubtful that he would have used such a colloquial figure of speech as skedaddling despite Benteen's and Godfrey's recollections to the contrary.

3. Captain E. S. Godfrey, "Custer's Last Battle," *Century Magazine,* vol. 43, no. 3, January 1892; "A Transcript of Benteen's Narrative," from Colonel W. A. Graham, *The Custer Myth, A Source Book of Custeriana* (Harrisburg, PA: The Stackpole Co., 1953), p. 180.

4. Graham, *The Custer Myth,* p. 180.

5. Martin to Camp, October 24, 1908, Camp Notes—IU. Interview.

6. Winfield S. Edgerly to Camp, n.d., Camp Notes—BYU. Interview.

7. Rarely before the 1970s had Benteen's conduct been criticized by historians of the battle. In the past, Benteen's deepseated hatred of Custer—due in part to Custer's refusal on

the 1873 Yellowstone Expedition to allow him to return to his wife and gravely ill child, who subsequently died that summer—has been negligently glossed over by historians. Benteen's personal halo has become somewhat tarnished in recent years in light of the following discoveries: That the Seventh Cavalry's so-called "Enlisted Men's Petition" of 1876, which sought the immediate promotion of Reno to lieutenant colonel and Benteen to major in the regiment, had been forged (in part) by Benteen's own first sergeant, Joseph McCurry; the bragging about his occasional "wet dreams" in his letters to his wife; the drawing of a penis on a few of his letters to his wife; and his court-martial in 1887 for, among other things, urinating against the wall of a tent when ladies were present.

8. Camp to Brigadier General Charles A. Woodruff, retired March 3, 1910, Camp Papers, CBNM. Camp is repeating here what Godfrey must have told him at an earlier date.

12. Reno Disgraced: Panic and Rout

1. Thomas H. French to Mrs. Alexander H. Cooke, mother of W. W. Cooke, June 16, 1880, Godfrey Papers, Library of Congress, Washington, D.C.; E. S. Godfrey Folder, Francis R. Hagner Collection, Manuscript Division, New York Public Library. Copy in the author's possession.

2. Hardin [Montana] *Tribune,* June 22, 1923, quoting John M. Ryan, former first sergeant, Seventh Cavalry.

3. Letter, Ryan to Walter Mason Camp, April 7, 1920, Camp Papers, CBNM.

4. E. A. Brininstool, *Troopers with Custer,* (Harrisburg, PA: The Stackpole Co., expanded ed., 1952), p. 51. Interview with William C. Slaper, former private, Seventh Cavalry.

5. Ibid., p. 51.

6. Ryan in the Hardin [Montana] *Tribune,* June 22, 1923.

7. There is confusion as to which trooper, Klotzbucher or Lorentz, Dr. Porter administered aid. That Lorentz was the

290

trooper, see Reno Court, p. 1180; Chicago *Times*. Account of the Reno Court of Inquiry, p. 423; Ryan in the Hardin [Montana] *Tribune,* June 22, 1923; and Fred Dustin, *The Custer Fight* (Hollywood, CA: privately published, 1936), p. 16. That the trooper was Klotzbucher also see Slaper in *Troopers with Custer,* p. 51.

8. Roman Rutten, former private, Seventh Cavalry, to Camp, Camp Notes—IU.; Ryan in the Hardin [Montana] *Tribune,* June 22, 1923; Judge William E. Morris, former private, Seventh Cavalry, to Robert Bruce, May 28, 1928, CBNM.

9. E. A. Brininstool, *Troopers with Custer,* p. 51. Slaper Interview.

10. Red Feather to Major General Hugh L. Scott, 1919, National Anthropological Archives, Smithsonian Institution, Washington, D.C. Interview.

11. Charles F. Roe, *Custer's Last Battle* (New York: Robert Bruce, 1927), p. 9.

12. Thomas B. Marquis, *Wooden Leg, A Warrior Who Fought Custer* (Lincoln: University of Nebraska, Bison Books' edition, n.d.), pp. 222-223. Originally published 1931. The two unfortunate troopers who were killed were among the following A Company men: Irish-born Private John E. Armstrong; Private James Drinan, also an Irish immigrant; Private James McDonald; Private Richard Rollins; and Private Thomas P. Sweetser. These men were chased by four Cheyennes and several Sioux. One of the troopers was thought by the pursuing warriors to have escaped across the river. Marquis, *Custer on the Little Bighorn* (Lodi, CA: privately published, 1967), p. 15. But on June 27, 1876, Private William H. White found the body of the trooper who evidently had been cornered and killed along the west bank of the river near the mouth of Reno Creek.

13. Reno Court, p. 124. These three unfortunate troopers were among the following G Company men: Saddler Selby Crawford; Private Benjamin F. Rogers; and Private Edward Stanley.

14. Marquis, *Wooden Leg,* pp. 221-222. This trooper was one of the G Company men listed in the above note 13.

15. Charles C. DeRudio to a friend, July 15, 1876, in the New York *Herald,* July 30, 1876. This letter actually was ghostwritten by Major James S. Brisbin, Second U.S. Cavalry, after a discussion with DeRudio. DeRudio admitted to Camp that the letter was not entirely accurate. See DeRudio to Camp, February 2, 1910, Camp Notes—DPL. Interview.

16. Henry Petring, former private, Seventh Cavalry, n.d., Camp Notes—BYU. Interview.

17. Thomas F. O'Neill, former private, Seventh Cavalry, n.d., Camp Notes—BYU. Interview. James P. Boyle, former private, Seventh Cavalry, n.d., Camp Notes—IU. Interview; personal note by Camp, Camp Notes—IU.

18. O'Neill to Camp. Interview.

19. Ibid.

20. Letter, Morris to Cyrus Townsend Brady, September 21, 1904, in Brady's *Indian Fights and Fighters* (Lincoln: University of Nebraska Press, Bison Books' edition, 1966), p. 403; Morris to Camp, n.d., Camp Notes—IU. Interview.

21. Rutten to Camp, Camp Notes—IU. Interview.

22. "Story Of The Big Horn Campaign of 1876: As told By Private Daniel Newell of Company M, 7th U.S. Cavalry," to John P. Everett, *The Sunshine Magazine,* September 30, 1930; Morris to Camp, Camp Notes—IU. Interview. *Troopers with Custer,* p. 65. Slaper interview.

23. Author. Research. This account of McIntosh's death is based on a handful of composite eyewitness accounts.

24. Collection, CBNM. Interview; George B. Herendeen to Camp, August 5, 1911, Camp Notes—BYU. Interview. McIntosh's notebook is at the Custer Battlefield National Monument, Crow Agency, Montana. The bullet hole in this memorandum notebook is still visible today. A copy of the notebook's contents is in the author's possession.

25. Luther R. Hare, former second lieutenant, Seventh Cavalry, February 7, 1907, Camp Notes—BYU. Interview; John C. Creighton, former private, Seventh Cavalry, to Camp. Creighton stated, however, that Clear was killed on the lower bluffs east of the river near where Company M Private William Meyer fell. Camp Notes—BYU. Interview. Ryan told Camp (letter, December 17, 1908, Camp Papers, BYU) that Clear was killed on the bluff near Dr. James M. DeWolf.

26. Hare to My Dear Father (Judge Silas Hare), July 3, 1876, printed in the Denison [Texas] *Daily News* of July 15, 1876; reprinted in the *Chicago Westerners Brand Book,* vol. 25, no. 11, January, 1969, p. 82; Hare to Camp, Camp Notes—BYU. Interview.

27. Eagle Elk to John G. Neihardt, November 27, 1944, Joint Neihardt Collection at both University of Missouri Library and the State Historical Society of Missouri, both Columbia.

28. John Burkman, former private, Seventh Cavalry, to I. D. O'Donnell, O'Donnell Collection, CBNM. Interview; Herendeen to Camp, August 5, 1911, Camp Notes—BYU. Interview.

29. Red Feather to Scott, 1919, Interview; Eagle Elk to Neihardt, 1944. Interview; Marquis, *Wooden Leg,* p. 224.

30. He Dog to Camp, July 13, 1910, Camp Notes—BYU. Interview; O. G. Libby, ed., "The Arikara Narrative of the Campaign Against the Hostile Dakotas, 1876," North Dakota Historical *Collections,* Volume 6, 1920, pp. 124-130. Interview with Red Bear.

31. From notes in the archival files of the CBNM; Jerome A. Greene, *Evidence and the Custer Enigma* (Reno, NV: Outbooks, 1979), p. 59 and accompanying fold out map. These two unfortunate troopers were two of the men listed in the above note 9. See also: Douglas D. Scott and Richard A. Fox, Jr.'s, *Archaeological Insights into the Custer Battle* (Norman: University of Oklahoma Press, 1987) and Douglas D. Scott, Fox, Melissa A. Connor, and Dick Harmon, *Archaeological*

Perspective on the Battle of the Little Big Horn (Norman: University of Oklahoma Press, 1989) for more recent discoveries of human relics on the Custer battlefield.

32. Petring to Camp, Camp Notes—BYU. Interview.

33. Hamlin Garland, "General Custer's Last Fight as Seen by Two Moon [*sic*] *McClure's Magazine,* vol. 9, September, 1898; Colonel W. A. Graham, *The Custer Myth, A Source Book of Custeriana* (Harrisburg, PA: The Stackpole Co., 1953), p. 102.

34. Marquis, *Wooden Leg,* p. 223.

35. Ibid., p. 223.

36. William G. Hardy, former private and trumpeter, Seventh Cavalry, n.d., Camp Notes—IU. Interview.

37. David Humphreys Miller, *Custer's Fall* (New York: Bantam Books, Inc. 1963), p. 84; Miller, "Echoes of the Little Bighorn," *American Heritage,* vol. 22, no. 4, June, 1971, p. 31; "The Sioux Version by One Bull" to John P. Everett, in *The Sunshine Magazine.*

38. Kenneth Hammer, ed., *Custer In '76* (Provo, UT: Brigham Young University Press, 1976), note 2, p. 134, confirms that Botzer was killed at the river; Douglas D. Scott and Clyde Collins Snow, "Archaeology and Forensic Anthropology of the Human remains from the Reno Retreat Crossing, Battle of the Little Bighorn, Montana," *Papers on Little Bighorn Battlefield Archaeology,* the recollection of former G Company Private Theodore W. Goldin; Douglas D. Scott, ed., *The Equipment Dump, Marker 7, and the Reno Crossing,* See above, pp. 207-230.

39. Eagle Elk to Neihardt, November 27, 1944.

40. O'Neill, Camp Notes—BYU. Interview. This interview indicates that Martin was killed on the retreat; Charles A. Varnum, *I, Varnum, An Autobiography,* ed. John M. Carroll (Glendale, CA: The Arthur H. Clark Co., 1982), p. 129. Varnum's autobiography reprints his testimony that he had seen a corporal of A Company being killed at the retreat crossing. The only A Company corporal killed in the battle was James

Dalious. The bodies of several troopers who were killed at the retreat crossing floated downriver and were swept onto a sandbar in a lower loop of the river; See also: Samuel Alcott, former sergeant, Seventh Cavalry, and Thomas Blake, former private, Seventh Cavalry, n.d., Camp Notes—IU. Interviews. These two witnesses supported the evidence regarding the death of Sullivan. The skeleton of one of the troopers killed at Reno's Retreat Crossing was uncovered in 1958. Partial remains of another of these unfortunate troopers was discovered near the retreat crossing in 1989.

41. Boyle to Camp, Camp Notes—IU. Interview.

42. DeVoto to Camp, July 24 and October 17, 1917, Camp Papers, CBNM.

43. Letter, French to Mrs. Cooke, June 16, 1880, Godfrey Papers and E. S. Godfrey Folder, Francis R. Hagner Collection.

44. Letters, DeVoto to Camp, July 14 and October 1, 1917. DeVoto recalled Mask as serving as Hodgson's orderly and that he and others looked unsuccessfully for Mask's body at the spot where Hodgson was killed, but could not find it. The fact that DeVoto looked for Mask at Reno's Retreat Crossing means that Mask was on duty with Reno's company when killed otherwise the Custer battlefield would have been searched for his body. DeVoto, a former private in the Seventh Cavalry, was on duty in Company B with the pack train at the Little Big Horn. His account of the battle is in the Camp Papers, CBNM.

45. William Heyn, former first sergeant, Seventh Cavalry, to Camp, n.d., Camp Notes—BYU. Heyn stated that Hodgson was shot and fell from his horse in the stream. Reno reported that Hodgson's horse was killed from under him in the river. (Major Marcus A. Reno, "The Custer Massacre," Custer Battlefield Study Collection, CBNM.) See also: Edgar I. Stewart, *Custer's Luck* (Norman: University of Oklahoma Press, 1955), p. 374; Bruce L. Liddic, *I Buried Custer* (College Station, TX: Creative Publishing Co., 1979), p. 20. The latter book con-

tains the diary of Private Thomas W. Coleman of Company B, Seventh Cavalry.

46. Military service record of Frank Braun, Seventh Cavalry, 1875–1876, National Archives, Washington, D.C.

47. "Story of the Big Horn Campaign of 1876: As told by Private Daniel Newell . . ." *The Sunshine Magazine.*

48. Ryan in the Hardin [Montana] *Tribune,* June 22, 1923; Brininstool, *Troopers with Custer,* p. 52. Slaper interview. Sometime before the battle, Hodgson had told fellow officers that if he ever became unhorsed in combat, he intended to catch hold of a stirrup of a passing trooper.

49. Morris to Brady, September 21, 1904.

50. Brininstool, *Troopers with Custer,* p. 52. Slaper interview.

51. Reno Court, p. 566.

52. Edward Pigford, former private, Seventh Cavalry, n.d., Camp Notes—BYU. Interview.

53. Morris to Brady, September 21, 1904.

54. Ryan in the Hardin [Montana] *Tribune,* June 22, 1923.

55. "Story of the Big Horn Campaign of 1876: As told by Private Daniel Newell . . ." *The Sunshine Magazine.*

56. Atlanta *Constitution,* May 24, 1897.

57. Varnum, *I, Varnum,* p. 67.

58. Libby, ed., "The Arikara Narrative," quoting Red Bear, who recalled Stabbed's words for Libby.

59. Letter, W. A. Falconer to Camp, February 22, 1917, Camp Papers, CBNM.

60. George W. Wylie, former corporal, Seventh Cavalry, October 16, 1910, Camp Notes—IU. Interview.

61. Colonel W. A. Graham, *The Reno Court of Inquiry, An Abstract,* (Harrisburg, PA: The Stackpole Co., 1954) pp. 160-161.

62. Stewart, *Custer's Luck,* p. 389.

63. Captain Frederick W. Benteen to Private Theodore W. Goldin, January 31, 1896, Benteen-Goldin Letters, Thomas

Gilcrease Institute of American History and Art, Tulsa, Oklahoma.

64. Luther R. Hare, former second lieutenant, Seventh Cavalry, to Colonel (later Major General) Robert P. Hughes, December 13, 1893.

65. Letter, Hare to Colonel Charles Francis Bates, June 11, 1929, Godfrey Papers.

13. Stragglers in the Timber

1. The left-behind-in-the-timber list is published here for the first time. It was compiled by crossing references of many sources over several years—author.

2. Ferdinand Widmayer, former private, Seventh Cavalry, October 7, 1910, Camp Notes—BYU. Interview. Widmayer was not present at the Little Bighorn and got his information secondhand, perhaps from Morris. See also: Judge William E. Morris, former private, Seventh Cavalry, n.d., Camp Notes—I.U. Interview.

3. John M. Ryan, former first sergeant, Seventh Cavalry, in the Hardin [Montana] *Tribune,* June 22, 1923.

4. John Foley, former private, Seventh Cavalry, n.d., Camp Notes—BYU. Interview. This head had tinges of red hair. The only G Company corporals killed were Otto Hagemann and James Martin. Both were killed in the retreat from the valley and neither had red hair. Private John J. McGinnis of G Company had red hair and it was not uncommon in the Old Army for privates to have been acting corporals and for corporals to have been acting sergeants, but McGinnis' head was said to have been on a pole in the village.

5. John G. Neihardt, *Black Elk Speaks, Being the Life Story of a Holy Man of the Oglala Sioux* (Lincoln and London: University of Nebraska Press, Bison Books' edition, 1961), pp. 127-128 (from original 1932 book).

14. Custer's Last Stand

1. Report of First Lieutenant John E. Greer, U.S. Ordnance

Department, U.S. Army, August 17, 1876, National Archives, Washington, D.C.

2. Dennis Lynch, former private, Seventh Cavalry, October, 1908, and February 8, 1909, Camp Notes—BYU. Interviews. Lynch was aboard the *Far West* at the time of the battle in charge of Custer's luggage. He later gave battle historians secondhand information and passed it off as if he personally had witnessed what he told.

3. The designation of the unit "troop" for a U.S. Cavalry company was not officially adopted until 1883.

4. Good Voiced Elk to Walter Mason Camp, July 13, 1909, Camp Notes—DPL. Interview. Good Voiced Elk, as a member of the Indian Police at the Standing Rock Agency, North Dakota, participated in the killing of Sitting Bull on December 15, 1890.

5. Helena [Montana Territory] *Herald*, July 15, 1876. Curley, the scout, before he left the area, saw two Gray Horse troopers drop into the river.

6. David Humphreys Miller, *Custer's Fall*, (New York: Bantam Books Inc., 1963), pp. 96-98; Miller, "Echoes of the Little Bighorn," *American Heritage*, vol. 22, no. 4, June, 1971, pp. 33-34. Miller interviewed both Bobtail Horse (who was still alive in the 1930s) and White Cow Bull (still living in 1938).

7. Captain Edward S. Godfrey, January 16, 1896, in the *University of Montana Historical Reprints*, in Colonel W. A. Graham's *The Custer Myth, A Source Book of Custeriana* (Harrisburg, PA: The Stackpole Co., 1953), p. 345; Soldier, n.d., Camp Notes—BYU. Interview; Private Peter Thompson, *Narrative of the Little Big Horn Campaign,* ed. Daniel O. Magnussen (Glendale, CA: The Arthur H. Clark Co., 1974).

8. Letter, Daniel A. Kanipe, former sergeant, Seventh Cavalry, to Camp, July 20, 1908, Camp Papers, BYU; Hairy Moccasin to Camp, February 23, 1911, Camp Notes—BYU. Interview.

9. First Lieutenant Charles F. Roe, "The Custer Massacre," *The Army and Navy Journal,* March 25, 1882, quoting Curley. Cur-

ley stated that the noncom was a Gray Horse man whereas Sergeant Daniel Kanipe stated that the noncom belonged to Company I. This man's body was found about 150 yards from the ford on the village side of the river. His dead horse was found nearby.

10. Colonel Charles Francis Bates, *Custer's Indian Battles* (Bronxville, NY: privately published, 1936), Preface. Bates was the brother-in-law of Godfrey.

11. Thomas Two Moons to Richard Throssel in the Billings [Montana] *Daily Gazette,* July 2, 1911. Interview.

12. Low Dog to Brigadier General William W. Robinson, Jr., n.d., Camp Papers, CBNM. Interview.

13. Miller, *Custer's Fall,* pp. 96-98; Miller, "Echoes of the Little Bighorn," pp. 33-34; Curly and Hairy Moccasin, September 18, 1908, and February 11, 1911, Camp Notes—BYU. Interviews; Helena [Montana Territory] *Tribune,* July 15, 1876. Interview with Curley; White-Man-Runs-Him to Major General Hugh L. Scott and Colonel Tim McCoy, 1919, interview, in Graham's *The Custer Myth,* p. 23; George Bird Grinnell, *The Fighting Cheyennes* (Norman: University of Oklahoma Press, 1956), p. 350. White Shield, et al to Grinnell. Interviews; Low Dog to General W. W. Robinson, n.d., Dog, Camp Papers, CBNM. Interview; John F. Finerty, *Warpath and Bivouac on the Conquest of the Sioux* (Norman: University of Oklahoma Press, 1961), pp. 130, 137. Finerty was a newspaper correspondent with Crook's command on the campaign; He Dog to Camp, July 13, 1910, Camp Notes—BYU. Interview; Statement of Horned Horse, n.d., Camp Papers, CBNM; Foolish Elk to Camp, September 22, 1908, Camp Notes—BYU. Interview; Two Eagles to Sewell B. Weston, December, 1908, Camp Papers, CBNM. Interview; Tall Bull to Camp, July 23 1910, Camp Notes—BYU. Interview; Two Moons to Richard Throssel in the Billings [Montana] *Daily Gazette,* July 2, 1911. Interview.

14. J. W. Vaughn Research Files, CBNM.

15. Standing Bear to Judge Eli S. Ricker, March 12, 1907, Ricker Collection, Nebraska State Historical Society, Lincoln. Interview; Standing Bear to Camp, July 12, 1910, Camp Notes—BYU. Interview.

16. Miller, *Custer's Fall,* pp. 97-98; Miller, "Echoes of the Little Bighorn," pp. 33-34.

17. Lieutenant Colonel Richard E. Thompson, U.S. Signal Corps, and George W. Glease (real name George W. Glenn), former private, Seventh Cavalry, February 14, 1911, and January 22, 1914, Henry Petring, former private, Seventh Cavalry, n.d., Camp Notes—BYU. Interviews; Edward G. Mathey, October 19, 1910, Camp Notes—BYU. Interview; Augustus L. DeVoto, "Description of Reno's Fight," 1916, Camp Papers, CBNM.

18. J. W. Vaughn Research Files, CBNM. Many cartridge casings from Indian firearms have been found in North Medicine Tail Coulee (Deep Coulee).

19. Low Dog, interview, in the Leavenworth [Kansas] *Weekly Times,* August 18, 1881.

20. Lights (also known as Runs-After-the-Clouds) to Sewell B. Weston, 1909, Camp Papers, CBNM. Interview.

21. Roe, "The Custer Massacre."

22. Jerome A. Green *Evidence and the Custer Enigma* (Reno, NV: Outbooks, 1979 ed.), p. 59 and accompanying map.

23. Dr. Marcello Del Piazzo, Director, Archives of the State of Rome, Rome, Italy, to author, February 25, 1972.

24. Ibid.

25. Monsignor Martino Giusti, Prefect, Vatican City, Rome, to author, November 18, 1968.

26. *The New Webster Encyclopedic Dictionary of the English Language,* 1980, pp. 18-19.

27. Robert G. Cartwright Research Files, CBNM. Joseph A. Blummer, Colonel Elwood L. Nye, Doctor of Veterinary Medicine, and Captain Edward S. Luce, Custer Battlefield

superintendent, found cartridge casings on this ridge in 1928, 1929, 1939, and 1943.

28. Author. Research. Company E suffered the loss of 37 enlisted men in the battle, one of whom was a Company E man on duty with the pack train who was later killed on Reno Hill. A Company E noncom (according to Curley) was killed when his frenzied horse carried him across the ford. This also was verified by Low Dog. This left a total of thirty-five enlisted men on duty on the so-called South Skirmish Line.

29. Indian chiefs directed—they did not command or order—their warriors in battle. War chiefs suggested battle tactics, but such suggestions were never meant to be obligatory for the warriors, who fought as individuals and often came and went in battle as they pleased.

30. Douglas D. Scott, Richard A. Fox, Jr., Melissa A. Connor, and Dick Harmon, *Archaeological Perspectives on the Little Bighorn,* (Norman: University of Oklahoma Press, 1989), pp. 103-113.

31. Thomas B. Marquis, "She Watched Custer's Last Battle," *Custer on the Little Bighorn* (Lodi, CA: privately published, 1967), p. 38.

32. Stanley Vestal, "How Good were Indians as Shooters?" *Guns,* December, 1956; Author, "The Marksmanship of the American Indian," *The West,* vol. 2, no. 6, November, 1969.

33. Foolish Elk to Camp, September 22, 1908, Camp Notes—BYU. Interview; Charlie Corn to William 0. Taylor, former private, Seventh Cavalry, September 5, 1909, Camp Papers, CBNM. Interview; He Dog to Major General Hugh L. Scott, 1919, National Anthropological Archives, Smithsonian Institution, Washington, D.C. Interview; Dr. Valentine T. McGillycuddy to E. A. Brininstool, April 28, 1931, University of Texas Library, Austin. Interview.

34. A note containing Reno's words is in the Camp Collection at the CBNM. Grace Aileen Harrington (Second Lieutenant Henry M. Harrington's daughter) to William J. Ghent, April

301

19, 1938, Ghent Papers, Library of Congress. Some teeth with gold fillings [Harrington had gold fillings] were found on the battlefield in 1884, but whether they were Harrington's isn't known. The teeth were sent to Harrington's dentist at West Point.

35. Stanislaus Roy, former sergeant, Seventh Cavalry, to Camp, n.d., Camp Notes—BYU.

36. Colonel Herbert J. Slocum, January 23, 1920, Camp Notes—BYU. Interview. In Camp notes is a statement that Turtle Rib, a Miniconjou, corroborated Gall's story to him [Camp] about Foley's suicide.

37. Daniel A. Kanipe to Camp, June 16-17, 1908, Camp Notes—IU. Interviews; Letter, Kanipe to Camp, July 20, 1908, Camp Papers, BYU.

38. Ferdinand Widmayer, former private, Seventh Cavalry, n.d., and Richard E. Thompson, February 14, 1911, Camp Notes—BYU. Interviews; Letters, Kanipe to Camp, July 29 and November, 1909, Camp Papers, BYU. In 1876 Thompson was a second lieutenant in the Sixth U.S. Infantry. He was aboard the supply steamer *Far West* at the time of the Little Bighorn battle.

39. Flying By, May 21, 1907, Camp Notes—BYU. Interview.

40. Scott, Fox, et al., *Archaeological Perspectives,* pp. 68, 80, 84.

41. Report of First Lieutenant Edward S. Maguire, chief engineer, Department of Dakota, to Brigadier General Andrew A. Humphreys, commanding the U.S. Corps of Engineers, July 2 and July 10, 1876, National Archives; Luther R. Hare, private, Seventh Cavalry, Reno Court, p. 257. Testimony; Brigadier General Edward J. McClernand, "With Indians and Buffalo in Montana," *The Cavalry Journal,* vol. 46, no. 36, January–April, 1927.

42. Hump in the Leavenworth [Kansas] *Weekly Times,* August 18, 1881. Interview.

43. Neihardt, *Black Elk Speaks, Being the Life Story of a Holy Man of the Oglala Sioux* (Lincoln and London: University of Ne-

braska Press, Bison Books' edition, 1961), p. 122; Miller, *Custer's Fall,* p. 103.

44. Good Voiced Elk to Camp, n.d., Camp Notes—IU. Interview.

45. Raymond J. DeMallie, ed., *The Sixth Grandfather: Black Elk's Teaching Given to John G. Neihardt* (Lincoln: University of Nebraska Press, 1984), p. 187.

46. Reno Court, p. 201; William G. Hardy, former private and trumpeter, Seventh Cavalry, n.d., Camp Notes—BYU. Interview. Hardy, who viewed the bodies, agreed with Moylan.

47. Reno Court, p. 477; Thomas M. McDougall to Godfrey, May 18, 1909, Godfrey Papers, Library of Congress, Washington, D.C. The stench and the sickening sight of the gore in the Gray Horse Ravine forced a mass burial of the bodies in this coulee because of vomiting on the part of the burial party. It is believed the remains of these men were still there at this writing (1990). Archaeological digs, supervised by the National Park Service in 1984 and 1985, failed to locate the remains of these men, although a bone fragment—which may or may not have been washed into the ravine from elsewhere—had been detected in this ravine in 1983. A geomorphology test in Deep Ravine (Gray Horse Ravine) in 1989 also failed to uncover any signs of these "lost" troopers.

48. Letter, George W. Glease to Camp, September 23, 1913; Letter, Camp to Charles A. Varnum, April, 1909. Letter, Ryan to Camp, April 7, 1920, Camp Papers, CBNM. Two heads were positively identified by Glease as those of Sturgis and A Company Private John E. Armstrong. Another head identified in the abandoned village was that of Sergeant Miles O'Hara. See also: First Lieutenant Holmes O. Paulding, Assistant Surgeon, to his mother, July 2, 1876, Bradley Tyler Johnson Papers, Manuscript Department, William R. Perkins Library, Duke University, Durham, North Carolina. Others to view the heads in the village were Godfrey, Herendeen, and Private John Burkman of Company L. See Godfrey to the Quartermaster General, U.S. Army, January 7, 1921, Godfrey Papers; Bismarck [Dakota Territory] *Herald,* July 8, 1876, quot-

ing Herendeen; Statement by Burkman, O'Donnell Collection, CBNM. Burkman saw three charred heads tied to a lodgepole in the village which had been strung together behind the ears with wire.

49. Ibid.

50. Red Feather to Douglas D. Scott. Interview; Waterman to McCoy, 1920, interview, quoted in Graham, *The Custer Myth*, p. 110.

51. Moving Robe Woman to Stanley Vestal, Walter S. Campbell Collection, Western History Collection, Division of Manuscripts, University of Oklahoma Library, Norman; Pinedale [Wyoming] *Roundup*, n.d., clipping, Agnes Wright Spring Collection, American Heritage Center, University of Wyoming, Laramie. Interview.

52. Respects (Fears) Nothing to Ricker, November 9, 1906. Interview.

53. Military service record of James Butler, Seventh Cavalry, 1870–1876, National Archives. Godfrey erroneously believed that Butler had served in the British Army prior to his service with the U.S. Army. A few historians of the battle have repeated Godfrey's erroneous opinion.

54. Charles Kuhlman, *Legend into History* (Harrisburg, PA: The Stackpole Co., 1952), p. 230. A horseshoe, circa 1870s, was found in 1948 about 300 yards from where Butler was killed and was said to have been fitted for a blooded animal with a faulty gait. Did it belong to Butler's mount?

55. John Stands-in-Timber and John and Margot Liberty, *Cheyenne Memories* (Lincoln: University of Nebraska Press, Bison Books' edition, 1972), pp. 207-208.

56. M. I. McCreight, *Firewater and the Forked Tongues: A Sioux Chief Interprets U.S. History* (Pasadena, CA: Trails End Publishing Co., 1947), p. 113.

57. Lieutenant Colonel Frederick D. Grant, March 22 and April 19, 1919, Camp Notes—BYU. Interviews. The son of Presi-

dent Grant saw the empty grave sites of these men in 1878. Camp also saw these same empty grave sites, as late as 1905.

58. Joseph A. Blummer to Robert G. Cartwright, Cartwright File, CBNM. Blummer discovered a foot bone in a rotted cavalry boot in North Medicine Tail Coulee (Deep Coulee) in 1904. The boot was initialed "J. D."

59. Foolish Elk, September 22, 1908, Camp Notes—BYU. Interview.

60. Lights, 1909, Camp Papers, CBNM. Interview. Lights told of the short-lived escape and place of death of this trooper. The body of Henry Bailey was found in this area. Douglas D. Scott and Richard A. Fox Jr., with a contribution by Dick Harmon, *Archaeological Insights in The Custer Battle, An Assessment of the 1984 Field Season* (Norman: University of Oklahoma Press, 1987), p. 124.

61. John P. Langellier, Kurt Hamilton Cox, and Brian C. Pohanka, eds. and compls., *Myles Keogh, The Life and Legend of an "Irish Dragoon" in the Seventh Cavalry* (El Segundo, CA: Upton & Sons, 1991), p. 150.

62. Ibid.

63. Kanipe to Camp, July 20, 1908, Camp Notes—IU. Kanipe identified Bobo's unmutilated body among Keogh's dead.

64. Ibid. (Refers to Kanipe letter of July 20, 1908.) Kanipe told Camp that he saw the bodies of a Company I sergeant and that of his horse across the river in the village; Roe, "The Custer Massacre." Curley saw a noncom on a gray horse carried across the river where he was killed; Winfield S. Edgerly, n.d., Camp Notes—BYU. Edgerly stated that Bustard's body was found near that of his company commander, Keogh. Company I rode bay horses. We know that when the regiment reached the Powder River supply base, it had a shortage of serviceable mounts. Did Bustard secure a serviceable gray horse to ride? Was Kanipe mistaken in later years as to the company of the dead noncom across the river? After all, the bodies were badly decomposed after horrible mutilation when found. Was Edg-

erly equally mistaken as to where Bustard's body was found?; William G. Hardy, former private and trumpeter, Seventh Cavalry, and James Flanagan, former sergeant, Seventh Cavalry, n.d., Camp Notes—IU. Interviews. Adding to the confusion, Hardy confirmed that the carcass of Bustard's horse was found in the village, but Company D's Irish-born Sergeant James Flanagan agreed with Edgerly that Bustard was found among the dead of Keogh's command.

65. Burkman to I. D. O'Donnell, O'Donnell Collection, CBNM. Comanche was a Company I horse and was not Keogh's personal mount, which had been left with the pack train.

66. Grinnell, *The Fighting Cheyennes,* p. 341.

67. William R. Logan to Camp, May 17, 1909, Camp Papers, BYU. Logan was a friend of Boyer. See also: First Lieutenant John G. Bourke, diary, 1877, United States Military Academy, West Point.

68. Scott, Fox, et al., *Archaeological Perspectives,* pp. 73-74, 81-82, 88. Diary of Bourke, July 21, 1877, West Point. Bourke visited the Custer Battlefield in 1877 and saw a civilian-clad skeleton sticking out of the dirt near Deep (Gray Horse) Ravine.

69. Patty M. Maddocks, Director, Library and Photographic Services, United States Naval Institute, Annapolis, Maryland, to author, October 8, 1982.

70. Hamlin Garland, "General Custer's Last Fight as Seen by Two Moon [sic]," *McClure's Magazine,* vol. 9, September, 1898; reprinted in Graham's, *The Custer Myth,* pp. 101-103.

71. Ibid.

72. Richard E. Thompson, February 14, 1911, Camp Notes— BYU. Interview; Letter of Thompson, August 14, 1876, Appointment, Commission and Personal File of George E. Lord, M.D., National Archives. The body of Dr. Lord inadvertently was listed as not having been found after the battle. Thompson, who was a second lieutenant of the Sixth U.S. Infantry, was attached to the Little Bighorn Campaign, identified the surgeon's body on Custer Hill after the battle.

73. Paulding, Godfrey Papers. Statement; Letter, Myles Moylan to Second Lieutenant Frederic S. Calhoun, 14th U.S. Infantry, July 6, 1876, Brice C. W. Custer Collection; Kanipe to Camp, June 16-17, 1908, Camp Notes—BYU. Interviews; Letter, Jacob Adams, former private, Seventh Cavalry, to Godfrey, January 2, 1927, Correspondence File, CBNM; Thomas F. O'Neill, n.d., Camp Notes—BYU and IU. Interviews; John E. Hammon, former corporal, Seventh Cavalry, to Charles E. Deland, February 28, 1898, Dustin Collection, CBNM. Statement; Hammon to Camp, n.d., Camp Notes—BYU. Interview; George R. McCormack, "A Man [Private Jacob Adams, Company H] Who Fought with Custer," *National Review,* March, 1934, Elizabeth B. Custer Collection, CBNM; Ryan, CBNM. Statement; Godfrey, "Custer's Last Battle," *Century Magazine.*

74. Miller, *Custer's Fall,* p. 113.

75. Left Hand to McCoy, 1920, interview, in Graham's *The Custer Myth,* p. 111. Left Hand erroneously thought this officer was General Custer. Custer was wearing only buckskin trousers in the battle—not full buckskins—and no Indian in the battle could have possibly known which officer was Custer. The Indians did not learn they had wiped out Custer until much later. The Cheyenne said this particular officer had blue marks on his skin above the arms (Grinnell, *The Fighting Cheyennes,* p. 353), which were an obvious reference to Tom Custer's tatoo.

76. Tall Bull, July 22, 1910, Camp Notes—BYU. Interview; He Dog, July 13, 1910, Camp Notes—BYU. Interview; Marquis, *Wooden Leg, A Warrior Who Fought Custer* (Lincoln: University of Nebraska, Bison Books' edition, n.d.), pp. 237-238; Stanley Vestal, "White Bull's Account of the Custer Battle," *Blue Book,* August-September, 1933.

77. Vestal, "White Bull's Account."

78. White Bull to Stanley Vestal, 1932, Walter S. Campbell Collection, Western History Collection, Division of Manuscripts, University of Oklahoma Library, Norman. Interview; Vestal,

Warpath: The True Story of the Fighting Sioux Told in a Biography of Chief White Bull (Boston and New York: Houghton Mifflin Co., 1934), p. 200; Vestal, "The Man Who Killed Custer," *American Heritage,* vol. 8, no. 2, February, 1957, p. 9; James H. Howard, *The Warrior Who Killed Custer, The Personal Narrative of Chief White Bull* (Lincoln: University of Nebraska Press, 1968), pp. 51-57. White Bull personally told Vestal of the fight with the blond-haired soldier.

79. Vestal, "White Bull's Account."

80. Thomas M. McDougall, former captain, Seventh Cavalry, n.d., Camp Notes—BYU. Interview. McDougall, who commanded the pack train escort, viewed the body of Hughes among the dead in Deep Ravine. Two Moons' reference to the man's braids on his sleeves was the man's chevrons. Garland, "General Custer's Last Fight as Seen by Two Moon [*sic*]," *McClure's Magazine,* vol. 9, September, 1898.

81. Lynch, October, 1908, and February 8, 1909, Camp Notes—BYU. Interviews. Everything Lynch learned about the battle was secondhand. He was left aboard the *Far West* with General Custer's baggage because Herendeen needed his horse.

82. James M. Rooney, former private Seventh Cavalry, n.d., Camp Notes—BYU. Interview.

83. Glease, Camp Notes—BYU. Interview.

84. Thomas F. O'Neill, former private, Seventh Cavalry, n.d., Camp Notes—I.U. Interview.

85. Turtle Rib to Camp, September 22, 1908, Camp Notes—BYU. Interview.

86. David F. Barry, *Indian Notes on the Custer Battle,* Usher L. Burdick, ed. (Baltimore, MD: Proof Press, 1937), pp. 27-28.

87. Father Peter J. Powell, *Sweet Medicine: The Continuing Role of the Sacred Arrows, the Sun Dance, and the Sacred Buffalo Hat in Northern Cheyenne History* (Norman: University of Oklahoma Press, 1969), vol. 1, p. 117.

88. Pinedale [Wyoming] *Roundup,* clipping, n.d.

89. Marquis, *Wooden Leg,* p. 239.

90. Graham, *The Custer Myth,* p. 110; Waterman to McCoy, 1920, interview; Marquis, *Wooden Leg,* p. 264. We know that this officer was Tom Custer because Wooden Leg told Dr. Marquis that the buckskin-clad officer when stripped was found to have colored writing (tattoos) on his arms and breast. Waterman erroneously told McCoy that this officer was General Custer, but it could not have been for two reasons: (1) Custer was not dressed in all buckskins and (2) Custer's head wound(s) indicates that his death was instantaneous and he would not have been on his hands and knees after being shot.

91. Kuhlman, *Legend into History,* p. 213.

92. Letter, Camp to Colonel George S. Young, October 5, 1911, Camp papers, CBNM. Camp secured his information from Charles F. Roe, former first lieutenant, Seventy Cavalry, who erected the present granite monument in 1881. Roe's description as to the location of Custer's body was accurate because the present granite monument was erected close to an earlier makeshift monument of cordwood—still present when the 1881 monument was erected—according to an 1879 report filed in the Department of the Dakota which gave the location of Custer's body to the cordwood monument.

93. John M. Carroll to author, July 19, 1982. There are two unpublished letters now in private hands, one of which was written by Godfrey—and both having been read by the eminent Custer scholar John M. Carroll—attesting to the mutilation of Custer's genitals. Godfrey, out of deference to Mrs. Custer whom he predeceased, publicly stated that Custer's body had not been mutilated. See also: Richard G. Hardorff, "Baliran, Honzinger, and the Custers: The Facts and Fictions of the Rain-In-The-Face Myth," *Research Review, The Journal of the Little Big Horn Associates,* vol. 2, no. 2 (New Series), December, 1988, pp. 2, 4.

95. Two Moons to Throssel, Billings [Montana] *Daily Gazette,* July 2, 1911. Interview.

96. Report of Second Lieutenant George D. Wallace, Seventh Cavalry, to the Chief of Engineers, Department of Dakota, in the *Annual Report of the Chief of Engineers to the Secretary of War, 1876,* National Archives. The mileage of Custer's trek from noon on June 22 was kept by Wallace, the regiment's acting engineer officer. Wallace's "best guess" estimation of Custer's total trek of June 25 was 26 miles at maximum. I have corrected Wallace's June 25 mileage based on Custer's farthest advance (to Monument Hill).

15. The Pack Train

1. Augustus L. DeVoto, "Description of Reno's Fight," 1916, Camp Papers, CBNM.

2. Ibid.

16. Movement to Weir Point

1. First Lieutenant Winfield S. Edgerly, interview in the Leavenworth [Kansas] *Weekly Times,* August 18, 1881; Edgerly to Colonel W. A. Graham, December 25, 1923, in Graham's *The Custer Myth* (Harrisburg, PA: The Stackpole Co., 1953), pp. 216-217.

2. Captain E. S. Godfrey, "Custer's Last Battle" (expanded and revised edition) in *Montana Historical Society Contributions,* vol. 9, 1921.

3. Colonel W. A. Graham, *The Reno Court of Inquiry, An Abstract* (Harrisburg, PA: The Stackpole Co., 1954), p. 107.

4. George B. Herendeen to the New York *Herald,* July 8, 1876. Chicago *Times* Account of the Reno Court of Inquiry, p. 293.

5. E. A. Brininstool, *Troopers with Custer* (Harrisburg, PA: The Stackpole Co., expanded ed., 1952), p. 136.

6. Captain E. S. Godfrey, "Custer's Last Battle," *Century Magazine,* vol. 43, no. 3, January 1892.

7. Chicago *Times* Account of the Reno Court of Inquiry, p. 566.

8. Ibid, pp. 374, 869.

9. Ibid, p. 300.

10. Ibid., p. 650; Reno Court, p. 967.

11. Chicago *Times* Account of the Reno Court of Inquiry, p. 73.

12. Ibid, pp. 566, 713.

13. Thomas M. McDougall, former captain, Seventh Cavalry, n.d., Camp Notes—BYU. Interview.

14. John Burkman, former private, Seventh Cavalry, to I. D. O'Donnell, O'Donnell Collection, CBNM. Interview.

15. George W. Wylie, former corporal, Seventh Cavalry, October 16, 1910, Camp Notes—IU. Interview; Walter Mason Camp to Godfrey, January 14, 1921, Camp Papers, CBNM.

16. Reno Court, pp. 764-765.

17. McDougall to Camp, n.d., Camp Notes—BYU. Interview.

18. Godfrey to J. A. Shoemaker, March 2, 1926, Godfrey Papers, Library of Congress, Washington, D.C.

19. John S. Gray, "Medical Service on the Little Big Horn," Chicago Westerners *Brand Book,* January, 1968, p. 82.

20. Hardin [Montana] *Tribune,* June 22, 1923, quoting John M. Ryan.

21. Report of Major Marcus A. Reno to Brigadier General Stephen V. Benét, Chief of Ordnance, U.S. Army, July 11, 1876, National Archives, Washington, D.C. In this report, Reno also stated that his regiment expended 38,030 rounds of carbine ammunition and 2,954 revolver rounds. Ironically, Reno had been a member of the ordnance board in 1872 which selected the 1873 model of the Springfield carbine for U.S. Cavalry issue.

22. Report of First Lieutenant John E. Greer, Ordnance Department, Springfield [Massachusetts] National Armory, August 17, 1876, National Archives. Greer reported that in firing the Winchester, the "attempt to get a target at 900 yards was a failure; 26 shots were fired without hitting the target . . . using different elevations and firing both left and right. The bullet strikes on the end of the chamber [and] is upset and sometimes wedged so as to require several minutes to extract it. A

sliding lid covers the opening in which the carrier block rises and falls; the gro[o]ve in which the lid slides weakens the side frame at [the] top so that a slight blow will bend it over the opening and prevent the working of the carrier block."

23. Hardin [Montana] *Tribune,* June 22, 1923.

24. Gray, "Medical Service on the Little Big Horn," p. 83.

25. Wylie, Camp Notes—IU. Interview.

26. Winfield S. Edgerly, n.d., and Luther R. Hare, former second lieutenant, Seventh Cavalry, February 7, 1910, to Camp, Camp Notes—BYU. Interviews.

27. Stanley Vestal, *Sitting Bull, Champion of the Sioux* (Boston and New York: Houghton Mifflin Co., 1932), p. 176.

28. Augustus L. DeVoto, "Description of Reno's Fight," 1916, Camp Papers, CBNM; Hardin [Montana] *Tribune.* June 22, 1923.

17. Night and Day

1. Billings [Montana] *Gazette,* 1926, clippings, Clippings File, Billings Public Library.

2. John M. Carroll to author, July 19, 1982. Three of these skulls were kept at the Crow Agency in Montana for a century and then buried. Carroll also has seen testimony relating to the torture-death of Second Lieutenant Henry M. Harrington and two other men. Reno also left a written record of this fact (memo of Walter M. Camp—CBNM).

3. John Foley, former private, Seventh Cavalry, n.d., Camp Notes—BYU. Interview. The Irish-born Foley—not to be confused with Corporal John Foley of C Company who was killed with Custer's battalion—stated that this corporal's head still had traces of its red hair.

4. Charles A. Varnum, *I, Varnum, An Autobiography,* ed. John M. Carroll (Glendale, CA: The Arthur H. Clark Co., 1982), pp. 73, 94.

5. Letter, Captain Frederick W. Benteen to Edward S. Godfrey, January 3, 1886, Godfrey Papers, Library of Congress. Wash-

ington, D.C.; Letter, Private Theodore W. Goldin, January 6, 1892, Thomas Gilcrease Institute of American History and Art, Tulsa, Oklahoma; Letters, to Walter Mason Camp, December 5, 1918, Camp Papers, CBNM; Godfrey to John G. Neihardt, January 6, 1924, E. S. Godfrey Folder, Francis R. Hagner Collection, Manuscript Division, New York Public Library; Godfrey to G. H. Asbury, January 26, 1926, Godfrey Papers; Godfrey to J. A. Shoemaker, March 2, 1926, copy, Godfrey Papers; Godfrey to the Order of Indian Wars, January 25, 1930, Washington, D.C. Talk.

6. Thomas M. McDougall to Walter Mason Camp, February 26, 1909, Camp Notes—BYU. Interview.

7. Reno Court, p. 991; E. A. Brininstool, *Troopers with Custer* (Harrisburg, PA: The Stackpole Co., expanded ed., 1952), p. 60. However, the Reno-hating Private John Burkman of Company L., Custer's devoted striker, who was left with the pack train, and thus had his life spared, stated in that Reno was drunk—Glendolin D. Wagner, *Old Neutriment* (Boston: Ruth Hill, 1934), p. 49.

8. "List of Persons and Articles Hired by First Lieutenant Henry J. Nowlan, Seventh Cavalry, April-September, 1876," National Archives, Washington, D.C. Churchill is referred to as "B. (or Benjamin) F. Churchill" in many books on the battle, but U.S. Army Quartermaster records of the Seventh Cavalry list him as R. C. Churchill. I have referred to this man by the name under which he enlisted as a civilian quartermaster employee.

9. Chicago *Times* Account of the Reno Court of Inquiry, pp. 607, 636-638.

18. Entrenchment Hill

1. Hunt, Frazier, and Robert, *I Fought With Custer* (Lincoln: University of Nebraska Press, Bison Books' edition, 1974), p. 103.

2. Ibid., pp. 103-104.

3. George W. Glease, January 22, 1914, Camp Notes—BYU.

Interview; John M. Ryan in the Hardin [Montana] *Tribune,* June 22, 1923.

4. Thomas M. McDougall to Walter Mason Camp, n.d., Camp Notes—BYU. Interview.

5. Ibid.

6. Stanley Vestal, *Sitting Bull, Champion of the Sioux* (Boston and New York: Houghton Mifflin Co., 1932), p. 178.

7. Henry Petring, former private, Seventh Cavalry, n.d., Hugh McGonigle, former private, Seventh Cavalry, October, 1908, to Camp, Camp Notes—BYU. Interviews.

8. Hardin [Montana] *Tribune,* June 23, 1923; "Story of Big Horn Campaign of 1876: As told by Private Daniel Newell of Company M, 7th U.S. Cavalry," to John P. Everett, *The Sunshine Magazine,* September 30, 1930. Both Ryan and Newell recalled that Private James J. Tanner was mortally wounded during Benteen's charge, which contradicts what some historians of the battle have previously written (e.g., Edgar I. Stewart, *Custer's Luck* (Norman: University of Oklahoma Press, 1955], p. 525).

9. Charles A. Varnum, *I, Varnum, An Autobiography,* ed. John M. Carroll (Glendale, CA: The Arthur H. Clark Co., 1982), pp. 93–94.

10. First Lieutenant Winfield S. Edgerly to his wife, July 14, 1876, in "Echoes from Custer's Last Fight," *Military Affairs,* vol. 17, no. 4, Winter, 1953, p. 173; Edward D. Pigford, former private, Seventh Cavalry, to Earle R. Forrest in "Fighting With Custer," *The Morning Observer* (Washington, PA), October 3-19, 1932. Interview.

11. E. A. Brininstool, *Troopers with Custer* (Harrisburg, PA: The Stackpole Co., expanded ed., 1952), pp. 59–60.

12. "The Battle of the Big Horn: As Related by Charles Windolph, Company H, Old Seventh Cavalry, U.S.A.," to John P. Everett, *The Sunshine Magazine,* September 30, 1930.

13. "Account of Edwin Pickard," *Oregon Journal* (Portland), July

31–August 4, 1923; *Winners of the West*, June 23, 1926; *Montana, the Magazine of Western History,* vol. 4, no. 3, 1954, pp. 17–29.

14. Augustus DeVoto, "Description of Reno's Fight," 1916, Camp Papers, CBNM.

15. Thomas B. Marquis, *Wooden Leg, A Warrior Who Fought Custer* (Lincoln: University of Nebraska, Bison Books' edition, n.d.), pp. 259-260. Since the circumstances surrounding the death of each man of Reno's command have been substantiated by eyewitness accounts save for Housen, he must have been the unfortunate water carrier referred to by Wooden Leg. This remark was overheard by William Slaper—Brininstool, *Troopers with Custer,* p. 59.

16. Brininstool, *Troopers with Custer,* p. 59.

17. Ibid.

18. Letter, William O. Taylor, former private, Seventh Cavalry, to Camp, December 12, 1909, Camp Papers, BYU.

19. Marquis, *Wooden Leg,* p. 269.

20. Respect (Fears) Nothing to Judge Eli S. Ricker, November 9, 1906, Ricker Collection, Nebraska State Historical Society, Lincoln. Interview.

21. Lone Bear to Sewell B. Weston, January 5, 1909, Camp Papers, CBNM. Interview.

22. Lights to Weston, 1909, Camp Papers, CBNM. Interview.

23. Captain John G. Bourke, *On The Border With Crook* (New York: Time-Life Books, 1980 reprint of 1891 ed.), p. 416.

19. Terry and Gibbon to the Rescue

1. Thomas H. French to Mrs. Alexander H. Cooke, August 6, 1880, Godfrey Papers, Library of Congress, Washington, D.C.; Francis R. Hagner Collection, Manuscript Division, New York Public Library. Copy in author's possession.

2. Captain Frederick W. Benteen to Private Theodore W. Goldin, February 17, 1896, Benteen-Goldin Letters, Thomas

Gilcrease Institute of American History and Art, Tulsa, Oklahoma. Edward Luce, the late superintendent of the Custer Battlefield National Monument, suspected that the so-called "Enlisted Men's Petition" of the Seventh Cavalry was, at least in part, a forgery. The petition requested the immediate promotion of Reno to lieutenant colonel and Benteen to major. It was signed on July 4, 1876, allegedly by 237 enlisted men of the regiment. But Luce had noticed that two of the men had signed twice, three men who had signed the petition weren't present with the regiment—one had been a deserter—and that 17 of the signatures were of men who were known as illiterates because they invariably signed their company payrolls with an "X." Luce suspected that Benteen's first sergeant, Joseph McCurry, had, on Benteen's orders, forged at least part, and maybe all, of the signatures on the petition. Luce enlisted the aid of the Federal Bureau of Investigation in an effort to determine the petition's authenticity. On November 2, 1954, FBI Director J. Edgar Hoover informed Luce of the following: (1) "It could not definitely be determined whether or not Joseph McCurry prepared any of the ... listed signatures because of the limited amount of comparable known handwriting of McCurry; (2) There is insufficient comparable known handwriting of any individual available in the known specimens to determine whether or not these [specific] individuals wrote the petition ... ; (3) ... Variations were noted in the signatures [of 79 individual signatures] and the corresponding known signatures which suggest in all probability that the signatures on the petition were forgeries."— Report of the FBI to the National Park Service, U.S. Department of the Interior, Washington, D.C., November 2, 1954, File No. 95-38 320, Lab File No. D-192503; Edward S. Luce to Hillory A. Tolson, Assistant Director, FBI, October 17 and November 8, 1950, and September 29, 1954; Tolson to Luce, November 3, 1950, and November 5, 1954, CBNM; Copy in the author's possession; J. Edgar Hoover, Director, FBI, to author, May 2, 1969.

3. Lieutenant Colonel George H Walton, "The Tart-Tongued

Bomb Thrower of the Seventh Cavalry," *Army,* August, 1964, p. 66.

4. Katherine Gibson Fougera, *With Custer's Cavalry* (Caldwell, ID: Caxton Printers, 1940), p. 272.

5. Bismarck [Dakota Territory] *Daily Tribune,* July 8, 1876.

6. Thomas M. McDougall, n.d., Camp Notes—BYU. Interview.

7. Hardin [Montana] *Tribune,* June 22, 1923. John Ryan interview.

8. Augustus DeVoto, "Description of Reno's Fight," 1916, Camp Papers, CBNM. DeVoto was one of the men who brought Hodgson's body to the hilltop. DeVoto stated that Criswell, he and three other men brought Hodgson's body to the bluffs. See also: Bruce R. Liddic, *I Buried Custer* (College Station, TX: Creative Publishing Co., 1979), p. 20. McDougall over the years recalled Criswell, Ryan, Moore, and Bailey as the men who rescued Hodgson's body. Private Thomas W. Coleman, also of Company B, stated in his diary that he buried Hodgson on the morning of June 27 on a knoll overlooking the river.

20. Taps

1. Brigadier General Edward J. McClernand, "With the Indian and Buffalo in Montana," *The Cavalry Journal,* vol. 46, no. 36, January–April, 1927, p. 192.

2. Marcus A. Reno, former major, Seventh Cavalry, died in poverty and a victim of oral cancer, and, needless to say, in disgrace.

3. Charles C. DeRudio, Camp Notes—IU. Interview.

4. Captain Frederick W. Benteen to Private Theodore W. Goldin, January 6, 1892, Benteen-Goldin Letters, Thomas Gilcrease Institute of American History and Art, Tulsa, Oklahoma.

5. Frederic F. Gerard, January 22 and April 3, 1909, Camp Notes—BYU. Interviews. Gerard did not reveal Edward S. Godfrey by name. He only told Walter Mason Camp that "an

officer in the Seventh Cavalry" had made this statement to him. But the identity of Gerard's officer is obvious when reading Godfrey's testimony at the Reno Court of Inquiry.

6. Thomas H. French to Mrs. Alexander H. Cooke, June 16, 1880. Godfrey Papers, Library of Congress, Washington, D.C.; E. S. Godfrey Folder, Francis R. Hagner Collection, Manuscript Division, New York Public Library.

Glossary

War Department—A division of the President's cabinet involving military affairs.

Division of the Missouri—A jurisdiction area of the U.S. Army's geographical command system.

Department of the Platte and Department of Dakota—Subdivisions of the Division of the Missouri.

Regiment (Cavalry)—twelve companies (or "troops" unofficially).

Battalion—Three or more companies.

Squadron—Two companies.

Platoon—One-half of a company.

Detachment—Less than a Platoon.

Detail—(Usually) five to ten men.

Chief—Indian leader of a band (any size) of Indians.

War Chief—Indian leader who fought in battle; may also be a chief when not fighting.

Warrior—An Indian who fought in battle.

Senior Captain—The ranking captain of the regiment from the standpoint that his captain's commission predated that of all other captains of the regiment.

Regimental Adjutant—A first lieutenant serving as the chief assistant or administrator to the regimental commanding officer.

Sergeant Major—The highest ranking enlisted man of the regiment.

Noncom—Any corporal or sergeant.

Chief Trumpeter—The senior bugler of the regiment; held rank of private.

Orderly—An enlisted man assigned to render personal service to an officer for a particular day.

Top Kick—A first sergeant.

Striker—A trooper employed as a personal servant to an officer; such employment was illegal by Army regulations, but regulations were universally ignored.

Shavetail—Army slang for a second lieutenant.

Selective Bibliography

Asay, Karol. *Gray Head and Long Hair, The Benteen-Custer Relationship.* Mattituck, NJ: John M. Carroll & Co., 1983.

Bray, Robert T. "A Report of Archaeological Investigations at the Reno-Benteen Site. Custer Battlefield National Monument, June 2–July 1, 1958." Crow Agency, MT: Custer Battlefield National Monument (CBNM).

Brininstool, E. A. *Troopers With Custer.* Harrisburg, PA: The Stackpole Co., expanded ed., 1952.

Camp, Walter Mason. Collection of Notes, Interviews, Letters, and Assorted Papers. Provo, UT: Brigham Young University; Bloomington: Indian University; Custer Battlefield National Monument; Denver: Public Library.

Carroll, John M., ed. *The Sunshine Magazine,* September 30, 1930; Bryan, TX: privately published, 1979.

Idem, ed. *I, Varnum, An Autobiography.* Glendale, CA: Arthur H. Clark Co., 1982.

Darling, Roger. *Benteen's Scout-to-the-Left—the Route from the Divide to the Morass (June 25, 1876).* El Segundo, CA: Upton & Sons, 1987.

Idem. *A Sad And Terrible Blunder, Generals Terry and Custer At The Little Big Horn: New Discoveries.* Vienna, VA: Potomac-Western Press, Vienna, VA, 1990.

du Bois, Charles. *Kick the Lion Dead, A Casebook Of The Custer Battle.* Billings, MT: privately published, 1961.

Idem. *The Custer Mystery.* El Segundo, CA: Upton & Sons, 1986.

Idem. Dustin, Fred. *The Custer Fight.* Hollywood, CA: privately published, 1936.

Dustin, Fred. *The Custer Tragedy.* Ann Arbor, MI: privately published, 1953.

Idem. *Echoes From the Little Big Horn Fight.* Saginaw, MI: privately published, 1953.

Ege, Robert J. *Settling the Dust.* Chinook, MT: privately published, 1974.

Gibbon, John. "Last Summer's Expedition Against the Sioux." *American Catholic Quarterly Review,* April 1877.

Godfrey, Captain Edward S. "Custer's Last Battle." *Century Magazine,* January, 1892.

Graham, Colonel William A. *The Story of the Little Big Horn.* Harrisburg, PA: The Stackpole Co., 1952.

Idem. *The Custer Myth, A Source Book of Custeriana.* Harrisburg, PA: The Stackpole Co., 1953.

Gray, John S. "Medical Service on the Little Big Horn Campaign." Chicago Westerners *Brand Book,* January, 1968.

Idem. *Centennial Campaign.* Fort Collins, CO: The Old Army Press, 1976.

Idem. Gray, John S. *Custer's Last Campaign, Mitch Boyer and the Little Bighorn Reconstructed.* Lincoln and London: University of Nebraska Press, 1991.

Greene, Jerome A. *Evidence and the Custer Enigma.* Reno, NV: Outbooks, 1979.

Hammer, Kenneth. *Men With Custer, Biographies of the 7th Cavalry, 25 June, 1986.* Fort Collins, CO: The Old Army Press, 1972.

Idem, ed. *Custer in '76.* Provo, UT: Brigham Young University Press, 1976.

Hardorff, Richard G. *Markers, Artifacts and Indian Testimony: Findings on the Custer Battlefield.* Short Hills, NJ: Don Horn Publications, 1985.

Idem. *Custer Battle Casualties: Burials, Exhumations and Reinterments.* El Segundo, CA: Upton & Sons, 1990.

Hunt; Frazier; and Robert. *I Fought With Custer.* Lincoln: University of Nebraska Press, Bison Books' edition, 1987; reprint of the original 1947 book.

King, W. Kent. *Massacre: The Custer Coverup, The Original Maps of Custer's Battlefield.* El Segundo, CA: Upton & Sons, 1989.

Koury, Captain Michael J. *Diaries of the Little Big Horn.* Bellevue, NE: The Old Army Press, 1968.

Kuhlman, Charles. *Custer and the Gall Saga.* Billings, MT: privately published, 1940.

Idem. *Legend into History.* Harrisburg, PA: The Stackpole Co., 1952.

Libby, Orin Grant. ed. "The Arikara Narrative of the Campaign Against the Hostile Dakotas, 1876." North Dakota Historical *Collections,* vol. 6, 1920.

Marquis, Thomas B. *Wooden Leg, A Warrior Who Fought with Custer.* Lincoln: University of Nebraska, Bison Books' edition; n.d.; originally published in 1931.

Idem. *Custer on the Little Bighorn.* Lodi, CA: privately published, 1967.

Meketa, Ray, and Bookwalter, Thomas; assisted by Henry Weibert. *The Search For The Lone Tepee.* Horn Press, 1983.

Miller, David Humphreys. *Custer's Fall.* New York: Bantam Books Inc., 1963.

Reno, Marcus A. "The Custer Massacre," Custer Battlefield Study Collection, CBNM.

Reno Court of Inquiry. Proceedings of the Court of Inquiry in the case of Major Marcus A. Reno concerning his conduct at the Battle at the Little Big Horn River, June 25–26, 1876. National Archives, Washington, D.C.; Reno Court of Inquiry. Chicago *Times* Account. William J. Ghent Papers, Library of Congress, Washington, D.C.

Sandoz, Mari. *The Battle of the Little Bighorn.* Philadelphia and New York: J. B. Lippincott, 1966.

Schoenberger, Dale T. "Custer's Scouts," *Montana, the Magazine of Western History,* vol. 16, No. 2, Spring, 1966.

Scott, Douglas D., and Fox, Richard A., Jr. *Archaeological Insights into The Custer Battle.* Norman: University of Oklahoma Press, 1987.

Scott, Douglas D.; Fox, Richard A., Jr.; Connor, Melissa A.; and Harmon, Dick. *Archaeological Perspectives on the Battle of the Little Bighorn.* Norman: University of Oklahoma Press, 1989.

Scott, Douglas D., ed. *Papers On Little Bighorn Battlefield Archaeology: The Equipment Dump, Marker 7, and the Reno Crossing.* Lincoln, NE: J & L Reprint Company, 1991.

Stands-in-Timber, John; Liberty, John; and Liberty, Margot. *Chey-*

enne Memories. Lincoln: University of Nebraska Press, Bison Books' edition, 1972.

Stewart, Edgar I. *Custer's Luck.* Norman: University of Oklahoma Press, 1955.

Taunton, Francis B. (in collaboration with Pohanka, Brian C. C.). *Custer Field: "A Scene Of Sickening Ghastly Horror."* London: The Johnson-Taunton Military Press, 1990.

Utley, Robert M. *Custer Battlefield.* Washington, DC: National Park Service, 1988.

Vaughn, J. W. *Indian Fights, New Facts on Seven Encounters.* Norman: University of Oklahoma Press, 1966.

Vestal, Stanley. *Sitting Bull, Champion of the Sioux.* Boston and New York: Houghton Mifflin Co., 1932.

Vestal, Stanley. *New Sources of Indian History, 1850-1891, the Ghost Dance—the Prairie Sioux—A Miscellany.* Norman: University of Oklahoma Press, 1934.

Vestal, Stanley. *Warpath and Council Fire: The Plains Indians' Struggle for Survival in War and in Diplomacy.* New York: Random House, 1948.

Weibert, Henry and Don. *Sixty-Six Years in Custer's Shadow.* Billings, MT: Falcon Press Publishing Co., 1985.

Willert, James. *Little Big Horn Diary.* vol. 1. LaMirada, CA: privately published, 1977.

Index

325

329

When Buffalo Ran
George Bird Grinnell

March 1995

5 1/2 x 8 1/2
SC
128 pp.
ISBN 0-88839-258-3
9.95

This 1920 classic is the story of Wikis, a Plains Indian who grew up in the mid-1800s. Wikis tells his own story, of how he grew from a child to a man, preserving the life and teachings of days that have long since passed away.

"...I dreamed that a wolf came to me, and spoke, saying: 'My son, the spirits to whom you have cried all day long have heard your prayers, and have sent me to tell you that your cryings have not been in vain.' "

Argilite:
Art of the Haida
Leslie Drew and Douglas Wilson
8 1/2 x 11
HC
313 pp.
ISBN 0-88839-037-8
40.00

The Incredible Eskimo
Life Among the Barren Land Eskimo
Raymond de Coccola & Paul King
5 1/2 x 8 1/2
SC
435 pp.
ISBN 0-88839-189-7
16.95

Indian Art and Culture
of the Northwest Coast
Della Kew and P. E. Goddard
8 1/2 x 11
SC
96 pp.
ISBN 0-919654-13-4

Indian Healing
Shamanic Ceremonialism in the Pacific Northwest Today
Wolfgang G. Jilek
5 1/2 x 8 1/2, SC, 184 pp.
ISBN 0-88839-120-X   16.95

Kwakiutl Legends
Chief James Wallas and Pamela Whitaker
5 1/2 x 8 1/2, SC
150 pp.
ISBN 0-88839-230-2
14.95

Guide to
Indian Herbs
Dr. Raymond Stark
5 1/2 x 8 1/2, SC
48 pp.
ISBN 0-88839-077-7
6.95

Eskimo Life of Yesterday
Hancock House
5 1/2 x 8 1/2, SC
48 pp.
ISBN 0-9199654-73-8
3.95

Native Lore

Totem Poles
of the Northwest
D. Allen

5 1/2 x 8 1/2
32 pp.
ISBN
0-919654-83-5
SC   4.95

Indians
of the Northwest Coast
D. Allen

5 1/2 x 8 1/2
32 pp.
ISBN
0-919654-82-7
SC   4.95

Art of the Totem
Marius Barbeau

5 1/2 x 8 1/2
64 pp.
ISBN
0-88839-168-4
SC   6.95

Iroquois—Their Art & Crafts
Carrie A. Lyford

5 1/2 x 8 1/2
96 pp.
ISBN
0-88839-135-8
SC   9.95

Guide to
Indian Rock Carvings
of the Pacific Norwest Coast
Beth Hill

5 1/2 x 8 1/2
48 pp.
ISBN
0-919654-34-7
SC   5.95

Indian Tribes
of the Northwest
Reg Ashwell

5 1/2 x 8 1/2
74 pp.
ISBN
0-919654-53-3
SC   7.95

Haida: The Queen Charlotte Island Indians
Their Art & Culture
Leslie Drew

5 1/2 x 8 1/2
112 pp.
ISBN
0-88839-132-3
SC   9.95

Coast Salish
Their Art, Culture & Legends
Reg Ashwell

5 1/2 x 8 1/2
88 pp.
ISBN
0-88839-009-2
SC   795

Tlingit
Their Art, Culture & Legends
Dan & Nancy Kaiper

5 1/2 x 8 1/2
96 pp.
ISBN
0-88839-010-6
SC   7.95

Modern Classics

My Heart Soars
Chief Dan George
Drawings by Helmet Hirnschall
5 1/2 x 8 1/2
SC
96 pp.
ISBN 0-88839-231-1
7.95

My Spirit Soars
Chief Dan George
Drawings by Helmet Hirnschall
5 1/2 x 8 1/2
SC
96 pp.
ISBN 0-88839-233-8
7.95

Robert Service
5 1/2 x 8 1/2,
SC, 64 pp.
ISBN
0-88839-223-0
5.95

**The Cremation of
Sam McGee**

**A Century
of Gold**
James and Susan Preyde
5 1/2 x 8 1/2, SC, 192 pp.
ISBN 0-88839-362-8   15.95

James and Susan Preyde have thoroughly researched this enjoyable book which covers the Klondike Gold Rush in detail.

The authors have included many photos for the readers interest.

**Crazy Cooks and
Gold Miners**
Joyce Yardley
5 1/2 x 8 1/2, SC, 224 pp.
ISBN 0-88839-294-X $22.95

A delightful story of two ambitious and resourceful people as they wrested a comfortable livelihood from the north.

A prim little girl who didn't want to finish school, Joyce went on to become a wife, a postmistress, a lady rancher, a lodge and restaurant owner, and a gold panner.

Robert Service
5 1/2 x 8 1/2
SC
64 pp.
ISBN
0-88839-224-9
5.95

**The Shooting of
Dan McGrew**

WESTERN GUIDES

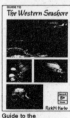